Part of a Long Story

By Agnes Boulton

Part of a Long Story
The Road Is Before Us

Part of
a Long Story

Agnes Boulton

Doubleday & Company, Inc.
Garden City, New York
1958

"Moon of the Caribees" by Richard Middleton,
from *Poems and Songs*. Reprinted by permission
of the Richards Press, Ltd.

Library of Congress Catalog Card Number 58-9374

Contents

Turn Back the Universe and Give Me Yesterday

1

It must have been in the late autumn because winter came before long and with it one of the coldest nights in many years. It was cold even then walking back late that night to the hotel where I had taken a room. The dark young man whom I had just met had on a thin suit and no overcoat, and I remember thinking that he must be very cold standing so long in front of the hotel talking to me. It never occurred to me then that we would be married by the following spring. . . .

2

I had left the farm behind, the little house on the hill overlooking the valley of the Housatonic and the blazing red and yellow hills of autumn. As the slow milk train wound along the river toward the city to which I was returning, stopping at each depot to take on the tall silver-colored cans of milk, I felt a certain nostalgia for the low dark hills and the stony fields, for the old barns where soon the manure from the cows would be frozen solid in the morning and the woodpile icy until it thawed in the sun, for the winter days which would soon be here and chunks of wood roaring in the kitchen stove. It was a yearning of the flesh perhaps for a beauty that I had known, a remembrance of the senses—of how the smell of snow was, and wood smoke, and the cold cow barn in the early morning and the cows rising to their feet as one came in; the touch of so many things, the feel of changing nature and of morning, noon and late evening, as one went in and out and felt the air against one's face and skin, the sound of branches splitting beneath their enameled coating of ice, and the drip-drip of water from the porch roof and the eaves of the house as the sun came up, and the sound of silence on the hills and in the long valley below.

It was not thought—because I did not think, nor consciously recall anything, but felt it; although as the train waited and the tall galvanized cans of milk were heard clattering in the boxcar, I did wonder if they could possibly send a can of milk every other day down to the depot. Thinking that, my fingers curled into the milkers' rhythmic grip and I remembered the rough warm feel of the cows' tits and the sound of milk swirling in a long stream into the pail. I closed my eyes as the train creaked and clattered along its three-hour journey. *Winter in New York* . . .

Well, I hoped doubtfully that my family would be happy on the farm and at the same time I had a feeling that the farm was no longer mine. . . . Something had happened to me, or to them, or between us; what, I didn't know, although I roused myself definitely to say to myself again that I was going back in the spring—the early spring! I had to go to New York for their sake and mine, to make more money, and I would return! I would return before that, if possible. . . .

But I did not return—not until many years later when for a few hours one summer I went back and walked again across the stony fields and looked down into the long valley and, with the permission of the aging strangers who owned it, went through the old house. The maple bough still guarded the window of the bedroom that had once been mine, but everything else had changed. Even the old town near which the farm lay was gone; there was no trace of it, not a house or a store or a tree nor a sign of the long main street where the village had focused its daily life, so that I felt like a ghost, and wondered what had happened and if I had only dreamed my past life. . . .

I had found the farm by following the river road, known so well so long ago when I took the cans of milk down to the depot. That road was unchanged except that one came upon it from a great cement bridge built across the Housatonic. But I found the town on my way back, a ghost town of disintegrating houses, forgotten, empty, without grass or living trees, for the sun never came there, silent except for the sound of the river flowing over the rocky channel stones under the bridge beneath whose great span the entire village lay, dead and forgotten.

I did not know, looking out at the passing hills that morning, that I would not return in the spring to the budding maples and the sugar sap boiling in the long iron trough; nor that a colder wind stung with salt spray and the smell of fish and sea and old rope, a midnight moon shining on icebergs, would be part of my life before the winter was over. Or that the sound of old trees in winter would not be ever again against the silence of the hills but against the low distant monotone of the ocean.

3

I had some money, about a hundred dollars maybe, and I took a small room at the Hotel Brevoort. Beautiful Mary Pyne, who had temporarily left her wild, kind, tramp poet, Harry Kemp, and who was living in the village in order to continue her long daily conversations with Hutchins Hapgood, had told me this was the best thing to do, and very cheap. She and Harry had spent the previous summer on the farm, taking sunbaths in the nude, at least so Harry boldly told us when they returned from their long walks. She and Hutch Hapgood were both interested in a new group, the Provincetown Players, and she told me something of Hutch, whom I had never met, and of the Provincetown Player group of whom I had never heard. The person *I* wanted to see was Christine, whom I had met and admired when she was running a small restaurant on some street whose name I do not now remember. But I have the impression, before this, of Christine serving meals in a basement, where the glory of her hair, skin, body, and spirit, and the no less warming and wise sound of her laughter was the magnet that drew to her tables less vital and more frustrated souls. . . .

However I was now directed to Macdougal Street, upstairs, number 139, and I went up two or three flights and entered a large, bare room, and at that hour, four in the afternoon, with very little light coming in through the two long dusty windows that faced on the street. There was no sign of life and, expecting to see Christine, I felt a lowering of my spirits. I wondered if I had come to the right place. Then, seeing an open door, I went through it and entered another room, square, around which were arranged tables and chairs. These were laid out with salt and pepper and sugar bowls—Christine's, obviously. A large clock in a wooden frame, hanging over an imitation marble mantel, ticked loudly—the only sound in the room— and I listened wondering, and then went to a door opening into the kitchen from which came the sound of heavy and spasmodic breathing.

A man was sitting at a table against the wall, reading a newspaper spread out before him, or at least staring at it. He looked up after a moment and then looked back at the paper.

"Is this Christine's?"

"Sure!" he said, not noticing me again until I brought his attention back by asking where she was, or when she would be here. It seemed urgent at the moment that I find Christine. Already two days had passed since I arrived in New York. "You can't tell!" he said. He was a large man with a great deal of magnetism which seemed to end in nothing as it came to you, just as his large hazel eyes, full of kindness and inquiry, ended in a blank stare. "She's out—evading me! She thinks I'm going after her. When she's been all the places she thinks I won't be at, and had a few beers, she'll probably be back here."

He got up, looked into some pots simmering on the stove, folded up the newspaper, and, taking a dog-eared book without a cover from his back pants pocket, sat down and began studying it, sounding each word over to himself as he read.

I left and sat on a bench in the nearby park, feeling very lonely and blue as the evening descended over the city. It was getting colder and at last I got up, unable to stand the chilly wind, and went back to my little room. I lay on the narrow bed, hearing the sounds of the city outside, and perhaps wondering what was going to happen to me. On a small table my typewriter stood with a half-typed sheet of paper in it. Looking at it I was unable to move; although all that was necessary was to add another, the finishing paragraph and the words *The End*. That was not bad. Finished, there would be a good chance of a check in two weeks from one of the pulp magazines. Not a large check, but it kept things going. But what kept me in a stupor on the bed was that *The End* was not the end. . . . Once this last page was removed from the typewriter another would have to be inserted with its black carbon paper, name and address in the upper left-hand corner, number of words in the right. Then the thing turned down one third of a page to the left of center. New title—what? *She Never Knew Why* fourteen thousand words. A novelette. A hundred and fifty dollars—and it was not even started. "*She Never Knew Why*." She never knew why *what?* And why not? I only knew that she had dark languishing hair, faint eyes—faint from pain or from too much sex? Or was she a blonde with hair like tabasco sauce and eyes like wine? Either way it was the body beautiful, very scantily clad, lying in bed probably, with silk sheets, with an eider-down puff fallen to the floor, and the bed of sin on which she had sold herself. She is waiting—for what? The telephone to ring? Or a knock on the door? Or perhaps this time instead of waiting she is thinking. But *could* she think? Is that why she never knew why?

That was why I wanted desperately to see Christine. The year before, she had told me of a place where she had worked for a while because she was tired of running a restaurant. I do not remember now at what she worked, unless it was a small factory of some sort, but the hours appealed to me; there were different shifts, the one she had was from two o'clock until six or seven. No experience required. . . . Some sort of place where one sat with other girls and occupied oneself with a monotonous job, doing it over and over, requiring, once one had learned it, no more than the constant surface attention of one's mind. And there was, also, as she told me about it, a strange, barren spirit among the girls, something that in some way, at some time, people should know about.

4

I looked at the telephone, which never rang because no one who might call me knew where I was, and then called the number that I had taken from the wall telephone in the restaurant. It was after seven o'clock now, but for a while there was no answer. Then the receiver was taken off the hook at the other end and a bedlam of noise, voices, and a clatter of dishes came over the wire, and it took a moment before I was able to convey my message. At last I got Christine, told her I was in town and wanted to see her and have a long talk, and that I had been over that afternoon and seen the man who was sitting in the kitchen. That, she told me, laughing, was her new husband. They had been married since last I saw her.

"He's trying to reform me. But, dear, isn't he handsome?"

I told her that he was, then she said she was still worried about him. But she seemed to take it very lightly, and after pausing a moment she suggested that instead of coming over now when she would be too busy to do much talking, I meet her that night about ten-thirty when she would be free. I asked her where and she said immediately at the Hell Hole. She seemed to think I would know where it was: but she had to explain to me that it was on the corner of Fourth Street and Sixth Avenue.

"It's the back room, dearie, of the Golden Swan. Everybody knows it."

I was quite excited at the idea of going to meet her in a place with such a name. Later on I learned that certain of a gang of tough hoodlums known as the Hudson Dusters often appeared there late at night or, rather, early in the morning. It was frequented also by a certain rather sinister girl with whose name Charles Demuth, the painter, was oddly infatuated, who consorted with one or perhaps all of the Dusters and whom we, or I at least, never saw; it was told that she came to a bad end in some way reminiscent of the girl in the "Frankie and Johnny" song.

When I opened the side door of the small and rather dingy saloon on Fourth Street it was a little before ten-thirty and Christine had not arrived. The place was rather dimly lighted and the walls, upon which a few nondescript pictures hung, receded into darkness. I seated myself at a table against the wall from which I could look into the bar and see what was happening there. It seemed, through the swinging door that separated the two rooms, even less interesting than where I was sitting, and I pondered as I had done outside on the street on the reason for the name of the place. No one came to take my order, for which I was glad enough as having gone this far I preferred to wait for Christine without having to order a drink.

The place smelled of beer and stale tobacco smoke. I took off my woolen gloves and my hat, which for some reason annoyed me, and smoothed back my hair. I found a cigarette in my bag and lit it. I thought of the old brown coat lined with lamb's wool which I had worn on the farm, and in the pockets of which I always found a package of cigarettes, usually left there by my mother, and I wondered if there was any reason for Christine asking me to meet her here at this hour instead of going to the restaurant to pick her up. I felt a little uneasy being in the back room of a bar, not being used to it, but I knew I should not mind, what with me writing about those girls lying beneath their eider-down puffs who never knew why and neither did I. . . .

Then I noticed that a man was staring at me from where he sat in a far corner of the room. He was so close to the stained darkness of the wall and so motionless that I had not seen him. He was dark and was wearing a seaman's sweater under his jacket. There was something startling in his gaze, something at the same time both sad and cruel. I longed for Christine, for I felt that here was something that I did not understand. His somber expression gave me the feeling that he had once known me somewhere. There was a poignant and expressive silence in the back room. I began to get uneasy, wondering if Christine was coming after all. She might have forgotten, and I thought that very soon I would leave if she did not come. This was not caused by the man looking at me. There was evident in him, to me sitting there, a reticence or shyness that was very noticeable, as if he wanted to absorb himself into the background of the room, become unnoticeable among the room's dark shadows, betrayed only by those dark and unhappy eyes. Then the door opened and the man that I had seen that afternoon stood there looking about with a benign but very determined air.

"Where's Christine?" he cried, seeing me. I did not know what to say and merely looked at him, astonished. He looked around and saw the dark man in the far corner. "All right, Gene—*you* here? Tell her I'm going to leave her—that's all!" And pulling his great buff-colored coat (which I found out later had been purchased by Christine, as a gift in keeping with his character) close about him he left, slamming the door. The barkeeper came in, hearing the noise, said something to the man in the corner and asked me if I wanted anything. I shook my head and he paid no more attention to me but wiped off a table or two and then turned on another light. At that moment Christine came in, and there was a moment of excitement while she embraced me, holding me tight, her Danish laughter gurgling, the barkeeper watching us. A comedy began, the center of which was Christine. Who can forget her? I don't remember what she wore or how she looked except that she was tall and voluptuous, with the ugliest face ever seen on a woman—forgive me saying that, dear!—and the most gorgeous, the most wonderful pile of red-gold hair, too heavy and too alive to stay properly on her head, always wanting to slip down to one side or the other. She, it seemed, knew Louis was after *her* now, when before she had been after *him*. She told us about it—the barkeeper, me, and the young man in the corner. Me and my job were forgotten—the main thing was that she was there. Soon Louis was forgotten too. Existence was in the moment and living was now and her husband didn't exist, not being there. Somehow the dark man was with us, and I saw that he was young and very interested in a silent way, speaking in a low and sometimes indistinct voice, that his suit looked as if he might have slept in it for a night or so and that his hands trembled a little. Christine ordered beer and then she said:

"Gene, tell me, is Jamie coming?"

I don't remember what Gene said, or I said or she said, except that when she said to me "This is Gene O'Neill" the name was a very pleasant sound to me, some impression just in the sound of it, though I had never heard it before so far as I remembered. Some names are like that and when they are, almost always something happens about that person. . . . And all the time I felt his dark eyes looking at me and I was wondering more and more. . . .

But pretty soon anyway Jamie came in, but not before Christine had an opportunity to explain something to me. Gene O'Neill had gone into the bar for a few moments to see someone there and during his short absence she told me that Gene was waiting here for his brother because he was completely broke and Jamie was going to give him some money. It seemed that their father, James O'Neill, the famed actor, gave each of his sons an allowance of fifteen dollars a week and Gene had run out of his and Jamie still had some left. Gene had told her about it that afternoon and Christine explained, laughing, *that* was why she had had me meet her here. She loved her husband, he was really just the man for her, but she was fond of Jamie too, and he was such a relief after those leonine embraces! *He makes love to every woman he meets, look out, darling, God, what a character! He's obscene too, but you don't mind. . . .*

Jamie came in and saw the three of us sitting at a table where Christine, who had the restaurant money in her big flat pocket-book, was buying drinks. I can't say that he swaggered in, though that word does occur to me, nor that he staggered, even though, as he was fond of saying, he was polluted, or on the way to where he wanted to go. He just appeared. He stood at the door, which he forgot to close behind him, not exactly unsteady but being careful of every movement, his face beaming through a sort of haze, a face so ordinary in some ways, so unlike his brother's, that it gave me a queer shock that first time, the face that had helped him make a success in *The Traveling Salesman* because it was just that, it gave exactly the idea of the traveling man, the "drummer." He was wearing a suit of loud black and white checks, a bowler, and a topcoat was over one arm. His collar was rather tight against his reddish neck, there was a small carnation in his buttonhole, and his tie was carefully tied. So what one noticed was his general natty appearance and the pleasure that he expressed at having at last arrived and seeing us there, for his gaze included me, indeed he almost seemed to single me out. . . .

But above all, perhaps, one noticed the quality of his voice when he spoke. It has been said of his father, James O'Neill, that he had the finest speaking voice on the American stage, and this voice was given to Jamie, too. It was penetrating—not big or deep, though he could make it that way. I remember now Gene once telling me with great amusement how when they were both on tour with his father Jamie, whenever bored, would take a taxi to the zoo of whatever city they were playing, stand in front of the lion's cage, and infuriate the lions and amuse the bystanders by roaring louder and better than the biggest lion.

"*What ho!*" Jamie said—his famous expression. "Late? Yes!" and here he quoted a line from Shakespeare which didn't quite seem to fit the situation, and then he added, moving carefully toward Christine, "I got lost in the subway, looking for a big blonde with a bad breath!"—leering a bit as he said it.

Yes, he leered but it was a kindly leer, with some sort of a Punch and Judy show behind it; yes, his smile was like the smile of Punch, with the lips pressed together and some secret behind it that he wasn't telling anybody. The dimples in Christine's face deepened and she became quite lovely, so gay, so warm. She led him on, it was a game of wits between them, a perfect contrast to her husband. His dark brother listened and watched her dimpling and gaiety as Jamie praised her hair, her eyelashes (she didn't have any that could be seen), her bosom, her teeth—which were perfect and which he said looked as if they could tear a man to pieces; and then he turned with a look at me, and asked his brother where he had found *this* beauty—more beautiful, he assured him, than anyone he had seen for a long time, a wild Irish rose, the one that would tear out a man's heart and make him cry out in his sleep with longing for her, and why hadn't he seen her first? That was his bad luck; for whenever his brother, drunk or sober, set his eyes on a girl there was no getting her to look at anyone else, and he looked at me sadly and took the wilted carnation from his buttonhole and handed it to me, but I don't think he even saw me.

We all laughed. It was something like watching the wrestlers in the arena put on their harlequinade of sound and facial expression which amuses but does not deceive, and yet somehow Jamie made us believe what he said when he said it. Then something strange happened again to me. . . . I saw that Gene didn't like the looks that his brother was giving me, or perhaps it was that he did not like my obvious enjoyment of the flattery which for quite a time I had not been hearing.

He and Jamie went out to the bar to talk together; Jamie may have given him the money and they had a couple of drinks. I asked Christine about the job I had been thinking about and she said the place had closed down. Now, why didn't I——? Then she stopped and ordered another drink for herself. I could see then that it was more important to her to talk about the two men and to my surprise she talked most about Gene. *Didn't I like him?* I said I didn't make him out, and she said, "Well, he's fallen for you, darling, I can see that. He's quite indifferent to girls—or rather he's ironic about their glances and their advances and that's as far as it goes. Although I think he'd miss it if it wasn't happening. He has a sorrow which isn't a secret, and Jim"—she called him that now—"has a secret which he won't allow to become a sorrow. Not yet. Not until next year."

"Why next year?"

She picked up her drink and looked across at me. If anyone told Christine anything in confidence she never repeated it.

"So—what do you think of Gene?"

"He's—strange, isn't he?"

"That's his genius! He's not drunk enough to really talk though. You should hear him when he does." Then she added thoughtfully, "He hardly ever talks when he's sober."

I asked her what Gene did and she said that he wrote plays. "I thought you'd heard of him. Mary Pyne and Hutch——" she began; but I explained to her that I wasn't interested in the theater and hadn't paid much attention when Mary was talking about the new group.

"He has a play uptown, done by the Washington Square Players—*In the Zone*" she said, "beside two they are going to do down here!" I was about to say that he looked more like a poet to me, but she had lost interest and, going to the swinging door, called in to them to join us.

I had intended to leave early, but instead I sat at the table, where we were now all together again, fascinated by Christine and the loquacious Jamie, and touched by the sudden engaging and warm smile that now more frequently appeared on Gene's face. But he soon became more silent; nor did he look at me as much as he had. I felt myself drawn toward him and I was aware of a curious and yet simple sensation—I must and I would see a lot of this man. Just why, I didn't know: it had never happened to me before. I remember that I also was very silent during the last of this evening.

At last we got up, and Jamie, as I remember it, wanted his brother to go uptown with him, but Gene shook his head. So we walked along Fourth Street together and Jamie took Christine down Macdougal Street, imitating, as they went off, the roar of a lion in order to warn the husband, should he be around, while the dark and silent brother walked across the deserted Washington Square beside me. I had been amused by the evening, particularly by Jamie and by the lion's reverberating roar, and felt quite gay and happy and young. But Gene said nothing until we reached the steps in front of the Brevoort and I put out my hand to say good night. Then he began to talk. I wish I could remember what he said but I can't. I don't think I quite knew—even then. He was sad, and when he looked away from me his eyes were dramatic. He had his hands in his pocket and he obviously felt cold. I began to worry about him and said I must go upstairs. But he kept me there a moment longer, his dark eyes looking at me directly now. His voice was low but very sure. "I want to spend every night of my life from now on with *you*," he said. "I mean this. *Every night of my life*."

I don't think I realized until I got upstairs to my room what a singular thing it was for him to say. I had not replied, or even smiled, which might have shown I just considered it a new way of paying me a compliment. We both just stood there silently and stupidly for a moment, and then I said, well, good night, or something like that and went into the hotel.

I closed the door behind me, looking at the typewriter and the narrow bed; then, still somewhat bewildered, I went to the window and pulled the shade aside a little to look down to the street below where we had been standing. I had a feeling that he might still be standing there as he was when I left him. But he was gone, and although I stood there for a while, looking down the street at the trees in the park I saw no sign of him. . . .

5

The next day, answering the telephone, I heard Christine's deep warm laughter. She told me she left Jim—as she always called him—downstairs waiting for Louis Ell and still roaring like a lion. When she got upstairs she found Louis sound asleep on the bed. Did I have a good time? How did Gene O'Neill behave? What did I think of him? There was to be a party Saturday night: *he* would be there and everybody else and I must be sure to come. . . .

After she hung up I went out and sat for a moment in Washington Square, observing the ghostlike trees through the mist which had arisen after the cold night. Then I had breakfast at the nearby drugstore and while I sat drinking coffee and eating a cruller I thought how nice it would be some morning just to telephone down while I was still in bed and have room service send up coffee and brioche.

The typewriter was waiting in my room and I sat down and began writing. Then I got up, lay down on the bed, and continued in longhand. The story had gotten away from me; it was not what I had intended but I continued for two or three hours. By then I had finished what I was doing and, reading it over slowly, was quite happy about it. I could not understand how the style of the typewriter and the style of the pen were so entirely different. Thinking about writing I began to think of Mary and Harry Kemp up on the farm that summer and Harry's great enthusiasm about his work and the way he went about it. (Was it then that he was writing the play about Judas or was that when he was in Ocean County?) I decided to call Mary Pyne and go over and see her and show her what I had just written, because she was a good critic and would like it. Then, too, I could find out more about these Provincetown Players, not Christine's angle but what Mary thought about them, for I knew that she was very interested, even going to act with them. I suppose I really wanted to ask her about Gene O'Neill, the sound of whose name still fascinated me, and about whom I really knew nothing. I kept thinking about the strange thing he'd said the night before, though of course I wouldn't mention that to Mary. . . . Men said things like that because they thought after a few moments more it might lead up to going to bed with the girl; but *he* had said it and departed. Or when they knew a girl well and meant it—it might be a sort of vague proposal. But he didn't know me and had given no sign of sudden love. But he *had* stared at me.

I thought him the strangest man I had ever met and could not stop wondering what would happen when I met him at Christine's party.

6

One has an idea, puts it off and thinks about it, and then nothing happens. I carried on an imaginary conversation with Mary Pyne in my room about the young playwright and other things also, for we had much in common, but I did not call up to see her before the night of the party. I finished the novelette that I'd been working on the day before and put it in the mail. Then I went over to see Bob Davis, who had bought some of my first short stories, and came back full of confidence—though, as he explained, he was now only publishing magazines for men.

Bob Davis, then editor of a string of magazines for Munsey—*The Cavalier, Scrap Book, Railroad Man's Magazine*—became a famous figure later in American literary history; a noted editor, a writer of books himself, a famous photographer, and a beloved gourmet and *bon vivant*.

It was always fun being with him, he gave so much to everybody, and I think he was fond of me, perhaps remembering the time when he had written me to come to his office in regard to a story titled "Lanigan—Lineman" which I had sent in to *The Cavalier* magazine and a girl of seventeen wearing a blue serge suit, her hair in a big bun under a straw hat, had appeared. I was trying to appear sophisticated but he just looked at me in silence. Then he had said: "Young lady, where did *you* learn about linemen?" and burst into a large boisterous laugh ending in an amused chuckle, for it appeared very funny to him—but not to me. He finally made me admit that my knowledge of them, or rather interest in them, came from seeing them climb poles along the road and thinking them very romantic men and even falling in love with one particular dark, bright-eyed one whom I never met, and whose only communication with me had been what they would now say was a wolf call from the top of a pole which I was passing on the way to high school, adding admiringly, "You for me when *you* develop!" which I pondered on, sometimes thinking he was fresh, but often thinking he meant something much more serious and wondering how we could meet.

But I had managed to assure Mr. Davis that I was a professional writer, having sold a story to the *Black Cat* and one to the *Evening World*, and that I very carefully looked up all the technical details of my story. He bought it for forty dollars. He was even more astonished when I sent him my next one, called "Past One at Rooney's," concerning what happened late at night at a gambling hall once visited by O. Henry. He had asked me how the h——I ever got the material for that and I told him I went there one night, of course.

I went back to the Brevoort, amused at his suggestion that I might see if I couldn't fall in love with a fireman so I could write for *Railroad Man's Magazine*. He would probably buy a story a month from me. When I got there I called up the magazine to which I'd sent the novelette and asked them if they could read it as soon as it arrived and send me a check by Friday. It was an order from them, but they told me no checks could possibly be mailed out until Monday. This upset me, as I had planned to buy a new dress to wear to the party—convincing myself that I needed one anyway, as one does when rather guilty about an expenditure. I found a letter from my mother saying that my little girl was doing fine and hadn't even seemed to miss me, but the cows weren't giving much milk and that William Jones, from whom I had bought the cows on the installment plan, said the last payment was overdue and he would take the cows away if I didn't send the money right away. However, the check coming Tuesday would cover that payment, which was only twenty-five a month for six cows. I wouldn't buy the dress; it would be too late to wear it to the party anyhow. Instead I went out and purchased a new blouse, and probably made some purchases at the cosmetic counter. . . .

When I looked at myself Saturday night I felt satisfied. The new blouse went very well with my suit, and I did not wear a hat. Christine, whom I called earlier, said just to come as I was, nobody bothered to dress, so I felt fairly confident as I climbed the stairs at Macdougal Street. Until, almost at the top, I heard the sound of laughter and many voices inside.

7

The room was very crowded, people talking and moving about in an atmosphere of excitement, some standing alone in self-absorbed depression. The tables had been pushed back against the wall. One silent group near the radiator was watching the others gloomily; I got the impression that they were trying to get warm, but it seemed that they were only waiting for a drink, for when Louis Ell came in from the kitchen carrying a tray with filled glasses they stepped forward eagerly. The air was full of cigarette smoke and as I stood at the door, someone got up and opened a window—for in spite of the depressed people there was such warmth and talking and humidity and enthusiasm that it seemed something must be done to let some of it out into the night and out over the city.

I didn't see Christine and for a moment I wondered what I should do, for no one noticed me. Then a thin, interesting, pallid and dazed young girl, who seemed for the moment as out of things as I was, who seemed indeed to be in or belong to another world, said, "You can put your coat outside!"

There was a long table in the outer room, which was in semidarkness. The table was piled with coats and wraps and I laid my heavy coat there, thinking the girl was beside me, for she had followed me outside. I turned to thank her but she was gone and it was a moment before I saw that she had pulled a chair up at the far end of the table and was just silently sitting there, her gaze fixed like the eye of a dazed camera on the open door of the crowded room. There was nothing for me to do but go back, for she did not see *me* any longer, and in truth I wasn't interested in her then, though later on in the year, before she suddenly and mysteriously disappeared, she had become of great interest to me (though all this time I never had any conversation with her, for few people did) and I had become one of her silent allies. . . .

I often thought of her later; but not for some years did I know that this girl whom I admired and even defended (for there was a certain conspiracy among the women against her) had become the brilliant photographer Berenice Abbott, whose photographs for many years have been on exhibition in New York and Paris.

At that moment I was tangled like a fly in flypaper in a thought or feeling that was depressing *me*. It wasn't that I hadn't seen Christine, whom I needed in order to orient myself, but that the man who had walked home with me to the Brevoort wasn't there. I went again to the door, and perhaps because I had taken off my heavy coat this time was noticed, for though everyone else was as absorbed in the talk and themselves as before, this time a bright-eyed man with slightly grizzled hair and an intensely alive face came and stared at me, led me to a chair and said to wait, he'd get me a drink. After doing that he stood by my side without a word, listening to what was going on and watching through his heavy-lensed glasses a group near the mantelpiece, over which hung the large clock ticking its moments away. A big man with thick white hair and fine and kindly eyes was talking and listening at the same time to two or three women; a couple of men edged in, listening. Nearer us an intense woman with a strong and fascinating face was also watching the big man near the mantel, paying no attention to a tall blond young man, still wearing his overcoat (which I later found he never took off), who was talking earnestly and quietly to her.

These people I came to know later: The big man with white hair was the great George Cram Cook, who organized and started the Provincetown Players, and without whose intense interest and devotion some people think Gene O'Neill would never have succeeded in reaching the theater; the dark woman was Ida Rauh, who, as an actress, was once compared to Duse; and the blond young man (Lawrence Vail) with the overcoat also had an interesting life, for he first married Peggy Guggenheim with all her money, and then later a distinguished woman writer.

At that moment Christine came in from the kitchen, laughing and dimpling and fortified with gin and food, Louis behind her, holding her arm. They were both happy now, not only because of the party and the gin, but because at a meeting of the Provincetown Players it had been decided that Louis should do the scenery for a play called *Ile;* not only that, but also play the part of a harpooner. Christine saw me at once; in fact she had been waiting for me, expecting, no doubt, that I would go out into the kitchen and find her. She pulled me to my feet and told me about Louis' good luck while he stood by, large and friendly, regarding me with his large eyes, which were quite bovine now; apparently he had forgotten all about the other night—it was as if he had never seen me before.

"That *Gene!*" she finished. "He was the only one that voted against him. He did his best to keep him out. He hates all big men, Louis! that's it. Where is he now—where is he now? At the Hell Hole, drunk. Big guy among the gangsters!"

Christine had not been malicious as she said this, but very kindly: at the same time giving the impression that it was the truth.

"Isn't he coming?"

"Maybe later. He'll make some sort of a sensation," she whispered to me, winking both eyes. "A lot of people haven't come yet. Come into the kitchen with me. I want to tell you—— Why don't you drink your drink?"

I wondered why she didn't introduce me to the man who had brought me the drink and who was still standing by. But this didn't happen, as she took it for granted that people got to know one another without the need of names. (*A name, a label, what did it mean except that it prevented your knowing the person behind it?*) Christine, among other things, was a mystic. Now she was listening to the general trend of the conversation that was going on, some sort of argument or opposition to something, whispered or determinedly voiced in guarded words. I had no idea what it was all about, but decided that the people who were drinking the most were having the best time. Then I heard someone ask where Gene was and people were silent; the question made a break in the clamor, which seemed to affect everyone so that in a moment all of them, indifferent or not, were wondering why he was not here when he *should* be here.

"Gene's all right. Leave him alone!" the big man by the mantel said, and then people went on talking and drinking and becoming more and more interested in each other. Christine went back to the kitchen and I with her, while Louis Ell remained to talk to a blond man, who, it seemed, was a portrait painter and wanted to help him with the sets.

There was no one in the kitchen and it was quieter there. The mixed punch, very strong, was in a granite pot on the table, but Christine had her good gin behind the stove. The man who had got me the chair followed us, so Christine took a drink from the big pot instead, and, after a minute, during which he also helped himself to a drink, he said: "Why don't you introduce us, Christine?" to her: and to me: "Are you going to join? You could get a part in the next play. You are an actress?"

I was secretly flattered, as in fact I have always been when once in a great while people who have just met me will ask that question, probably because of having been married to a playwright.

"*No!* She's a writer and wants to write about factory girls." Not write about them, I explained, I wanted to work there. "Well—let's say you want to write about something," said Christine vaguely, for she did not want to hurt my feelings. "This is Otto Liveright, God bless him!"

"Be careful—writing destroys a woman's looks!" said Otto Liveright, looking me over again, as if from a new angle. But I could see that he had lost interest, and a moment later he sauntered out into the other room.

8

I, too, was beginning to get bored. I felt very much out of things. I was not particularly interested in the people there, or in the Provincetown theater, and this in itself was enough to dampen my spirits. I tried to recall exactly what Christine had said about Gene O'Neill. Someone else had come in and was claiming her attention now. He might come over—*maybe later*, that was it! She wasn't sure, then. Also, it seemed to me definitely that she was taking a different attitude. The other morning she had taken such interest in Gene and me, almost as if there was something brewing, as she would phrase it. Tonight she acted as if it should make no difference to me if he were here or not. I began to think that I should not have come.

Mary Pyne had told me that she was coming tonight—she was not here either. Christine, no longer busy, and perhaps noticing my rather forlorn expression, took my arm and we went back into the other room. It was just then, as we came in one door, that Gene O'Neill appeared at the other. He stood there with a peculiar, slow dramatic glance that seemed to take in everything, without really noticing anyone. Everyone in the room stopped talking and looked at him, and he moved inside, with a laugh and a gesture both mocking and defiant. There was another man with him who waited at the door like a shadow—someone I never saw before, or saw again.

There was a sort of general movement toward him, laughter and greetings. I don't think he said a word. He just smiled. Jig Cook came forward and clapped him on the shoulder, and somebody brought him a drink of the punch, which he ignored. I don't know what he was wearing, probably the same things as when I saw him before, but there was something about his appearance that started and held the attention. Was it intensity? No, perhaps a quality of romantic somberness. If there *was* intensity, it was that of being himself—an awareness on the part of others of his being always intensely aware of himself. Now I am getting at it, for this would account for his shyness or whatever it was—which was really an intense self-consciousness.

His eyes moved slowly, in a peculiar manner, resting for a moment on something or someone, but he gave the impression that he was only cognizant of something that went on inside himself. And all the while there was the mask or echo of a sardonic laughter, at times ribald and again becoming painful, etched on his restless face.

I saw all this but it did not seem to affect me, for what I was seeing was the person I wanted to see—the person he was. *Judge not by appearances, but judge with true judgment.* The man who had kept his eyes steadily on me the night we met, saying without words something that was true; he who had walked home with me through Washington Square, and standing in front of the Brevoort had said something that he seemed to feel deeply—it was *he* whom I saw. . . .

But this man (though it was he) would not look at me. He saw Christine, made a gesture, saw me standing with her and ignored me. It was not obvious to anyone except Christine—but it was obvious to me.

Somehow this did not upset me, but aroused a rather excited and firm determination to make him acknowledge that he saw me. It was as if a battle, out of sight of everyone, was going on, an unseen and psychic combat, though outwardly I still gave the appearance of being rather quiet and uninterested. Christine, glancing from him to me, looked uncomfortable.

Some music was turned on and one or two couples began to dance. Gene watched them as if there was forming in his mind an image of some bizarre dance that he would in a moment execute. His inner attention was obviously still on himself. Christine moved away from me over to where he was standing and I saw her put her hand on his arm. She said something quietly. He refused to reply. She said something more and he took a pint bottle from his hip pocket. With a laugh he threw some of the contents into the back of his throat and swallowed it. His eyes roamed abstractedly, then came back to Christine. He looked across the room at me.

I didn't wait for Christine to bring him over—that was evidently what she had in mind. Perhaps I knew better—that she would be unsuccessful. But I didn't even think. I walked across to where they were standing. "Hello!" I said to him. "Remember me?"

After we were married I came to know too well that, no matter what his inner feelings, Gene O'Neill in a moment of embarrassment, or crisis, would dissemble and give quite a different and often opposite impression. Now he just looked at me vaguely and, without answering my question, gave me a most polite smile.

"It's quite a party," he said, continuing this politeness in the tone of his voice. Christine looked at him, then at me, and moved away, leaving me standing there beside him, while, before us, dancing couples passed, holding each other closely.

"It's a cold night—good night for a party! The iceman cometh!" he said, and I saw his eyes fasten on Nina Moise, who was sitting with a plate of food on her lap. He smiled with a warm and yet diabolic expression—at *her*. Then—he was gone.

Someone came up and began to talk to me, but I didn't hear a word that was being said. I saw Mary Pyne come in with another woman and stand near the door, talking, but I was not even interested in speaking to her now. I was watching Gene. It was only a moment later that I saw him take the bottle again and drink from it. I was the only one who saw it, for he went outside into the other room, which was dark, stood there, and then tilted the bottle quickly. I, alas, was watching everything he did. . . . Then, returning, he really *did* something. He crossed dramatically to the end of the room and with a violent, sardonic, and loud laugh, pulled a chair up in front of the mantel over which the big clock ticked away the minutes. Everyone stopped talking. He stood on the chair and looked about at his audience. Then he quoted—it may have been a popular song at that time, I don't know—in a dramatic chant, full of meaning:

> *"Turn back the universe,*
> *And give me yesterday.*
> *TURN BACK——"*

Turning back to the mantel, he leaned over and opened the glass face of the clock, and slowly and carefully with his sensitive spatulate fingers he pushed back the long hand of the clock, watching the small hand follow it. . . .

There was silence—then sudden laughter. He got down, still singing or chanting in his low voice, looking a little dizzy but pleased. He seemed to see no one now but Nina Moise, who was gazing at him, her plate untouched, fascinated and amused. Nina was the new and very capable director at the Provincetown Players, a dark and trimly plump girl with a keen kind face, later to become one of the most important people in her field in Hollywood. He went over to her and sat down on the floor at her feet. Her face grew tender and understanding, and then he took her hand and placed it for a moment on his forehead.

He did not look at me again as far as I knew. His eyes grew more violent, and although he devoted himself to Nina more or less, he also became involved in some sort of an argument that was going on among those people who seemed to be at the head of the theater group to which he belonged. His talk, though it seemed rather incoherent to me, was about the future of the Provincetown Players and he was evidently opposing some of their ideas very strongly.

Now his admiration for Nina Moise did upset me, and I quite lost the feeling of combat with him that I had had before. I tried my best to appear gay and indifferent, but I did not feel that I was succeeding very well. Even the few men who had cast eyes in my direction before left me alone. I have noticed, particularly at parties that what really attracts people is a certain vitality. Fame or beauty or an interesting mind do attract and hold for a while, to be sure, usually for reasons of self-interest; but it is vitality, a spontaneous giving forth of itself that people seek and need and gravitate toward. My inner temperature was burning very low indeed. All I did was try to hear if anyone was talking about Gene O'Neill. . . .

He was with Nina and some others, but no one made any comments now on him or his actions—it was as if there was nothing more to be said. I didn't even feel like talking to Mary Pyne, but, deciding it was time to go, I went over to her. She was still talking to the woman who had come to the party with her. Calm and beautiful, with her lovely, smooth red hair, Mary saw me coming and smiled; and then she kissed me and asked me how I was? She introduced me to her friend—Susan Glaspell. Susan had been glancing around the room with her expressive eyes. Her wavy hair was fluffed under a seal cap, and her sensitive face was pleasant and even rather gay, though she appeared pinched from the cold, which she felt even in that warm room.

They had been talking about Gene O'Neill, and Susan continued this conversation, praising a short play which he had written the past summer in Provincetown—adding that it was a pity he ever had to come to New York. She had given me a brief smile, but now she was observing me with a certain interest and turning to Mary Pyne she asked her if I didn't remind her of someone?

Mary was puzzled, until Susan said, "*Louise, of course!*" Mary looked at me thoughtfully then frowned slightly, as if an unpleasant thought had occurred to her.

"Well—perhaps! But she's not like her, really. Though I do see what you mean. We're speaking about Louise Bryant," she explained to me, "who went to Russia this fall with her husband, Jack Reed. You've heard Harry and me talking about Jack. . . ."

I felt awkward being discussed like this; and vague, too, about this person whom I resembled. Miss Glaspell glanced over at Gene, who at the moment was silent, looking at the tall, dusty window near him with a very melancholy expression. Then she caught Mary's eye and shook her head.

"Poor Gene is still suffering about it, I'm afraid," she remarked. "I think that up to the last he thought she would not go to Russia with Jack!"

Mary Pyne somehow gave the impression that she did not want any of this to touch her. She may have seen something that disturbed her in my reaction to Susan's words for she said very dryly: "I don't think its very important one way or the other. Certainly after the exhibition he put on in front of all of us here tonight he can't be very sensitive about it! '*Turn back the clock—and give me yesterday!*' When a man makes a public gesture like that to convince us that he's still unhappy about some woman, it's being rather blatant, isn't it? One would say that he's now dramatizing it and not feeling it—don't you think so?"

"I don't understand it," Susan said. "Of course, he's been drinking very hard tonight! I think he had it in his mind to oppose some of our plans—probably got himself well loaded in order to do it. We need him here, and yet I wish often that he would go back to Provincetown. We'd like another short play of his for the last bill."

I felt empty and exhausted and suddenly so depressed at being here at all that I was unable to say anything—about anything. Why had I ever come? Mary Pyne said, putting her hand on mine, "You're tired! Why don't you go home?" Susan looked at me curiously again. I managed a smile and said I *had* better run along—and then I could not resist glancing over to where Gene O'Neill was sitting. This time he was looking at me—with that same absorbed contemplation that had so stirred me the night I met him. For a moment we looked into each other's eyes across the noisy room.

Susan had the gift of pointed and significant gaiety; it was a part of her that helped make her play, *"Suppressed Desire,"* so well known. She laughed now, and looked at me rather archly:

"I believe *Gene* is the one who sees your little friend's resemblance to Louise," she said to Mary Pyne: "Maybe that's what's wrong with him tonight!"

9

I lay in bed for a long time the next morning, not caring about my typewriter, which was waiting on the table by the window, or the letter I had to write about Oscar Swanson's note to my mother, or even about getting dressed and going out for breakfast. I was very confused, and yet, looking back, it seems to me that I was happy—happier than I had been for a long time. Confused and troubled, too, because I knew that a new and obsessing emotion had taken hold of me, and from the strange and contradictory actions of the man on whom this feeling centered, I didn't know where it would lead to—or to what.

It didn't occur to me that he was influenced by alcohol, and that what I had observed was not his normal self. It was

obvious that at the party he was tight—or "blotto," as he used
to call it. I put the impression I had had of his slow movements
and gestures and fanatical eyes down to this: but I did not
seem to think of what he did or what he said as being influenced
by liquor. As he moved back the hands of the clock and quoted
"Turn back the universe and give me yesterday," to me that
was *him;* that was reality. Just as that night after first meeting
me, what he said when we parted was real—the truth. I saw him
as a whole human being from the first. Dark, morose, yet with
something childlike in his sudden smile; ironic, somber, romantic, tender and yet alien to other people in some way. I saw that
he was deeply attached to *something*. To the fabulous Louise,
whom I had never seen? No, I was sure it was not that, though
there was no doubt that was an important thing. To what, then?
It was, rather, to something that he held, quivering, within
himself. *Was* it himself—and what part of himself?

(*I am not sure even now, but perhaps as I write all this down
as it comes back to me, it will become clear. I hope so.*)

I only know that this image I had of him was very important
to me. Something had happened between us, some recognition
or unspoken communication. That I knew. But was it just a
passing thing—however real? Would I ever see enough of him
to find out? Would he ever *see* me and that recognition come
back?

Well! I made up my mind to eat dinner every night at Christine's! And (I'm a little ashamed of this now) I took the bus
up Fifth Avenue to Forty-second Street, climbed the steps
between the two passive lions that guarded the Public Library,
and took a big pile of books about Ireland to the reading room.
I had read Synge and Yeats and knew that my mother's father
had known Lady Wilde and the group that surrounded her
and I had heard stories about it all, but now I wanted to know
all about Ireland—and the revolution. Wasn't there a revolution
—a new one, or was it one of the old ones? I wasn't sure.
Looking back, I realize that two things I felt strongly about

Gene were: that he was Irish: that he was revolutionary. Though I see I have not mentioned this so far.

I didn't go up to the library because I wanted to be able to talk to him on these subjects, or impress him. My mind didn't work that way. It was to find out more—to understand, to share somehow in his own being. Leaving the library after some hours of reading I was in a state of exaltation—really excited! And, really not about *him*, for I wasn't even thinking about him, but about dark Ireland. *Uprisings, poetry, beauty and revolution.* . . .

Though I knew, of course, that he wrote plays, I didn't connect this too much with Gene when I thought of him. Perhaps because I'd never been interested very much in the theater, knew little about it, and thought of it not at all. I had read plays of course, Synge and Ibsen and Wilde. We had been brought up on Bernard Shaw and I remember going to my mother at a tender age and telling her I liked *Mrs. Warren's Profession* and *Widowers' Houses*— but what sort of houses were they? But to me a play was something that came alive as one read and I never saw them as being acted in the theater. It would have been logical (as I was foolish enough to leave my work, probably not eating any breakfast either, and go up to the library) to have taken books of plays, or books about plays to the reading room; or found out more about what *he* had done. But I must have seen him more as a poet then—not as a playwright, or so it seems. . . .

I went back to Christine's for dinner that night and listened to the conversation around me and was more or less unnoticed, except by Christine. It was very quiet after the night before and Christine was tired. Nina Moise came in and smiled at me pleasantly; and later I saw Jig Cook and Susan Glaspell both very preoccupied. But no one spoke of Gene O'Neill—much as I was longing to hear that romantic name. Nor did he appear. Nor did I dare mention him to Christine.

After a while she came over to the table and whispered to me that she was going to close the place early and asked me to wait. Thinking of what I had read up in the library, while I was waiting I outlined on the back of some large card of invitation that was in my pocketbook an idea for a novel. I saw this card the other day, the pencil marks so faint you can hardly read them, among some other old notes and letters. It was not about the Irish, but about a clam digger who revolted, no doubt, against the clams and the mud. . . .

Christine and I went over to the Golden Swan—this was the real name of the Hell Hole. It was only ten o'clock, and very quiet in the back room. Christine pushed the buzzer and said she was glad it was quiet, she needed a rest after last night. Gene O'Neill, she told me in an offhand manner, had a room upstairs over the saloon. I was more fascinated than ever by this, and kept looking at a closed door, imagining that it opened on a stairway and that at any moment he might appear. But Christine said no more about him, talking instead about some sort of intrigue or split among the Provincetown group which seemed to interest her. Christine never took sides but was always amused and kindly. Then she talked for a while about her mother, who was always an important part of her life and whom I was to meet later that winter. Next she asked me why I didn't take the little apartment on Seventeenth Street near Gramercy Park that I had had the winter before, and I told her I hadn't been sure of staying in New York. Last winter I had my small child and one of my sisters staying with me. I wouldn't want an apartment alone. . . .

At last the barkeeper appeared and we ordered two beers. There was a lot of noise and talking going on in the front room at the bar, and it sounded as if someone was getting into a fight. That was old Wallace the owner, Christine told me, and his cronies getting tight as they did every night, and later they would all go upstairs to bed, each with a pint under his pillow for the morning. I sat looking at the glass case on the wall, which held a stuffed, moth-eaten white swan who appeared to be floating in a very reflective mood on painted lily pads. In the dim and rather sinister light the swan began to have some sort of significance—and I began turning over in my mind how to ask Christine about what had happened last night. In fact I thought it strange that she had not spoken of this before. But she was thinking of the past winter and wanted to keep on that subject. It never occurred to me until later that she realized that I was almost in love with Gene O'Neill and she didn't want to bring up anything to hurt or upset me.

But he must have been in her mind, for she began talking about Louis Holliday, who, it turned out, was a friend who was very close to the young playwright. Louis, she said, should be back in New York very soon, and she looked at the door almost as if expecting him then. I had met Louis once or twice the winter before at Christine's old restaurant, but never knew him well, recalling mostly some fight in which he had been involved one night at Christine's. She brought me up to date with the story, adding: "I think that's one reason Gene's staying round New York—to see Louis when he gets back!"

This splendid young man had for some reason let himself get into bad shape, and couldn't seem to escape from it. Then he met a girl and really fell in love. She too fell in love. They talked everything over. She was firm about one thing; he must leave the village, go somewhere and regain his full health and mental stability. He promised to do this, and he did it. He gave himself a year; went out to a ranch in the West somewhere; didn't drink at all, nor did he see his girl during that time. When he came back, which would be soon, they were to be married.

I listened, bored and empty, as Christine told me all this. It wasn't what I had come to the Hell Hole for and I began to wish that I was back in the hotel alone. Christine may have sensed this, for she repeated after a moment (almost as if we had been talking about him), "Gene told me he really wants to get back to Provincetown. But he's going to wait until Louis gets back."

10

Then I heard his voice out at the bar, talking, and Christine said: "That's him now!" I felt suddenly very foolish and out of place and began to wish that I had not gone to Christine's for dinner or come with her here. I became cold and without any feeling, only aware that I was pursuing the man who was standing at the bar drinking—instead of attending to my own business. I had no connection, really, with any of this group of people, nor any particular interest except in this man. I became angry with myself—particularly when I realized that all my attention was on the sound of that low voice in the front.

Christine sighed. "Well," she said, probably still thinking of Louis, "it's a strange world!" At this moment the door from Fourth Street was pushed open by a tall girl in a tweed suit. She was followed by two seedy, tough, middle-aged men who stood looking about, abashed and unsure. I saw at once that this girl was a personality, an unusual one, but . . .

May I write about you, Dorothy? I'll have to ask you if I can. I saw your picture only last summer in a newspaper article, and I heard lately that you have been written about in Time *and elsewhere. Do you remember "Frankie and Johnny," and how, some weeks later, you and I went together to that deserted restaurant at dawn and saw Louis Holliday, dead, sitting at a table, while the wind from an open window ruffled his hair, and his empty eyes stared into space—those eyes that had been so sure and joyous on his return the afternoon before? It's a strange world, Dorothy, as our friend had just said. I must pay you one compliment among many, which is that—although I don't think you were more than tweny then—and you could sing "Frankie and Johnny" in a way that it was never sung before. . . .*

I watched her take the two men to a table and make them sit down: "I said I'd buy you a drink, didn't I? Don't you need it? Hello, Christine! Where's Gene O'Neill?"

Christine dimpled and laughed, full of life again. "Well, Dorothy, you ought to know!" Dorothy took this as it was meant, went to the door and called the waiter. Then she said, "Oh, there you are, Gene O'Neill!" She ordered three straight ryes, then went inside to the bar for a moment and came back alone.

"He'll be out!" she said to Christine, sitting down with the two men, who I found out later she had found sleeping on the steps of a church where for some reason she had gone to pray. She was extremely attractive in a strange way and gave rather the impression of being a sort of genius herself. Almost immediately she began to sing "Frankie and Johnny were lovers." The two men were fascinated, but she paid no attention to them, stretching out her long legs and for a moment closing her eyes. She ordered another drink for them; then one of them, making for the toilet, stumbled over her legs. It wasn't long before all at once the back room was filled up with the people who'd been drinking at the bar; and that was the first time I saw any of the Hudson Dusters, some of whom had been drinking with Gene outside and came in with him; and they all began singing "Frankie and Johnny," swinging and making a big emphasis at some of the verses. A girl named "Grapes" came in with another girl and they sat down. One of the girls had just come out of jail for no less than shooting *her* man, and the Hudson Dusters seemed very proud of this and one of them went off somewhere with her after a few minutes.

II

This was my third meeting with Gene O'Neill, and it has all come back to me as I write: I haven't thought of any of this for a long time, therefore it is perhaps more clear, like a coin that has been buried in the rushing channel of a river and comes up brighter for being long submerged. Christine and young Dorothy and the singing and the girl called "Grapes" seem in retrospect more easily visualized and known than I am, and even more than Gene O'Neill himself. I can only remember him as moving slowly around, his dark eyes alive and pleased, admiring Dorothy's strange almost staccato singing; drinking, laughing, and feeling that he was with friends; not, as I recall it, paying any particular attention to me, or maybe he did, I just don't remember. I suppose Dorothy was closer to the people who surrounded him that night—the people there, who he felt accepted him as one of themselves. Dorothy was beginning to be accepted too, because of her songs and her complete lack of fear about anybody or anything. It was odd, because she looked and dressed like a well-bred young college girl. But I believe it was also that she had a sort of desperate quality beneath her extremely cool manner.

Christine was tired, and left and Dorothy suggested that she and Gene and I go to a place nearby that she knew and get something to eat. We walked along the silent street together in the cold night and went down some steps to a place that was crowded with people eating at long tables. Everyone seemed more or less to know one another; and Dorothy would say, once in a while, that she had to catch a train to go and see her mother; and after a while I left with some sort of a journalist, who walked me home and was very hurt because I wouldn't sit in Washington Square for a while, while he explained to me about Rosicrucianism. . . .

12

Those first few days come back in a sequence. After that, there seems to be very little sense of order or relation in some of what I remember. Perhaps this is explained in Albert Einstein's words. "The experiences of an individual appear to us to be arranged in a series of events; in this the single events which we remember appear to be ordered according to the criterion of 'earlier' or 'later'. There exists, therefore, for the individual an I-time, or subjective time. This in itself is not measurable." Certain events stand out and I can place them in time because I can relate them to where I was living and what happened afterward. But I am not too sure of just when and where other things happened. I may have forgotten to put down some amusing or interesting episodes; I do not know if this happens with other writers or not, but when I talk about something that is past and bring it back to life, it is then very apt to go back into the oblivion where perhaps it belongs.

I close my eyes now against the pale, faintly luminous March sky and the tangled dark branches and black trunk of the tree outside the window and try to remember again those days in New York. . . .

There comes to me a panorama, a *montage*, such as a very modern play or motion picture might show. This is not exactly right, either, and I think of it as music, about which I know very little. There is a hurdy-gurdy (yes, there was one somewhere, outside a window); a lute, a piccolo: no drums, I wonder why? They may have been beating in Gene's mind and I did not hear them, for even then he had conceived the idea of the *Emperor Jones*. There is, too, somewhere the melancholy music of Tchaikovsky's *Symphonie Pathétique* . . . and clearly now as I write I hear an Irish ballad. *Mon dear, I remember . . . when comin' home the rain began. I wrapped my great-coat round her and she swore I was the only one . . . that ever she could love.* There is the melancholy piping of Pan, half man and half animal; and sea chanteys; and always "Frankie and Johnny." Sad music that has the sound of the sea, and behind the hurdy-gurdy and the mechanical piano comes the strains of the violin in Sibelius' Concerto in D Minor, introspective and somber, breaking into a mad dance.

Alas, the Pan that can never really be Pan, aping with futile gestures the abandon of life, punching the bag to keep the blood moving, staring into the mirror with haggard eyes to see if Pan's still there and if not—what is there? Secretly aware, perhaps, of some inner sickness of the blood, which one day, Pan or not, will take hold?

43

13

Nothing had been said that night about the legend of Gene's enigmatic love—even I had forgotten about it. It did not seem too important after I met Dorothy and saw Gene again and felt more confused than ever. The present, with its intense interest, mattered—not the past. I was aware that, though he paid very little attention to me that night, he was doing this as it were with a purpose. I knew that, though he was trying to avoid it, there was on his side as strong an attraction as there was on mine. This made my feeling for him even more poignant. This man was partly himself—and partly acting a part. Why? I did not understand. I had seen him sad and poetic. I had seen him pagan and ironic and darkly gay. I had seen a cruelty about his mouth that night that I had not noticed before. On what or on whom was he trying to revenge himself?

I cannot remember who told me about what had happened between him and Louise Bryant.

Louise was a young and ambitious newspaper woman—and beautiful. She was married to John Reed, who had already achieved some fame as a reporter in doing a daring story of Villa in the Mexican revolution. The idea of revolution stirred in John Reed's blood; today he is buried at the Kremlin in Moscow in a grave honored by the Russian people. Louise and Jack (as everyone called him) were among the group who organized the wharf theater in Provincetown, later to become the Provincetown Players.

Nothing too much was told me, as nothing too much was known. Only that he and Louise had been violently in love for a year or more—that there was a familiar triangle. She had gone off to Russia with Jack Reed that fall instead of (as everyone had expected) leaving Jack for Gene O'Neill.

Later, through Gene, through his mother, through friends, and even through Louise herself, though I never even spoke to her, and only saw her once, sitting at a table with her husband, I got to know all about it. Now it seems to be forgotten, people never mention it, but it was then and for some time afterward certainly a dramatic episode in his life.

One thing was brought out—that I looked like Louise. This must have been the story that at last reached her in Russia and started immediate action on her part. (For, if I looked like her, she must have thought, what was Gene doing but still clinging to *her* image?) This resemblance had rather an obnoxious effect on me. The main thing I wanted to find out was what she looked like. Perhaps I felt it was a good thing. For if each man carries in his heart an image of the woman he can love, then at least I bore some resemblance to that woman! Actually no two women were ever more unlike than Louise Bryant and myself.

Was I really in love with him that night when I left him in the restaurant with Dorothy? I don't know for sure, for I don't know what love meant to me at this point; certainly it had not arrived at that point which it later reached. I do not remember there being any great physical attraction in the ordinary sense, except that I liked to look at him—but this only satisfied a certain romantic part of my being. It was something stronger than that. A sense of destiny perhaps, or mutual need, or fulfillment? I learned afterward that he felt the same thing.

14

People moving like shadows along streets, in bars and stair-ways, feet crunching on frozen pavements, walks in the night and freezing bitter cold, bare trees, and distant cries in the night. (Who was Becky? She, too, loved Gene.)

Against all this I myself do not seem to stand out with any importance, though so far I've been writing more about myself than anyone else. (But that was necessary to me; it was the only way I could get back into it, and get started on remember-ing.) There were many people moving in and out of those winter evenings and nights—Hutch Collins, who played in *Ile* and died a year later: tall, possessive Scotty, who had a strange fascination for Gene; Hippolyte Havel, the little anarchist; the Irish fellow who mysteriously disappeared and whom I have never forgotten—it was he who sang, in the most beautiful tenor voice I have ever heard, "*I wrapped my greatcoat round her*," sitting at a table in the Hell Hole, and at my request, for it was a favorite of my father's.

Many people moving around here and there, but all in a small orbit. . . . From Macdougal Street to Waverly Place; north a few blocks; south a few blocks . . . I could draw a circle around it on a city map, and the center of the circle would be the point where two streets meet—there was a saloon there which had a certain glamour because John Masefield had once lived there, or spent much time there drinking at the bar.

15

There was another place where two streets met, with a tall building on it like a little Flatiron Building, dark and empty at night, with small factory rooms and offices above. I remember this very well, and I will try to locate it if I go down again to the Village. Perhaps the building will not be there, or will not look as it used to look, but the streets must be the same—or do they do away with streets, too, and build new ones?

I remember so clearly the two meeting streets, the tall, triangular building looming up through the darkness, and silence of a very late night . . . rain changing to snow, dim street lights, the wet and cold of the pavements soaking through my thin shoes as I stood there one night with Gene, fascinated and thinking what a strange, mad, great person he was, while he gestured at the building, speaking with slow intensity, the whites of his eyes showing as he moved his glance upward and from window to window, and told me (and himself) that this was the spot, the location, for the revolution . . . the two streets meeting, the tall building: and he would be up there in that building, with machine guns at every window commanding the two streets below; able to shoot them down as they came to attack—those forces of the reactionary law and order of the land. . . . He explained it all in detail, and at first it seemed to me that he would be alone up there, leading the revolution; and I asked him if he could handle all those machine guns; I guess it came down to there being six of them up there; but I know that they were going to hold it for a long time, maybe a week even, and then the ammunition gave out and law and order shot them down, every one, with machine guns of their own. . . . But that made no difference; this would be the symbol, the proud banner of the spirit and glory of free man with Gene leading them on, men shot down in cold blood; and this spot in Greenwich Village would for that reason never be forgotten. I saw his face, silent and intense, as he stood there when he had finished speaking, and I saw that he was deeply moved and convinced of something that meant a great deal to him.

16

This endeared him to me more than ever, and thinking what great manner of man is this, the dark poet and understander of everything? I held to his hands as we went down the slippery icy steps into a small, faintly lighted coffee shop that was in the basement of that very building that was to start or end, I've forgotten which, that fine revolution, and drank coffee out of tall glasses at a table lit only with candles. It was in this small place that something happened that broke up something else, and brought me and Gene together; and I mention the light of the candles because that was, in a way, the cause of it. . . .

Yes, it is important because I thought it was the first time after that meeting when he had said that he wanted to spend every night of his life with me that he saw me and became absorbed in me, and couldn't take his eyes off my face. Dorothy was there, too, of course, as we knew she would be, but the candlelight only brought out the long classic line of her jaw and the ends of her tousled short hair. Gene stopped listening to her and looking at her, as he always did under more normal light. Even when she sang "Frankie and Johnny" with a new verse added he paid little attention, for he was looking at me. . . . How do I know that it was the soft radiance of the little candles, set in a row along the table, casting their light upward on my face, that did it? Was there a mirror on the wall in which I saw myself romanticized in this light into some sort of perhaps unreal beauty? No, because if there had been a mirror Gene would have been observing himself in it as he talked, as he always did when there was a mirror around. Did he tell me? I doubt that, as I am sure he thought it was really me, and not any effect of the candlelight. Could I have done this deliberately, leaned nearer to the candles than was necessary, thinking: *I am more beautiful than Dorothy, even though I can't keep a tune! Please look at me?*

Those, as I remember it, seem to have been my sentiments: perhaps I took off my hat if I wore one; or loosened my hair; or just sat there, trying to look like The Blessed Damozel, leaning on the gold bar of Heaven— I don't remember. I only know that I knew, because I saw it in his eyes, that I looked beautiful; and that I was silent, and that I loved him . . . and that he wasn't looking at Dorothy now, but at *me*.

48

Death at Dawn

During this time Gene was going to the Provincetown Theatre on Macdougal Street almost every afternoon and evening, and often I was with him. *Ile* was produced, and *The Long Voyage Home;* and there was much happening that may be of importance to those interested in the theater, particularly in the early days of the Provincetown group, that I am not going to put down here, even though Gene was a pivotal part of it all. People I knew and liked, some of whom I grew to love—*Jig and Susan, Jimmy Light and dear Sue Jenkins, Nina Moise, Donald Corley and Dave Carb: Teddy and Stella Ballantine, and of course, young Saxe Commins.* Jimmy Light later became director of the Provincetown Players, giving everything he had to it. Don Corley visited us frequently, a poetic and whimsical man, not quite of this world; Dave Carb, one of the original group in Provincetown, became outwardly conventional and wrote about the theater in *Vogue:* Teddy Ballantine—everyone knows his fine acting and excellent parts in motion pictures, although now I understand he has returned to his painting—and Saxe Commins, later Gene's closest friend, standing by him in a period of despair, was to become a well-known editor and one of the partners in Random House. All that went on, the excitement, the rehearsals, the talk, the audiences—so much and so interesting and yet were I to put down even a part of it here, this would not be part of a long story, but the first volume of an epic. A play was produced by Maxwell Bodenheim; another play of Susan Glaspell's—*Outside; In the Zone* was up at the Comedy Theatre: and the Provincetown put on a play by that talented young writer Michael Gold. . . . The winter grew colder and colder and Gene bought a nubby blue overcoat, which he was to wear until the late fall, when Shane was born.

2

This overcoat was thrown over me, and I think it covered part of Gene, too, the first night we spent together. *White Nights*, Gene used to say of such occurrences, and I will use the expression though I am not quite sure what it means. Perhaps the white and dazzling cold of the night streets suggested it— a cold that penetrated into the rooms and the apartments and which, I am sure, caused the gas—or was it the water mains?—to freeze. Walking along the streets became a perilous interlude between places where one sat and talked and ate; there was ice below and white sky above, and the air was so sharp that it hurt as one breathed. . . .

Sometimes Gene carried a thin leather portfolio with him, though not often, and this night he had it clutched tightly in one cold hand while the other held my arm. We had left Polly's restaurant and were going to a small apartment that belonged to some friend of Hutch Collins. Hutch had phoned us while we were eating dinner, and said to come over after we finished. "It must be like this in Russia," I said on an outgoing frozen breath, and then knew I had made a mistake, for under the passing street light I saw Gene's mouth turn cruel and scornful.

Hutch opened the door for us and took us into a dingy and sparsely furnished front room. There was a smaller room behind it, seen through a partly curtained arch, much the same as the other except that one could glimpse an unmade double bed. Gene took a pint of Old Taylor from his overcoat, and Hutch got glasses and we all sat down. Hutch tried to make me some coffee but the gas was frozen, so he found an old can of Sterno among some debris in a cupboard, and some was made over that. Gene was in a dark and pensive mood, expressing himself at intervals about what went on at the theater. I think that *Ile* was in rehearsal, and *In the Zone* (of which he spoke scornfully) was a success. Hutch Collins, warm and simple and quiet, was not saying much. Someone knocked, and he went to the door again and came back with a tall, bleak, hardfaced character whom I had seen several times at the Provincetown Theatre, not understanding exactly why he was there . . . *Scotty!* . . . I had also met him with Gene several times, drinking and giving his opinion about this and that.

Scotty did not like me. He already felt that I was (or would be) interfering in his relationship with Gene. I wondered how he had found out where Gene was—but he was always very smart about that. Gene now addressed most of his remarks to the newcomer, who in turn gave advice, sided with Gene, and urged him on to taking action in whatever it was all about. I began to get bored with his talk on subjects which I was sure he knew nothing about, and this feeling was shared by Hutch, who would look at me silently once in a while, in understanding or perplexity. Scotty was encouraging Gene in his bad mood, with a shrewdness which was obvious to us but not to Gene, and implying that the young playwright was always right about everything. He was very much the center of things now that he was there and he emphasized this by glancing constantly at a large flat cardboard box, which he had brought with him and had placed beside him on the couch: as if to say that *this* was important, too, keeping us meanwhile in suspense.

After talking with Gene for a while he got up and opened this box, spreading out on the couch some exquisite tablecloths and bureau scarves, made of batiste, with fine lace and drawn work. He wanted Hutch Collins to buy one to take home to his wife, telling him he could have it for ten dollars, whereas it was worth nearer seventy-five, but not explaining how he got these things. . . . Afterward he devoted himself to Gene, whose intense excited eyes were now fixed only on him.

Hutch Collins got restless and I began to get sleepy, thinking it was time to get back to the Brevoort, but I didn't want to leave Gene. While they were talking, Hutch and I went through the back room to a sort of wall kitchenette that they had in small apartments then and, standing talking to me, Hutch tried to get what was left of the Sterno going for more hot coffee, for the apartment was getting colder and colder. When we returned Scotty had produced from somewhere a quart of liquor and had poured out two large glasses for himself and Gene. (I think that this legerdemain of producing a bottle when it seemed that there was no more to be had was one of Scotty's greatest charms.)

Hutch Collins, who drank a great deal but never showed it and was very quiet, poured himself an even larger drink and sat down on the couch. Scotty, who observed everything, gave him a derogatory glance, implying that Hutch was unwanted. He managed to convey to us, without a word, that Hutch Collins and I were outsiders, that he alone understood and was the intimate companion of the young playwright, and what were we doing here?

Hutch sat on the couch, saying nothing, and I, taking a creaky willow chair, also silently waited and was watched covertly by Scotty—though he was careful to give Gene the impression that he was giving *him* his complete attention. Then there came one of those long silences that so often followed a speech of Gene's and which those who understood him and were his friends did not break—for one knew that it would be breaking into his continued (though silent) stream of thought. Scotty said nothing, but I knew he had me on his mind—how to get rid of me. When Hutch and I were in the kitchen we had heard Scotty suggesting that he and Gene leave and go elsewhere but Gene had ignored this and evidently intended to stay where he was; which, of course, seeing it was Gene's wish, Scotty was too wise to oppose. Hutch Collins, he knew, would

go before long, for he had a wife and children somewhere uptown. But me——?

I was watching Gene's face, as one does when one is in love
(probably with a foolish expression on my own), when Scotty
came to my side, holding a kitchen glass two thirds full of
yellow liquor and for the moment pretending that I was a little
queen—but with quite other ideas in his mind.

"Here—drink this," he said solicitously. "It's the best—got it
off a boat!"

I shook my head, for one smell of the stuff was enough to
knock me over, and Scotty, unable to suppress a baleful look
at me, went back to his conversation with Gene. I sat there
in a sort of daze, listening. Hutch, sitting erect on the couch,
dozed off for a moment, holding his glass in his hand. He
looked tired and unhappy. It was nearly four o'clock. There
was a long silence, and at last Scotty seemed to sense that the
topic they had been discussing had come to an end, at least for
Gene. He didn't like this and began fishing around in his pockets
and at last brought out a clipping, at which he stared.

It was not until he began to read it aloud that I realized the
morose look was his idea of expressing a sudden poetic mood
that had overcome him. Gene listened silently. It was a poem,
cut from the *Journal-American* . . . something about craving
a ship . . . and long furrows; and I remember perversely thinking that the furrows reminded me more of those on Scotty's
face than on any sea.

Scotty began the second verse, and Gene's face hardened:
he regarded Scotty with malevolence.

"Tear it up!" he exclaimed. Scotty folded it carefully and put
it back in his pocket, conveying angrily at the same time that
Gene was *not* in a state to appreciate good poetry.

Gene stood up; he filled his empty glass with the yellow
liquor, and held it insecurely in his hand. It was as if he were
searching for something in the past, his eyes moving vaguely
around the room, perhaps on that same search. After a moment
he began to recite a poem:

"Ah,—the wind on my forehead that might not blow
on the earth. . . .
I saw the lights of a ship march slowly over the sea.
And the land fell away behind me, and into the night
That covereth all things and passes no more for me.
My heart went dreaming . . ."

"Swinburne!" Scotty said scornfully. He was clever enough to combat Gene at times. " 'My heart'—ha-ha-! 'Dreaming'! Good old stuff!" But he'd made a bad mistake—for Gene was quoting Richard Middleton.

But Gene did not hear him; again he paused; again that absent search. . . .

"I am only a dream that sings,
  In a strange large place,
  And beats with impotent wings
  Against God's face,
  The darkness is all about,
  It hides the blue,
  But I conquer it with my shout
  And pierce it through.
  And the golden cities rise up,
  Till I am as space,
  And the earth is my drinking cup,
  And my resting place. . . ."

Scotty was hurt, staring gloomily at his feet while Gene recited. But Hutch woke and listened and I saw real love in his eyes. Hutch had an inner integrity, a sort of inner purity under his tough newspaperman appearance. He worked on one of the big newspapers uptown during the day, supported his family, but at night came down and rehearsed at the Provincetown Theatre. He died very suddenly the following year and I remember what a great shock it was to Gene and to me too.

It was about this time that the door opened silently and the owner of the apartment came in. I cannot remember his name, or who he was, hard as I try, for we never went to his place again. He was quiet and dark and moved noiselessly, and I remember getting the impression that nothing that happened made any difference to him or interfered with what was going on in his mind. He spoke to Gene and Hutch—but pointedly ignored Scotty, who then rose up and took his box and left with sarcastic dignity.

I felt the cold coming through the chair, through the floors and the walls, through my coat and into my bones, and must have shown it, for Hutch asked me if I wanted more coffee, and went in to try and make it. Gene and the other were seated, speaking to each other only at intervals, and so I got up and went back to where Hutch was, and sat on the bed watching the little blue flame heating the pot. . . .

Suddenly Gene, tall and menacing, stood in the door between the two rooms. Then I felt his hand heavily on my shoulder and I was pulled to my feet and pushed through the door to the other room and left standing there, dazed, not knowing what had happened. The quiet dark man raised his eyebrows slightly, then lowered them.

"Have a drink?" he said, rising and holding a glass toward me. Gene had seated himself again. This time I gulped some of the awful stuff, shivering. I could feel it warming me as it burned its way down my throat. A moment later Hutch came in with a cup of coffee, and I swallowed that also and then sat down in the willow chair.

Gene sat there expressionless, without saying a word. Hutch was calm, as if nothing had happened. He didn't say anything to Gene except that he had to get uptown. In spite of our host urging him to stay and sleep on one of the couches, he took his hat and turning up the collar of his overcoat, left us. The quiet dark man picked up a newspaper and started to read it.

Gene was silent. He looked tired and bitter and sick, and after a moment he got up and went into the next room. I heard the bed creaking as he lay down. I just sat there, feeling the temporary warmth of the liquor and the coffee, not able to think. The dark man offered me a cigarette, saying nothing; I said something about this being very inconvenient for him but he told me it was all right, he was used to sleeping on the couch. He pulled out an old, moth-eaten bearskin carriage robe from a closet and sat regarding it, and then Gene called me and I went in.

He was lying under a tumbled quilt that he had tried to pull about him unsuccessfully. His overcoat was on the floor beside the bed. I lifted it up and placed it over him. "Lie down!" he said, and I did, not even taking off my coat, for the cold was penetrating everything, and I could see my breath in a faint vapor as I lay there, hearing Gene breathing beside me. The only light came from the next room, and I could hear the dark man groan as he wrapped himself in the bearskin robe before he turned the light off.

Gene was motionless lying beside me under the heavy cotton quilt, which seemed to have an unpleasant quality of its own, damp and smelling of mildew and spilled beer. He turned over, without saying a word, his face to the wall. After a while I pulled the overcoat that covered him partly over myself and got as close to his back as I could, for I was suffering from the cold, and that must have warmed me a little, for before I knew it images of places, and faces of people that I had never seen were forming behind my eyelids. Then I was asleep.

A faint light was coming through the window when I awoke. I could see Gene's head close to the wall, as if he had not moved during the night, and as I slipped out of the bed I tucked my part of the overcoat against his back. In the next room, completely covered by the bearskin robe, the dark man slept, snoring. There was no mirror; I combed my hair as best I could, straightened my coat, and put on my gloves. I was not sure of just where this place was or just how to get back to the Brevoort and I hesitated, wondering if I should awake the man on the couch and ask him. Looking out through the window to the street I saw that it must be ten or eleven o'clock. I stood there in a sort of daze, wondering what I should do. I did not want to wake Gene, and he would probably sleep for another couple of hours.

I couldn't stay here either; the same restless nervousness that had wakened me made me want to leave. I wanted to walk along the street and feel the snow crunching beneath my feet and yet something made me long to stay. *If only he was awake*—— And, standing there in miserable indecision I felt I could not leave until I had spoken to him—at least to tell him that I was going. . . .

"*What are you doing?*"

I turned and saw Gene standing in the doorway. His eyes were burning; he was pallid and he needed a shave. I remember that he was wearing his dark blue high-necked sweater, salvaged from his trip to Southampton as an able-bodied seaman, under his coat. He gave me a dark look. "Where is my portfolio?"

I did not know and somehow I felt panicked by this question. We looked around the room, and then I saw that it had slipped down behind the end of the couch. I picked it up and handed it to Gene. He looked inside, smiling scornfully to himself, threw it in on the bed, and then picked up a glass, two thirds full of liquor that had been left on the small table. He stared at it —and then with a shudder he drank it. I had my hand on the door but I did not open it, wondering what he was going to do. I only had to wait a moment until after the liquor had burned down his throat.

He began talking and I stood there listening to him, amazed and shocked and yet somehow untouched. He began a tirade against me, couched in language that he had learned at sea and in the dives of the waterfront and I listened for a while and then opened the door and went out.

3

In looking back over what I have written and trying to place events in the order, more or less, that they occurred, nothing much has been said of what we talked about when we were together, either alone or at intervals between the conversation of others. It was, among other things, the charm of his words and voice that tightened the net in which I was being caught. His speech was often hesitant; pauses or intervals in which, if one listened, one caught the meaning of what he could not put into words.

The war was going on and he talked about that—or rather against it. With bitter sarcasm he told of how he had taken long lonely walks across the Provincetown dunes and had been arrested by two Secret Service men and held for a short time as a spy. There seems to be a suspicious attitude in the United States against people who take long walks. A year or so later when Gene and I spent the winter in the Old House in Ocean County one of the old neighbor women with whom I was friendly hesitated and then confidingly asked me if Mr. O'Neill didn't take drugs?

Gene retained not only a certain scornful bitterness tinged with humor about the Provincetown episode, but a certain defiance as to what he would or would not do if any similar encounter turned up. It was wartime and he was not in uniform and looked of draft age. He was secretly conscious of this, which, looking back, seems a queer streak in him. I don't recall if he had a draft card exempting him because of his tuberculous record or not, but because of that he certainly would have been exempted. I think the only disillusionment about him at this time (which of course I put quickly out of my mind) was when one afternoon two officers in uniform came into the back room of the Golden Swan and began looking around—obviously they meant business. I was sitting with Gene at a corner table and somehow expected he would rise up and denounce these people, as he had often said he would do should they approach him.

They did approach him and began questioning him, or asked for his draft card, I forget which, and with a queerly disappointed feeling I saw him immediately become overfriendly—

although when they first entered I had seen a somber tightening of his lips, accompanied by a quick swallowing. . . .

He was ashamed of this, I know, though he did not try to explain it, and it was that night he got very drunk and some of the Hudson Dusters gang having come into the back room he decided to join them and become their leader. It all ended in a big fracas, with Harold de Polo "bottling" someone in Gene's defense.

He talked also about people, about Hutch Hapgood, Mary Pyne, and Terry Carlin, whom I hadn't met yet and who was to be a part of our life for a long time; and about Jig and Susan, and others who were members of the Provincetown Players group: but again this is strange, it does not seem to me that he spoke too much about those who were really closest to him. For his conversation about people would often seem to be the release of a certain sarcastic enjoyment of their actions and motives—perhaps he was following out some pattern about life or people which was working in his mind. Life was a dark, sardonic thing, lit with alcohol and bitter dreams, and he was the poet, with "vine leaves in his hair. . . ."

Thus Spake Zarathustra . . . This book had more influence on Gene than any other single book he ever read. It was a sort of Bible to him, and he kept it by his bedside in later years as others might that sacred book. In those early days in the Village he spoke often of *Zarathustra* and other books of Friedrich Nietzsche, who at that time moved his emotion rather than his mind. He had read the magnificent prose of this great and exciting man over and over again, so that at times it seemed an expression of himself. I have some copies of Nietzsche that belonged to him, which he bought and read before I knew him, and which are copiously marked. . . .

Gene often carried in his pocket a small blue volume of poems he had purchased that fall, for I found that book too, recently, with *Eugene O'Neill, 1917*, written on the flyleaf. The cover had been chewed by a mouse, and there is a cigarette burn on the outer edge. Some of the pages are clean and white, others have been much read. . . . This book brought back much to me, and with a certain sadness . . . and there was a sense of discovery too, for as I read them again, after this long time, it seemed to me that those poems he loved best in the book really dramatized something of himself as he was then.

He would read and quote these poems often, and now it gives me a strange and rather disturbed feeling—as if I see Gene himself, know him again as he had once been. It disturbed me because I began to wonder which *was* Gene and which was the poem—was it that the poem expressed him and what he felt? Or had he read the poem and from it created an image of himself?

This is not exactly fair to him, because it happens to most of us—that we find or read something at times which expresses to us what we *are*, or exactly how we feel about something, about which before we were inarticulate. These poems of Richard Middleton's—how many people know about them, or read them now? They seem beautiful to me, and then again I am not able to judge, because I am influenced by their being so much a part of O'Neill. . . .

It was from these poems of Richard Middleton's that he quoted that night, while Hutch, Scotty and I listened. . . .

4

After returning that morning to my room at the Brevoort, my confusion was worse than it had been after the party where Gene turned back the face of the clock—but of a different nature. I was too tired to even try to think. I took a bath and lay down on the bed to try and get together, into some shape, my feeling about what had happened. . . . When the telephone rang I was not going to answer it; then, alas, did there not come some hectic feeling that maybe *he* was calling, that he wanted to tell me that he was sorry?

But it was Christine. . . . I listened, wishing I had not answered. She had tried to get me the night before because she was anxious to tell me about a place she thought I should take—

a small two-room apartment—but I'd have to decide right away. (I had told her that I didn't want to stay at the Brevoort any longer, and to see if she couldn't find a place.) I listened but it didn't make too much of an impression on me—perhaps I was too tired.

I lay there thinking of many things Gene had said to me—about people, about himself. A colder and more realistic picture of him seemed to come to me, and this frightened me and made me very unhappy, for I didn't want it to be so. A part of me kept saying, *This isn't true, this isn't so, he is all you think he is.* Yet I thought of many things. I remembered too vividly the time the two men in the Hell Hole asked him about his draft card. I recalled a remark he had made in the same place, mockingly perhaps—but was it true?—what he wanted in a woman was mistress, wife, mother, and valet. I recalled his ironic and unkind comments about supposed friends—people to whom he was charming when face to face.

I thought about his work—what had I seen of it? *Ile, In the Zone* . . . a small volume of plays called *Thirst*. Why had I been so certain and confident of his genius? Was I wrong? Had my feeling for him deceived me? Then I remembered the poetry he had quoted the night before and how he had moved me. I recalled things he had told me about his Honduras trip, and about being at sea . . . and I weakened.

Then I thought of last night again—that speech, those bitter, exacerbating words. Where had they come from—what did he mean? He was full of spite—even of hatred. Looking back over the evening I could find no reason in what I had said or done for the way he treated me. I wept. . . .

I can't take this sort of thing from him, I thought fiercely, getting up from the bed. The thing to do was to move out of here, get the apartment that Christine had mentioned and not see him again.

It was after four o'clock when I dressed and went down to the desk after calling Christine. I had definitely decided to take

63

the apartment anyhow, though, to be truthful, I had not, I'm afraid, made up my mind as to Gene.

Before I could tell the clerk that I was planning to leave he handed me a bulky manila envelope, slightly soiled. I opened it, and seeing that it was a typed copy of the *Moon of the Caribbees* I took it upstairs, forgetting to tell the clerk my intention of leaving, and took it from the envelope. There was no letter—only a poem by Middleton, written in pencil on a small piece of paper.

> *I am only a dream that sings*
> *In a strange, large place,*
> *And beats with impotent wings*
> *Against God's Face.*
>
> *No more than a dream that sings*
> *In the streets of space;*
> *Ah, would that my soul had wings,*
> *Or a resting place!*

5

The Moon of the Caribbees. . . . I saw now an enchanted double of the man I knew. An image removed and lonely—surrounded by color, lights, and strange beauty, so that I, reading the words of the script, which seemed more a poem than a play, was a part of that luminous light and color and sound. . . . Outside, the snow, pale and wet, fell damply and pointlessly through empty city air, and the walls of the small room shut me into a new claustrophobia, and I knew I did not belong there; there was another world, something . . . Yet there was something luminous and excited and full of wonder within me, in my body as it were, and without thinking I pulled on my coat, and still without thought crossed Washington Square through the aimless snow, over the wet soggy pavements —to Fourth Street. I went into the Golden Swan, knowing he would be there.

I opened the door quietly: he did not hear me or look up. There was a small empty shot glass on the table before him, at which he was staring; and beside it a glass of water in which bubbles broke. Then he raised his eyes from the glass and fixed them on the flyspecked white swan floating in the painted lily pads. With sudden pain I observed the uncertainty and restlessness with which he looked at the passive symbol of that somehow sinister place.

"*Gene!*"

He saw me and the sadness vanished with his sudden surprised smile, as if doubt and unrest had suddenly been blown away. I went over and sat down beside him.

"I just finished reading *The Moon of the Caribbees*. Oh, Gene——"

I could not say any more, but perhaps what I felt showed in my voice, for he caught my hand and held it in both of his. Then the uneasy, tortured look came back into his face, and he said uncertainly: "You're sure you didn't come here to see me about what happened last night?"

"I never thought of it after I read *The Moon*. . . . I had to come over and find you and tell you how wonderful it is. You don't know how it has affected me, Gene—you've got to get away from New York. You've just got to get away to some-place where you can write."

I remember now his long pause, wondering if I had said too much, what he was thinking about. At last he spoke, but it was without looking at me.

"I have been sitting here fighting something out with myself. I don't want to go anywhere alone. I can't go anywhere with-out you. I *know* that now—since you came in. Since I saw the look in your eyes."

I was unable to speak. What did he mean? For as he finished speaking his lips pressed together in a solemn, almost stern look.

"Last night—this morning, wasn't it really?—I hated you. You with your great eyes that half the time are looking at something that I can't see! Jealousy is nothing but hatred. I'm very jealous—I've found that out recently. I was sore about your going into the room and sitting on the bed and talking to Hutch. I——"

"He was making me some coffee. The bed just happened to be there. It didn't mean anything." For a moment I thought Gene imagined I'd sat on the bed with the idea of luring Hutch to sit beside me.

"No—the bed didn't mean anything!" he continued, with a sort of mocking bitterness. "Not later, either!"

"Listen," I managed to say at last. "It's not that you mind Hutch, who's one of your best friends and who's never given me a really personal glance and you know it. You call it jealousy, but it's really that you aren't sure of yourself!"

He looked up from the empty glass, watching me with that same uncertainty.

"You aren't even sure about *me*. And that's the most ridiculous thing that ever happened in the whole wide world! Haven't I *shown* you? I've been chasing you, idiot! If you really knew me you'd know that's something I've never done before. And will never do again!"

He said nothing for a moment. I saw his face soften a little. "You are the only one who can make me sure of myself—sure about everything."

He looked at the envelope with its rubber band lying beside me on the table. He was leaning back against the chair now, away from me. "There's something else. Do you remember what I said that first night? I haven't forgotten what I said then—because I meant it."

"I haven't forgotten either."

An old woman stood at the door. She came in silently and crept past the table where we sat. She pulled out a chair and emptied the contents of an old tarnished embroidered bag on the beer-stained table.

"The next day I went to Christine's, thinking you might be there with her," Gene went on. "I didn't tell her this, but she started talking about you. She has great intuition. She seemed to think you were a wonderful person. I kept watching the door, thinking you might walk in and wondering what I would say to you. Then Christine got up—we were sitting at a table, nobody else was there, and she was drinking a cup of coffee—and went into the kitchen. I heard her pull out a drawer, and the sound of her searching through papers. She came back with an old *Evening World* in her hand. It had that article about you on the second page, with your picture. The picture made you look like a washed-out nincompoop! *'No money in milk cows says woman dairy farmer who's made a brave fight'!* Woman dairy farmer—Ye Gods!" He gave me a hard look. *"Down in New York to help the poor farmers win a milk strike—young widow has supported herself, a baby, and a herd of cows by her pen——"*

I remembered something and laughed, rather wickedly.

"That picture got me eleven proposals by mail, one handsome young milkman called on me with a box of candy and his bankbook, and a man in one letter said that he had eleven children and knew I was a fine woman because I looked like Abraham Lincoln!"

"Your mole, no doubt," said Gene sardonically. "It's in the same place as *his* was!"

But my little attempt at reprisal didn't help much; I saw Gene's face grow heavy and his low voice had a note of contemptuous self-pity.

"A dream came back to me that night when I first met you. It was a dream of my childhood—when I had to dream that I was not alone. There was me and one other in this dream. I dreamed it often—and during the day sometimes this other seemed to be with me and then I was a happy little boy."

"But this *other* in my dream"— he paused, looking at me, —"this other I never quite saw. It was a presence felt that made me complete. In my dream I wanted nothing else—*I would not have anyone else!*"

As he hesitated, I could see him watching his thoughts, trying to be sure. His fingers tightened unconsciously and clenched in the palm of his sensitive hand. Then he said: "I am right. I would have resented *anyone else*—this other was so much a part of myself."

I was listening, aware and almost identified with him, and it seemed as if I knew and understood the child he had been.

"*You* brought back this dream. No other person ever has. No other person ever will. You were the *other* in my dream. . . . I felt, after I left you that night, that I had always known you and that you were a part of me. It was the same the next morning. But I didn't want to go to the desk at the Brevoort and ask for you. I didn't even want to telephone you." He gave his sudden boyish smile again. "Maybe I just wanted it to happen that we—well—ran into each other! Without my having appeared to have done anything about it. The point however is—I wanted it to happen. That was why I went to Christine's. . . .

"After that I felt that the dream was impossible. You had seemed to me alone and virginal and somehow—with nothing but yourself. I wanted you alone . . . in an aloneness broken by nothing. Not even by children of our own. I don't understand children, they make me uneasy, and I don't know how to act with them."

This long conversation, which had confused and almost frightened me, for I could not see where it was leading, had the effect now of making me speechless. I looked over at the old woman, who with bony hands was picking out and separating the assortment of trash that she had emptied on the table before her. She took up a small stone, stared at it for a while with her rheumy eyes, and put it aside.

Gene got up and came back with two drinks and sat down again. I had the feeling that he didn't even know what he had done—or that he had left the table.

"There's more to it," he said. "God damn it, I want to get this over with! I've just been through a year and a half . . ." A pause—this was not finished. "That is all over now. It was torture to everyone concerned. That day at Christine's when

68

she showed me the article I made up my mind I would not go through anything like *that* again. I felt immediately a terrible jealousy of this farm—this other life of yours, and the fact that you had been married to another man and had a child by him. I looked at your picture and the caption over it and I laughed. Christine looked shocked. She didn't understand that I was laughing because it would be easy now—pretty damn easy —to forget you! She told me that you'd be at the party Saturday night. I decided I wouldn't be there, but after getting potted that night I changed my mind, thinking it wouldn't make any difference to me whether I saw you or not. I got myself into a state where it seemed nothing made any difference. Then I deliberately and drunkenly turned back the hands of the clock and sang that goddamn song because I saw you and wanted to hurt you. Everyone thought I was thinking of Louise. I wasn't—I was acting a part. I knew they'd whisper about it—some kindly soul would be sure to tell you that I was suffering because of Louise. They saw the way you looked at me when I came in. Nothing is ever missed. I wanted to hurt you—but after I got back upstairs here and lay on the bed and couldn't sleep I saw that this action of mine pointed to a truth!"

The old woman had picked up the stone and was turning it over in her fingers, peering at it as if she was looking for something. *Where did she get it? I will give you a stone and on it will be written a new name.* She pushed it beside two letters that looked as if they had been read many times; she held up a tattered clipping printed with bars of music. Among burned match ends and bits of broken cigarettes, she found some change. She carefully pushed two dimes and five pennies in a small pile at one side of the table. . . .

"If I had convinced myself that you were nothing to me, if I had felt nothing, I wouldn't have made a fool of myself that night. But I couldn't escape you. I tried to pay no attention to you, to absorb myself with other people, with other things."

He looked at the drinks on the table before us, which had not been touched.

"But you crept into my soul, and at night, alone, I heard your voice and thought of your hands being laid on my forehead. Last night I wanted to seduce you, to possess you—though under the circumstances, and in that place it would have meant nothing to either of us. I wanted to consummate the physical act because I thought it would free me from you. I hoped that then you would be just another woman. But I could not bring myself to this low subterfuge. And when I saw you leaving this morning, saw you even had your gloves on, I hated you with a fierce hatred. You were unattainable—because I saw that, I tried again to hurt you."

I put my hand over his. His face grew pale and I could feel his flesh trembling.

"I have thought of nothing but you since then—of you and me. Again I've gone down into my private inferno. For all your sweet ways I am not sure of you. How can I be sure of myself when I am not sure of you? I want it to be not you and me, but *us*, *one* being not two. I want you to feel that as deeply as I do. And this must be my life—*our* life—from now on. I will build my house not on sand, but on a rock."

The old woman made a swift movement. Her toothless mouth working, she swept all the objects which she had been sorting back into the tarnished tinsel of her bag.

"Now I have no choice. What *is*, *is!* I'm going back to Provincetown after Christmas. Is it possible for you to get away—to go up there?"

"Yes, it is," I said.

In the silence that was between us Lefty appeared, a dirty towel over his arm. He signaled to Gene. "Want a drink?"

"Not right now—we're going for a walk."

He looked down and saw that my shoes and feet were very wet from walking across the square. I was shaking, or shivering, but not from the cold.

"Your feet are wet! What's the matter—haven't you got any other shoes? Those look as if they had danced all night in all the sordid places of the world."

"I'll get some others," I said, wondering how. Gene looked away, toward the swing door of the bar, but he was seeing something else.

"The snow is very deep at Provincetown. Often it lies in the streets for weeks. . . ."

6

I moved over to Waverly Place. There was a large room, rather dusty, with a double bed and a couch along the wall, a boxed-in kitchenette, and another small room hardly more than a closet. The bed was covered with a faded blue spread. The only light was a bulb in the center of the ceiling, and I put my typewriter on a small table near the dingy window which looked out on a small empty court. I remember a feeling of happiness when I got my things in and was alone there, perhaps it was the little dingy kitchenette, for I went out at once and bought coffee, sugar, and milk and other things, and made myself a cup of coffee and sat there alone, drinking it.

Among my first visitors was Mary Pyne. It would have been too much of an effort for her to visit me at the Brevoort, for she was not well then but here on Waverly Place she felt I was a neighbor, and she wanted to see me and, I found out, talk about Gene O'Neill, for it seemed that the story of what was happening to Gene and me had spread around the Village.

"I only want to ask you this," she said. "I want to help you to see things as they are." Mary Pyne had a deep vision and peace within her. She never spoke with hurry or pressure. I realized that it was only because she felt close to me and concerned that she spoke at all. "You are in love with him, I suppose?"

"Yes, I am."

"I know what that would mean to you," she told me. "But you have to protect yourself in some way. I hear that you are thinking of going back to Provincetown with him when he goes. Do you know what that means?" No, I said, I didn't, not understanding what *she* meant. "I can only put it this way," she said. "Gene, here, is not the person he is in Provincetown. In other words, if I met a man under the circumstances you have met him, seeing him as you are seeing him, I could not persuade myself to believe or take seriously anything he said, any plans, however definite and urgent. He, now, is not exactly Gene, his mind is running around in a hot circle, and I don't know if he even sees what he thinks he sees. . . ."

"It's not as bad as that."

"I have seen him when he is not drinking and you have not. To begin with—how do you know that he is not still in love with Louise Bryant?"

"I don't know. He has never talked to me about her—not yet."

"She will come back from Russia and want him back. She is much more clever than you, and they were very much in love. That is"—Mary smiled—"if torture is love. I sometimes think Gene enjoys being tortured. What you will give him is something else, but he may want to go back to the pleasure of being tortured."

"I don't know anything about it," I said, feeling empty, and yet sure that my friend was wrong. It comes back to me that the point Mary Pyne was making was how could any woman take seriously what a man who was constantly under the influence of alcohol said to her. I protested to her that this was not so, that it was only *sometimes;* that he went to the rehearsals of his plays and was usually very quiet, if not a little bit somber; that having the room available at the Hell Hole—— But she interrupted me to say that I had not seen Gene when he was not drinking, and that she was thinking of me, not of him; that she had talked it over with Hutch and they both thought she, being really detached from everything, should talk to me about it. I think she saw me as having spent the past few weeks in and out of bars with Gene, up all night, and so on, becoming involved in Gene's loneliness and self-torture. *But it isn't all like that!* I tried to explain, and then she asked me if I could really believe that Gene loved me, for I had no doubt implied through all this that he did. I could only think about the shoes, and that I must get some if I was going to Provincetown, and she told me of a place on Sixth Avenue where they were cheap. . . .

Perhaps there is no point in my putting down this conversation with Mary Pyne at all. But it has remained strongly in my memory of these past days when other things, more interesting, perhaps, are obscure and much is forgotten. I think it made an impression on me then because of what she said; the advice she gave was so wrong and there was no way I could explain this to her. She was so fine a person, so sincere in her judgment, the fact that she was trying to help me made it much more important than it would have been coming from anyone else. I think it shows that the convictions of the heart are the right ones; one *knows*. There was no question of choice; no planning or plotting, putting one advantage against another disadvantage. One acts without choice, without the pain and delay of thought, for there is no choice.

She gave me a picture of Gene O'Neill that I did not understand, although to her it was the true one. The only advantage she had was in knowing him at other times, a fact which she repeated several times. This did not bother me, if anything it filled me with expectation.

7

Waverly Place remains indistinct in my mind, though there should be a sort of halo around it; but there is an element of the ludicrous which overcomes other memories. I was trying to finish a novelette, so as to get a check. I would get up, make a cup of coffee and propped in bed, continue at the point where I had left the troubled heroine the day before.

After an hour or so of this, I would sit at my typewriter and, with two fingers, type what I had written. I could not hear the noises of the street; everything was quiet. I silently cursed writing, remembering that I had said the year before that I would rather scrub floors than do what I was doing.

No doubt any interruption was a pleasure to me though I had the need of the check firmly in my mind. So when Dorothy appeared about ten o'clock one morning, I greeted her with warmth. She had not been seen around for a few days; but now she told me she had not been to bed all night and needed sleep. I remember she brought a great big yellow grapefruit in a bag. For, no matter what happened, she always ate a grapefruit in the morning and urged others to do so. She looked gaunt but firm, and rather annoyed me by treating me in a superior way, telling me to get along with my typing. She would lie down and sleep. This she did, but not before telling me she had just left a church that she found open at an early hour that morning.

Gene had been over the evening before and stayed until after eleven. He hadn't said anything about drinking or going out for a bottle, but had a cup of coffee and sat there telling me about a play he was going to write. He had done some work on it before leaving Provincetown; now he talked about it and his face became alive as he spoke of his characters and the meaning behind the play. He talked for a long time, sometimes getting up from the couch to walk up and down the room. I had become excited by the story of the play and did not notice, in that quiet room, how late it was, until he suddenly stopped and said he'd have to have a drink—we would go over to the Hell Hole. I hesitated, thinking of my work the next morning. Not expecting that even for a moment would I consider the matter, but that I would be only too eager to go with him, he said; *Oh, all right!* gave me a slow sarcastic look, as if to say I didn't understand anything, didn't understand at all; and before I could stop him the door closed and he was gone. I almost put on my coat and followed him; but, following some old pattern of inhibition, I had stayed there, lying on the big bed and wondering what he was doing, until at last I had fallen asleep.

I sat at my typewriter, determined to impress Dorothy with the fact that I was a professional writer and had work to do. I was thinking of how I had not gone with Gene the night before. Suddenly there was an emptiness inside me; I said: "How did you know I was here?"

"Oh, Gene told me!" Dorothy said, closing her eyes. She opened them after a moment and looked at me with strong calmness. "He's going to meet me here this afternoon around four o'clock. . . ."

It is beginning to bore me, thinking of this, although when first recalling it, it struck me as very funny. I have to tell about it because in a sense it leads up to Louis Holliday's death. Dorothy at first suggested that she stay with me and pay half of the rent. I was adamant and used my writing as an excuse; then she said she could give a lot of ideas.

But her only idea was a deep and increasing and, I am sure, a very real and important interest in Gene O'Neill. She could no more resist this than she could resist those sudden and unexplainable impulses to go into any nearby Catholic church and sit there. She had no religious background, and probably this impulse was as obscure to her then as it was to her friends, who only considered it amusing—Dorothy's way of dramatizing herself when she was not singing "Frankie and Johnny."

Who knows what strange elements or signs or portents were working in her? Only a few months ago I saw her picture in a newspaper article—a strong and benevolent face. She has become a renowned mother to the poor and destitute, giving them food and shelter within the fold of that religion which must have been beckoning her in those empty churches, where the Eucharist symbol of purity and love was always on the quiet altar. I could not recognize much of my Dorothy of the "Frankie and Johnny" days but sometime I shall go down and see her and ask her if she minds my bringing all this back. . . .

My little place became a *ménage à trois*. Gene did not give up his room at the Golden Swan, of course, but he began to spend more and more time with me. Dorothy would appear, often very late, and lie down on the bed fully dressed and go to sleep. I would lie down beside her after a while, and Gene would still be sitting on the couch, still talking. Dorothy once said Gene just *had* to have someone to listen while he talked and he never stopped talking. . . . In the morning Dorothy would ask where he was, as if I had secreted him somewhere. This went on with many variations. I don't know what Gene thought —but he was drinking less and talking more about his work.

Another play of his was going on; and after that he insisted that he wanted to go back to Provincetown. The idea of *Beyond the Horizon* was occupying his mind, and he wanted to get to work on it. I told him about the farm where I had lived for a while. He asked me many questions about it, and it seems to me now that *Beyond the Horizon* is laid in that countryside although he never went there, and the idea for the play, as Harry Kemp had told, originated on the beach of the harbor of Provincetown.

Once he left behind him a volume of Strindberg's plays that he had been reading in the apartment. Gene considered the author of *A Dream Play* and *The Dance of Death* a greater and much more profound playright than Ibsen, whom he liked to belittle as being conventional and idealistic. He lost that copy of Strindberg, but in the spring of 1920 (after he won the Pulitzer prize for *Beyond the Horizon*, with its check for one thousand dollars) he bought, among other things, a new copy of the book containing these two plays.

Gene was very impressed by Strindberg's anguished personal life as it was shown in his novels (*The Son of a Servant* and others, all autobiographical); particularly of his tortured relationship with the women who always seemed to be taking advantage of him—even his cook, who maliciously boiled all the good out of his food. These novels Gene kept by him for many years, reading them even more frequently than the plays. I don't know—but I imagine he had the same feeling of identification with the great tortured Swede up to the time of his own death.

I knew nothing about this playwright, but when one night, a little drunk, he read *Miss Julie* aloud, losing himself in the sound of the words and their haunted meaning, I was able to understand what Gene meant. He read passages from *The Confessions of a Fool,* smiling with sarcastic sympathy. Dorothy, interested, came with a tale of Madame Strindberg herself being in town (and was it then or later on that she managed to meet her and told Gene of her impressions . . . ?)

Dorothy would sit in a sort of trance when sometimes Gene would recite *The Hound of Heaven.*

> *"I fled him, down the night and down the days;*
> *I fled him, down the arches of the years;*
> *I fled him, down the Labyrinthine ways*
> *Of my own mind; and in the mist of tears*
> *I hid from him . . ."*

She even managed to get him to recite the poem one night from beginning to end at the Hell Hole while the Hudson Dusters listened admiringly.

8

Sometimes Jamie would come down looking for his brother; sometimes Gene brought him over to Waverly Place, and they would sit down and talk about their past life and of their adventures with women and wine. Often they would refer, with humorous, tolerant fondness to "the old man," as they called their father, James O'Neill. Jamie was always trying to get extra money from his father by some cleverly worked-out scheme—which never worked. Once in a while they would speak of their mother with affection—they called her "Mama." Jamie told of how she would get up at five-thirty in the morning, take a bath and get dressed without a sound, afraid of waking "the old man," slip out of the room and down the elevator at

the Prince George and go to early Mass across the street—
praying (as Jamie said, "on the side," but implying to us that
it was her most important prayer, and diverted her attention
from Jesus himself) that her husband would be asleep when she
returned, for he disliked being parted from her for a moment.

I got an impression of Gene's mother that was never to
change and I longed to meet her—and wondered what she
thought of her two strange sons. For Jamie I had a real fondness.
No matter what he had been through in one of those long
nights of his, longing for a bottle, or even having it there, he
showed up the next day with that smile of the sardonic Punch,
and a loud "What ho!" neatly dressed, well shaven, and,
though his hands were shaking and there might not be a quarter
in his pocket, viewing life as a stale joke that still intrigued and
held him—a joke that he wanted to share with others.

I had an impression of strength from Jamie. He never com-
plained, he never intrigued against others, he never looked sad
or blamed himself or anyone else, and if he lived in the past, it
was with irony. The world was his oyster and he had eaten
it, and that was that! He was all of a piece, unique, not vulnerable any more, exactly what he had made of himself and what he
was. Never did the Punch mask drop—but never did he make
you feel a mask was there.

Gene was happy with him and lost much of the somberness
that at times overcame him. I never thought of this before,
but it comes to me now and it may be significant, that Jamie
was the only male human being with whom Gene felt completely at ease *all the time*—without self-consciousness. Without
self, as it were.

*And this leads me to realize that I don't, even now, know
what, in his unspoken thoughts, was Jamie's idea of his own
brother, or what he really thought of him. . . .*

He had ideas, of course, of what Gene should do or not do;
that superficial and mocking advice that he loved to give him,
then and later. He appeared to like me very much and urged

Gene to give up any memories of any other females and cling to and cherish this new wild Irish rose. Nor did he seem to feel that I was interfering in his relationship with his brother; but when Dorothy appeared he would gaze at her with silent, baffled curiosity.

9

The cold continued and even grew worse, and my mother wrote me that they were completely cut off by the great piles and drifts of snow, but managed to get the mail and groceries sent up to the letter box at the foot of the hill. But she was taking care of everything and I mustn't worry, they were keeping warm, using up the pile of wood outside the shed door: best of all, as the road wouldn't be passable for a month or so, William Jones couldn't come around and raise the devil about that note—not till a thaw came. She wished, however, that we had never bought the other cows, for even though they were dry they had to be fed, and the manure froze behind them before she could get it cleaned out and they were now standing at an angle of nearly forty-five degrees. Foxes were coming close to the house at night and once they thought that they heard the howling of a wolf in the distance. She told me that the baby was fine and hadn't even missed me, it was much better for her there, and again, not to worry. She was going to write a mystery story herself and send it out, about a strange woman who lived on a big farm across the Housatonic River.

My mother said that she could see across the valley the light that was on at this house all night, illuminating the garden and the grounds; and the tale was that the woman had driven her husband away with her cold behavior and was living there with the hired man in sin. But rumors had reached her that her husband had returned and was lurking in the hills, and so she kept the grounds bright with the new electric lights that she had strung up outside; she had even had the evergreens around the house cut down so they would not be surprised, and the lover had to sit all night with a shotgun, instead of the lady, in his arms.

She would, she thought, end it with the neighbors—who were a little in awe of the whole ménage and also disgruntled and obnoxious about what it was costing to burn all that electricity whereas most of them had only kerosene lamps, becoming aware after several more months had passed that it was now the husband who sat at night with the rifle across his knee or on his arm, waiting for the strange and aloof wife and her hired-man lover. It now turned out that the wife and the lover had disappeared—no one knew where or how or even when, or if the husband had killed them and buried them under the wisteria vine which that spring began to grow and bloom prodigiously though it had never bloomed before; or if the husband had simply taken over and installed himself one night when, driven by desperation or perhaps boredom, the lovers had gone for a walk in the woods. And the husband was now waiting for them to return—would they? Or perhaps the woman would return alone? If that was to be the case, what, my mother wondered, would be the motivation for this return? Nothing, of course, but the love of the austere lonely house and the farm felt by the strange and aloof woman who was willing (perhaps glad, who knows? my mother added) by this time to sacrifice both men to her moods and needs. She could go inside after all was over and the two corpses had fallen side by side on the ivied lawn to be picked up and buried by the county, for there was neither murdered nor murderer any more and she was free. She could go inside, where she would turn out the electric lights and cut the wires and draw the bolt across the door, never again to look on the face of a man. . . . They might find her, my mother added, tranquil and full-blown, with a strangely satiated look on her strangely satiated face—like a female Dorian Gray.

But there were too many complications to *that*, she wrote,

unless she did it as a macabre tale—she rather preferred the strange and luxurious vitality of the wisteria vine. This could point out to the husband after a number of dazed years that there was no point in sitting there any longer with the shotgun. . . .

But my mother never wrote it, of course, which was a shame as she was really interested in it. Particularly when a year or so later, the lights having been burning all the time in the farm across our valley, she heard that the bill for the electricity got so enormous that a collection bureau that had taken over the account went to collect, broke in the door, and found the place had been deserted for months.

Do you remember, she added, how the vine at the end of the Old House suddenly began to grow after never growing for fifteen years?

I laughed, remembering her strange, almost pixyish way of liking to scare us just to laugh at our fears. I was relieved, too, for I had neglected writing to her and was beginning to feel guilty about it, but not guilty enough to sit down at the typewriter and do it. I had not told her, nor did I like mentioning it now, about Gene. They had not heard of him, nor of the Provincetown Players, I was sure of that, for the theater did not figure in our lives. Mary Pyne would not have written about it; probably she thought that it would all blow over and I would see the light. My reasons for not mentioning Gene or my plans when I did write had been rather obscure; but I think that they were based on the fact that a year or so before, I had, in some fit of madness or romance, allowed myself to become engaged—engaged, no less, because he insisted on it, and talked of being married in St. Patrick's Cathedral—to an odd young man with a distinguished and romantic Irish name. He had been in the war since the beginning and had been gassed. A few years later I received a telegram telling me that his plane had crashed and mine was the name he left to be notified. They had not cared too much for him, and somehow I was reluctant to mention to them that I was interested in someone else with an Irish name. . . .

10

I did not go back to the farm on the hill for Christmas, and I do not recall much about that Christmas in New York, except a general impression that people were moving in and out of the Village. Harold de Polo came down for one hectic week from Woodstock, where he had left his wife Helen and their two children. I met Lottie O'Neill, who later that year came to visit us in Provincetown. Saxe Commins was there, and Charles Demuth arrived for a visit from his home in Pennsylvania—both of these men later became the greatest of friends. Harry Kemp . . . Edith Adams and Hutchins Hapgood, who was writing a book about her, appeared more frequently. Many others . . . I was with Gene a great deal and these people were all friends of his.

I managed to get a lot of writing done, though this often meant leaving earlier in the evening than the others, many of whom liked to stay up late—as Gene in those days always did. It was necessary that I have at least some money ahead when I left New York, and that wasn't too easy. I wasn't spending too much money. I went to the place that Mary Pyne had told me about on Sixth Avenue and sitting there bewildered by a whole assortment of fantastic shoes (which would have suited a demi-mondaine better than me), I finally chose two pair which I later had to discard. I'm afraid I wasn't too practical—but I was happy.

One day I went up to see an old friend of the family who liked me to keep in touch with her. She was a charming stout old lady, widely read and amusing, and she had lived for many years quite alone in one of the few beautiful old houses left on Twenty-third Street in the Chelsea district, taken care of by the two trimly uniformed maids whom she had had ever since I first remembered her. She poured tea for me in her long drawing room and gave me kindly advice about my writing; she felt that I had talent, but that I should devote it to doing something serious and important. She had known Talcott Williams, dean of journalists, in his Philadelphia days and through him had met my mother, and my mother's sister, who at the age of nineteen had astonished the literary world with a brilliant and promising novel about a revolution in South America. She had not particularly approved of my first marriage, her idea being that a woman who wanted to write should go off somewhere by herself, study and write and do nothing else. She explained that it was different with men—they could always find women who would devote themselves, give them good meals, keep visitors away, and see that no household or even business details bothered them. The only other answer to the problem of a woman really interested in the literary life was to attach to herself another female who would take everything off her shoulders just as a wife did when it was the man who wrote. She looked at me with such kindness and affection when she said this that for a moment I thought she was going to suggest that I come and live with *her*, not realizing that not for anything would she have given up her solitary life. What she did was to suggest (to my great surprise) that she subsidize me for two years while I devoted myself to nothing but writing a book—*any* book, although she thought if I had nothing definite in my mind I might do a lot of research and find it most amusing and interesting to write an intimate life of Dean Swift.

I was deeply touched by this and her way of expressing it, and tried to show my gratitude, at the same time explaining rather lamely that I was involved in other things and couldn't very well accept her offer. She told me that she kept part of her income untouched every year in order to use it for something she was interested in: she did not urge me any further but said as she kissed me good-by to let her know if I changed my mind. . . . I hurried back to Polly's restaurant where I was meeting Gene for dinner—I don't think I ever told him of our old friend's kindly offer.

11

Polly's restaurant . . . it must be a familiar memory to many people who went to Greenwich Village in those days. Writers and painters went there to discuss their problems as well as to eat the good food that was served at a reasonable price. Polly Holliday dominated the scene—tall, dark-eyed, and calm, with an interesting and receptive mind, she gave her place the air of a club, and the people who went there didn't think of it as a restaurant. . . .

It seems to me that the Holliday family were in some way connected with the O'Neill family in the sense of being old friends. Adele Holliday had been a protégé of Otis Skinner—who was probably a friend of the elder O'Neill. She had been on the stage for a while, then given it up to marry and to give birth to two children, Polly and her brother Louis. Polly, at some time when money was scarce, had started a restaurant. Her brother Louis had been a friend of Gene's for years.

It was Louis' return to Greenwich Village that put an end to what had become an almost static time for everyone . . . a doldrums where nothing happened and action of every sort was being put off. It was, as I remember it, after the holidays, and everyone became excited and alive when the news came that Louis would return and there would be a celebration. Gene was very pleased and gay when he heard it and went to the Hell Hole the day Louis was expected back and started celebrating in the late afternoon. Unexpectedly Charles Demuth came in, bringing Eddie Fisk, another painter, then others, and when I went there to meet Gene at six o'clock there was a very convivial crowd.

We were supposed to go to Christine's that night for dinner. Christine also knew and loved Louis Holliday and she was starting a celebration at her place and with many nips of gin getting herself very happy, flushed of face, and moist-eyed, for she loved to cry with happiness when she was drinking. Gene, Demuth, and I arrived there and had dinner. Gene talked and did not eat. Dorothy and some others came in, and everyone was waiting for Louis, who at last arrived—a beautiful strong young man, full of health and vitality, tanned and clear-eyed from his year in the open air, good food and hard physical work. I have never seen anyone so at the peak of life, so confident and happy. He had conquered. He had come through—and tonight he was going to see his love again and this coming week they were to be married.

He had called Louise, his girl, on his arrival, but she said not to come up to her apartment—she would meet him later in the Hell Hole. Louis told about this jokingly—it did not bother him at all, for he knew Louise! She was testing him—she wanted to be sure! If, with the drinking and the memories and the old friends, he still stuck to his promise and did not drink, then she would know that the future was secure for them both. Louise had been testing him all along—and this was the final test, and of course she could depend on him.

It is to the credit of all of Louis' friends that not one of them offered him a drink; not even a final toast was drunk to the ending of the past and the beginning of a new life. They were all deeply pleased that he had accomplished what he had set out to do. From then on, the evening began to take on a pattern of movement and confusion. We all went back to the Hell Hole—other acquaintances of Louis' were already gathered there, some of them rather sinister-looking. Louis was having a wonderful time, not taking a drink, and as the time drew near for the arrival of Louise, he kept watching the entrance.

She came at last. . . . I remember seeing her and Louis sitting alone at a table, talking, while the noise and crazy songs and conversation went on around them. I can see them, even now— Louis eager, holding her hand, pressing it in both of his across the table while the dark girl listened and smiled with a curious sort of detachment. I remember, for it was the last thing I saw there that night. I had waited because I did want to see Louise. It was now after twelve. It was all too much for me—even before this I had felt that I must go home. Gene wanted me to stay but it was impossible, I was beginning to be overcome with a sort of uneasy fear, a sense of frustration and despair. He walked to Waverly Place with me and then left—saying he wanted to go back and be with Louis again.

I was lying in an exhausted sleep some time later when I was aroused by Gene's voice. He stood at the door a moment, as if groping and afraid—and my awareness of this was deepened when he did not reply to my questions. "Turn out the light!" was all he could say, and without even removing his overcoat he lay down on the bed, reached out to me when I lay down again and held me tightly, his head on my shoulder. *He is just very drunk—can't manage,* I thought, going off to sleep again myself, but I don't believe he slept at all. For, about three o'clock, I was awakened again (the door was left unlocked) and Dorothy stood there, looking down at the two of us— Gene crumpled in his overcoat, clinging to my hand like a lost child who has found its mother.

There was a strangeness about Dorothy's appearance; she gave the impression of being disheveled, as though she had forgotten about herself and even who she was. Her coat was unbuttoned, her hair damp, her face very pale. Something had happened, I knew that at once; and as she stood there, something was happening to her again. For a moment she looked at Gene as if he were a stranger; there was an emptiness in her face, as if some sudden knowledge had shocked her into awareness.

"So you're *here!*" she said. It seemed as if all her young vitality had left her. Gene just stared at her gloomily. "I tried to get you at the Hell Hole. Louis is dead," she added emptily. "I knew he would die."

Gene got up, then sat down on the bed, fumbling at the edge of horror, refusing to be aware of it. I could not understand,

86

but I could see he knew exactly what Dorothy was talking about.

All at once calmness—purpose and some deep understanding —came from the young girl standing there.

"I came to get you," she said to Gene. "You must go back with me to Romany Marie's. The police came. The coroner was there. But I," she said, taking a small container of some white powder from her coat pocket, "have this. The verdict was death from a heart attack." I got somehow into my clothes, longing to understand some part of what had happened. Dorothy became even paler and I saw her grimly wiping tears from her eyes. But she refused to say anything more. I gave her a comb and she ran it through her hair. Then the three of us went along the empty silent street, with Gene holding tightly to my elbow. I was bewildered and shaky, still not knowing just what had happened. Dorothy strode silently beside us, and Gene said not a word. Then at the corner he stopped and stood there. He did not look at either Dorothy or me, but there was suddenly something strongly belligerent about him.

"I'm going back to the Hell Hole!" he said in an anguished and now firm voice, as if he expected us to oppose him. "I'll see you later."

But Dorothy did not answer him. She held to my arm as if she could not now be any longer alone, and we watched him walk swiftly away. Then, crossing the street, we went without any words between us to Romany Marie's restaurant and up the flight of steps. The first thing that I noticed was that there was complete silence in the building, instead of the usual noise of talking and the clatter of dishes. When we went in the room appeared to be empty. There was no one at the long tables, and we stood a moment at the door. Dawn was just breaking outside and the pale light of day was already coming through the windows. I followed Dorothy to the other end of the big room where two policemen stood nonchalantly watching us. On a chair, with his legs stretched out before him and his head bent forward on his chest, was Louis Holliday. I thought he was asleep, and it was a moment before I realized from the motionless rigidity of his body and the translucence beneath his tanned skin that he was really dead.

One of the policemen greeted us, and Dorothy began talking to him in a low voice. I saw again how strained and unhappy she looked. I stood there silently regarding the dead man. A window had been opened by someone to let the cold fresh air into the room, and a breeze blowing in stirred his hair, and the dark damp curls over his forehead moved as though they at least were alive, so that for a brief moment it seemed to me that he must be aware of the wind and the dawn outside, until I realized again with added poignancy that he *was* dead, that the joy and confidence had left; that the flesh was in some unseen way preparing itself for dissolution.

After a moment Dorothy turned toward me, and we went back down the steps to the street. It was light by now, the thin silent daylight of a winter morning was all that the dawn had left and we walked down to the corner of Fourth Street and Sixth Avenue where a few cabs were lined up in front of the building owned by old Wallace. The doors were closed, but Dorothy knocked, saying she heard voices inside. No one answered. The cabbies slept in their seats, waiting for the bar to open, and Dorothy suggested that we get some coffee in a small cafeteria nearby while we too waited. As we turned to go, a certain shifty, rather elusive friend of Gene's appeared at our side and insisted on going with us. He had been there the night before, and he tried to talk to Dorothy, but she neither saw nor heard him, being absorbed in some inner world of her own.

Spilling tepid coffee into his saucer, P—— told me that after I left the Hell Hole the evening before, Louis got up suddenly from the table where he had been sitting with Louise, and with his face adamant went into the bar and ordered a double brandy. Louise rose too, and left at once, without saying anything to anyone. She had broken the news to him that she was going to marry another man. After two more brandies Louis announced this fact to everyone there and bought drinks for the house for an hour or more, or until closing time, using the money that he had saved for Louise. The party had grown very noisy and confused, and Louis sent out for some shifty character that he had done business with when he was in New York before, and a certain narcotic had passed into Louis' hands. He had concealed this carefully from everyone, and when the bar closed they all went upstairs to finish the evening in Romany Marie's restaurant. Gene and Dorothy and Louis and Charles Demuth were sitting together—Louis drinking, and passing from a blatant forced gaiety into a deep and introspective silence.

P—— had finished his tale, rather aimlessly, at the point where they had all arrived at Romany Marie's; and Dorothy, perhaps aware of my unspoken inquiry, began to tell me what had happened then (still ignoring P——, who sat there with rabid excitement on his thin face).

Louis had suddenly seemed to be quite himself, as if he had solved some problem; he half smiled at Gene, and, glancing at Dorothy as if sure she, too, would understand, he removed a small glass container from his pocket and quickly swallowed some sort of white powder. They did not understand, at first, what had happened.

"What—about Gene?" I was still confused. "He left. It was obvious that Louis was dying. Everyone left except Demuth."

That was why Gene had come to me. . . .

"He died in my arms!" said Dorothy, with awe and a questioning wonder in her eyes, and then she wept briefly and went to the door to wait for us. She had not mentioned that without thought of her own safety she had jeopardized herself by concealing the drug from the police, so that if there was any suspicion, no proof was ever found. When we joined her she was calm and there was a strange peace in her eyes.

12

When we got back to the Golden Swan the door was unlocked and Gene was sitting in the back room, drinking Old Taylor. He had a pint bottle of it, half empty, in front of him on the table. There were others there, but I saw only him, and with consternation, for he was in very bad shape—the worst I had ever seen him. He looked through us with torpid coldness and then took another drink from the bottle. He did not want us there, he did not want to leave, he did not want to be disturbed, and when Dorothy asked him to come with us and get a grapefruit and a cup of coffee he only gave a sardonic laugh, for he was unable to talk. After leaving us, Gene had come back to the Golden Swan and started drinking with old Wallace; he was drinking still and nothing was going to stop him. He did not want me or anyone else around. He was going to drink himself into oblivion and no one was going to stop him or penetrate the alcoholic barrier behind which he was determined to be alone. We sat there in helpless silence, not wanting to stay and yet afraid to leave, for it seemed that, in spite of the somber and unnatural quiet that he was maintaining, at any moment something violent and destructive might break forth. . . .

As the news of Louis' suicide leaked out, others came in, some of those who had been there the night before, and there was a subdued excitement and painful and furtive questions asked. It seemed to me that there was fear, a sense of being complicated or involved; a certain movement toward getting away and keeping out of sight—a feeling that the question was going to come up as to where and from whom Louis had got the narcotic that he had so fatally taken. Polly appeared, sinister and cold, and stood staring around in search of something that she did not find, and went out again, without a word, and without even looking at Gene. . . .

There seemed nothing to do and I left, accompanied by Dorothy, who walked a couple of blocks with me and then

suddenly left me, going off down a side street. I do not know
if she went back to where Gene was or not. The sunlight was
bright and hard now, and objects and people seemed to me like
falsely colored pictures, pasted against empty space. It was
after ten o'clock. I got back to my place, unlocked the door,
locked it again, and, pulling a blanket up, lay down on the cold,
empty bed. I did not dare remove my clothes and I did not
want to go to sleep but, exhausted, I slept. When I awoke I saw
from the fading light in the thinly curtained window that it was
evening again.

13

The suicide of his friend and what led up to it did something
to Gene; brought to him more than grief and the usual images
and words of destiny, Fate, *life's a tragic blot on the fabric of
time*, and so forth, that lesser things evoked in his mind. He left
the Hell Hole and stayed for a while with his brother at the
Garden Hotel. He became gentler and more quiet, and one
day he came to my place and suggested that he and I arrange
to go down to City Hall and get married. I thought it over and
told him I thought we should wait. I believe my feeling was that
it would not be fair to him or to me to get married just then—
that we should wait until we were both in a more serene and
marriageable mood. I saw him becoming more and more irked
against whatever it was that prevented him from leaving the
city. He was in very low spirits, and for the first time I saw him
object to anyone whom I might see or be interested in. Once he
packed his bag and brought it over to leave with me, saying he
was going to get tickets on the Fall River Line boat. He had just
received an unexpected check and he left in a taxi to do this, but
I did not see him again until the next afternoon. He was still
drinking and I realized that he would not be able to stop until
he got to Provincetown, and wondered if he would ever get
to the point where he would not allow some unexpected event
to interfere with his departure, either something that occurred

at the theater, or some need to help a friend. He decided one morning to stop drinking—then he would get away.

He bought the tickets and again packed his bag, borrowing another which he packed with books. He helped me close my suitcase, and went out to say good-by to a few people while I straightened the apartment and put a few things I had forgotten in my handbag. He came back and we got a taxi and started for the pier where the Fall River boat docked. It was a long and, for me, upsetting ride, with Gene sitting beside me, his lips pressed together, very silent and strange—and I feeling that he was a stranger whenever I managed to look at him. I did not realize what was wrong until we got on the boat and to a state-room, where he produced a bottle of Old Taylor, and with shaking hands swallowed a large drink. The ordeal of the ticket office and the packing and saying good-by and ordering the cab—all of it had been too much to face: perhaps in the taxi he did not want me to know, or perhaps he was oblivious of me and concentrating on himself.

At last the lines were cast off and the boat turned in the river and we were leaving the shore. . . .

Flight into Snow

That word *flight*. . . I wonder about that word, and why I used it. It came to me, and it sounded and looked all right, and seemed to express something I felt about this trip to Provincetown. But, considering it, there seemed to be something wrong about it, and I found that there was an implication of running away, or escaping. That was not true in any sense, and I was puzzled, as one finds in writing that the spontaneous word or sentence, coming without conscious thought, is often the right or true one.

Thinking about it, and how we both felt at the time, I realized that the word itself, "*flight*" had another meaning; the flight that has purpose—such as birds make in migration, or the sea gulls winging against the wind and sleet, beating their wings to get back to shore. So, let it stay. We were human beings and could not fly. Although sometimes I thought, as I saw Gene watching the sea gulls, that he envied them their oneness with the wind, and their freedom.

We arrived at the little Provincetown station, weary, and yet, when the train finally did stop, excited. The trip in those days (though one could also make it via Boston) was from New York to Fall River on the old Fall River Line, where one waited for the slow train that seemed to stop at every station on the Cape. It seems to me that Gene must have written to John

Francis, his landlord of the previous summer—it was Mr. Francis who met us at the train.

He was a big, kindly man, and I recall his look of chagrin and embarrassment when he saw that I was with Gene. But this changed to relief after he had inspected me, though for a moment he seemed lost in thought, as if deciding what to do. He was too tactful—particularly in dealing with artists and writers—to say to Gene, "I thought you would be alone." He got us and our bags into his small car, Gene in front, and in a couple of minutes we were at the studio apartments, which I believe some cousin of his had put up the previous year to accommodate artists at a reasonable price, many of whom used to go to the town's one hotel, which now had on the veranda the famous sign, *Dogs and Artists Not Allowed!*"

"Here, Gene," said John Francis, inserting a key and opening the door. "It's just what you want!" He went for the bags while Gene and I looked around the room. It was not large—perhaps sixteen feet square, with windows high on the north side, and none beside the door, giving privacy. There was a couch covered with an Indian blanket beneath the windows, a small kerosene stove for cooking, a tiny sink, and wood stove, a long deal table.

"I can put up shelves for books," said John Francis, returning. "And—look!" He glanced upward, and we saw a balcony with solid railings that one reached by a narrow flight of steps at the end of the room.

"Comfortable bed up there, and so on. Here's where you work—down here." Then, looking embarrassed at having made a suggestion, he added shyly, "unless you like to work there and sleep here on the couch. It don't make no difference to me."

"It's wonderful, Mr. Francis." Gene's dark eyes were glowing. In spite of the strain of the trip, he looked happier than I'd ever seen him look. He unbuckled a strap, opened one of the two valises filled with books. I noticed that John Francis had not brought my bag in.

He said: "There's a place exactly like this next door—except the couch cover's different, and no cookstove. I could get one—but maybe she'd like to cook in here. Won't be no offers to rent till spring, so I'll let you have both for the price of one. Or," he added philosophically, "maybe you'd rather move the stove in there. Then you won't be disturbed at your work by no cooking odors." He beamed—innocent, childlike and wise. . . . "I just as soon not have to buy another stove right now."

Gene put a match to the papers and kindling in the little stove and added some of the wood piled neatly on the floor beside it. Mr. Francis showed me the adjoining studio and put my bag on the floor. "That Gene is a wonderful fellow—a real genius. I never seen anybody work like he does—when he's working." I, too, was included in John Francis' aura of kindness. I have a feeling that he regarded us as sort of babes in the wood. . . .

Perhaps in spite of everything we were—who knows? Anyway, John Francis took care of us; he left to bring back a box of groceries and some meat, after inquiring gently of me what to get. He filled a five-gallon kerosene tin and brought that back too, and then tactfully said he'd see us later. When he closed the door behind him we looked at each other and then Gene came over and put his arms around me. We felt new and innocent—childlike, with all that fresh happiness of an exciting adventure that children have. . . . Outside, the snow had begun to fall; we saw the large flakes falling silently on the window, and we clung together, but not like the babes in the wood to be covered gently by the snow, and never awaken.

"Come on, cookie—cook!" Gene said, laughing. "How about a prune omelet—how's that for an idea?" And he began unpacking the groceries and arranging them on the shelves over the stove. . . .

2

We never moved the cookstove into the other studio. Gene's hours for work, once he started, were so regular and his absorption in it so deep that, propped up on the bed in the balcony, a writing board on his knees, he never heard or noticed what went on below him; he liked to come down the narrow wooden stairs when he had put down the last line of his morning's work in that small, firm handwriting, sometimes with the last written sheet in his hand, and talk to me about what he had done, while I fixed the lunch. The typewriter we did move over, and as I recall it, most of his clothes were in my studio too, although when later on he began typing on his script he moved the typewriter back, and, borrowing a secondhand card table from John Francis, worked in the lower room.

The snow fell silently all that first afternoon and night. Once in a while we would open the door and look outside at the small houses of Provincetown, half hidden by a blanket of white snow, and breathe in the mingled odor of fresh dampness and the water smell of the harbor, which we could not see now, but which Gene told me, his arm around my shoulder, was just beyond another street. There was a subdued excitement and love in his face as he spoke of it, and he said he would take me to see it as soon as it stopped snowing. I think his only regret was that our place was not right on the bay, on the other side of Commercial Street, where he could hear the waves lapping at night when the tide came in.

But the snow did not stop; it piled silently against the door, and only a pale and translucent light came through the north window, and the little stove needed few logs, so warmly and with such quiet was the snow covering us and the town.

John Francis came by about six o'clock, and we heard him shoveling away the snow from the door and path before we heard his gentle knock. Gene got up and turned on the light. We had fallen asleep on the narrow couch, his arm around me and my head on his shoulder, watching the wet flakes build a ledge against the window, tired out from the long trip on the train, and for a moment I did not know where I was. . . . John Francis brought us extra blankets, and a shovel, and a Boston newspaper—at which we never even looked, not even the next day. He stayed a moment, worried because he was afraid Gene had wanted to go out and couldn't, and said he himself had a bad time getting down Commercial Street, the snow was so high there. He left us after asking again if we had everything we needed, and if we would be all right. After he'd gone, Gene stretched his arms high and throwing back his head gave a loud cry of joy that startled me.

"God!" he said. "My God—how wonderful to *be* here!"

I was to get to know that cry well—that shout of mingled triumph and relief, because when at last a play or work of his was finished, always during all those years when he wrote so many, right up to the finishing of *Strange Interlude*, that sound would announce his satisfaction and joy. . . .

3

Let's cook, cookie. . . . *Let's eat.* . . . What we had came out of cans, and he opened them and set two places at the table, and then, solemnly, he took a large drink from the pint he had brought along on the trip, making a face as he did so. That and one other pint, which I think he got somewhere in town, was the last of the drinking. He spaced these drinks meticulously, and considering the four or five months he had spent in the village, not eating too much, it seems remarkable that within two or three days this man was no longer shaky, or ill in the morning from the effects of the quart or more he must have been drinking each day. Nor, when that pint or so was gone, did the thought of another drink enter his head. . . .

The next day after breakfast he finished arranging his papers, his work, and unpacked the big carton full of books that John Francis had held for him at the store. I, too, did the same thing, and then we began the joyous adventure of deciding what we had to buy—typewriting paper, yellow sheets too, carbon paper —black. Erasers, ink—oh, all of it! And *he*, it seems, must have at least a dozen number 1 yellow pencils—and a pencil sharpener, the kind you put on the wall. He thought that he had left one among his books and papers in the box at Francis', but it wasn't there, and after we were married and moved into Francis' Flats he found it on the wall, where he had left it the summer before. . . .

We made out a list, and then Gene looked over the groceries on the shelf and put down some ideas for more things we might get in that line too.

"We better get some cans of soup—plenty of soup now, for me. Then—in a couple of days we'll really have some good fish— oh! Right out of the briny!"

He couldn't get the door open, so completely were we snowed in. So we heated water and poured it on the snow, getting an opening for the shovel. The sun was out, but the snow had stopped falling, and before long we heard a snowplow coming along the street. . . .

4

There is a saying that a happy country has no history. . . . This period of our first few weeks in Provincetown does not now bring me many incidents or happenings to tell about. I recall as in a dream, the long main street of the town—and icebergs. Yes, if no one believes it—I have found some old photographs, showing them edging up along the main street, having floated in from the harbor.

It was a long walk from where we were to John Francis' store, but it seems to me we took it nearly every day. On one side was the harbor and the icebergs, and the smell of the sea and fish and salt hay, little houses or wharves and beyond them the spars of boats; and beneath our feet the pavement was rigid with ice, and great old trees creaked and moaned as we went along. . . . Gene wore some sort of a combination woolen muffler and cap that came almost to his nose, and coming back with a bag of groceries and the paper we would hold onto each other to keep from slipping.

I remember, too, walking alone along the street one night, with the moonlight lying over everything, and in my mind composing a sonnet—about something far away. . . . I remember walking back one evening from the nearby part of town with Gene, and he hesitating and halting in his talk, and saying there was one thing he wanted to tell me about, or something he should explain to me, that would make everything perfectly complete between us, or add to his pleasure, but I can't remember what this was, only that he was very halting and hesitant and unsure. . . . I don't remember any worries or troubles or anything that interfered in any way with the work that was going on in that small place. I suppose I was getting to know a different Gene and loving him more than I had in New York, and he seemed every day and all the time to love and care for me more and more, and I know he wrote a most enthusiastic letter about me to his father and mother in New York; for he read it to me, after spending an afternoon writing it, and I was completely taken aback at his description to them, of this wonderful girl-creature whom he wanted them, before too long, to meet.

I, too, wrote to my family; but as I recall it, everything was all right everywhere and there was nothing to take us out of this co-operation of work and living.

Gene had worked out more completely his outline for *Beyond the Horizon*, even making little drawings and plans for the sets, and was now writing the play, walking in the afternoon, and either reading or working (preparing the next day's work) in the evening. We went to bed about eleven and got up early so that after breakfast he was at work by nine or nine-thirty; and after doing a few little things around, probably deluding myself that I was keeping things tidy, I'd get to work too, writing on something or other.

This thing of "work" was truly co-operative; and I don't think there was a single flaw or holdup in it anywhere. Gene thought that what I was writing was too good for pulps—and wanted me to do something else. But the big and important thing to me then was Gene and his work; and although I had in mind, and started working on a piece called "The Philosopher's Night," I was really entirely absorbed in and held by Gene's play. . . . He discussed it, made changes sometimes, and read to me every day what he had written.

I wish I could remember now what books he was reading in the evenings, but I don't. Nietzsche, Strindberg—he kept these always with him, discussed them and quoted from them. . . . But I mean what other, newer books?

We got a periodical called *The Freeman*; perhaps even then we subscribed to the *Manchester Guardian*, which we enjoyed for several years.

5

I don't think at this period he read quite as much in the evenings as he did later on. Usually, besides the books to which he was devoted, he read in connection with his plays, either the one he was doing, or one he had in mind.

We had a lot to talk about, but it was not until later (that summer) that he really began to talk about his past. . . .

I have a photograph of Gene and myself, taken outside the door of our place. It must have been one of those fine warm days that come sometimes in the Provincetown winter, for he is wearing a sweat shirt, and I, my hair blown about, am seated on the step in the sun. He looks happy and contented, and I think he must have put on some weight; but even this snapshot does not show his charm and unusual good looks. His great dark eyes were unusually expressive, and I had never seen or touched such beautiful hair. . . .

It seems to me that I must have been finishing some novelette or other, or maybe got a check from one of the saucy pulps before I left. I remember at that time Gene's income consisted of fifteen dollars a week, sent by his father.

But money does not seem to enter into any of my memories of this time, neither lack, nor thought of it at all. . . . Except when, unexpectedly, *In the Zone* went into vaudeville and our intense excitement at the unheard-of wealth of fifty dollars a week. I don't remember if this was before or after our marriage.

I must have counted on selling—or did sell, let's say—a novelette every month or so. . . . I do remember wishing I could spend all my own writing time on "The Philosopher's Night" and I'm ashamed to say now that I just don't remember if I typed any of Gene's manuscripts for him. I probably didn't, as I have a feeling he was better at typing than I was. . . .

It was about a week after we moved into the studios that there was one abrupt knock on the door, and then silence—as if to say, *if you're busy or occupied at something interesting, don't bother.* . . . However, we weren't; and I think the young man who stood there when I undid the chain latch knew this, so convenient a moment had he chosen to present himself. When he introduced himself as our neighbor in the end studio, we understood this, and Gene and I laughed about it later . . . for the partitions were very thin, and I am sure, although this was the first time we had really seen him, he knew as much about us as we knew about him. He was tall and thin and brightly colored, like a Frans Hals. His nose was a bit red from the cold, and he seemed rather meager of flesh inside the large overcoat which he pulled about himself. Just at that time—though we didn't know that about him—I don't think he was getting quite enough to eat, although he was always more than generous to the little Portuguese boys that ran errands for him. He came in and we had a lot of fun talking to him—he was witty and amusing and regaled us with some wonderful local gossip.

It was he who, a year or so later, painted a large portrait of the two of us, during a Provincetown winter, with Agnes sitting on a sort of gilt sofa, and Gene standing morosely behind it.

Lytton, for that was his classic first name, was very tactful, and, though we did not see him too often, we always smiled understandingly when we passed him on the street or ran into him making purchases in John Darrell's drugstore. So when he suggested that we meet a very pretty and bright-looking lady, with charming blond-gray hair and a gay, kind little face, we agreed. We had seen them together several times. At least, that I think is how we met Alice Woods Ullman, who later was to be the solitary witness at our wedding. . . . Lytton told me afterward that one reason she wanted to meet us was that she felt *she* at least could and would do something about our getting married; giggling, Lytton told me privately (I think he was always a little in awe of Gene) that he had already confided to her the gist of some conversations he had overheard through the wall. "I heard Gene talking about you getting married, but nothing seemed to happen! And Alice was *so* interested—she felt you were meant for one another!"

This was true, and I think one reason we delayed was that it seemed so complicated when we were so busy. Gene longed now to get married, but I think he may have dreaded the sort of detail and personal exposure that it would put him through; probably having to take a pen and write something when his hand always shook, and having to utter *yes* or *no*, or answer a lot of questions. Or, perhaps—which is likely—it was that he—or we—were embarrassed at trying to find out how, in that town, to go about it.

However, Alice Woods was, like Lytton, most tactful, and we were soon dropping in for tea at her charming small house and more or less confiding in her. She was, I think, at that time writing a novel of her own. She had been married to a famous painter, lived in Paris a long time, had two boys away at school, and had lived a most interesting and vivid life, after being brought up strictly as the daughter of a well-known and conservative judge. She gave us the warmest and most disinterested friendship, and we in no way felt that she intruded on our privacy.

7

Our privacy *was* broken at this time by a most unexpected visitor from New York. Actually we both enjoyed it, as it did not interfere with Gene's work at all, and I was interested and somehow touched. I still can't imagine how she happened to come to Provincetown in the dead of winter—and alone at that.

I can almost see her now—poor pretty, fragile Lottie O'Neill. Where is she now, I wonder? What idea or impulse made her leave the warm and chaotic nest of her small ever-welcoming bedroom in New York, and take that long and lonely trip to the land of fish and icebergs.

She only stayed a few days, stopping at the Atlantic House in a state of constant concern over "bugs" and "flies" and dirty towels, or Portuguese men peeping over her transom at night (though there were no Portuguese peepers, and the reason for the famous sign about dogs and artists was because dogs had fleas, and artists soiled the towels by using them as paint rags). I do not want to give the impression that Lottie was an agitated or concerned person—she wasn't at all. She was in a sort of detached, even mysterious, vacuum all the time.

She was not only pretty, she was lovely, like a bell made of glass which gave off a tinkling sound when you touched it. She told us about the imaginary bugs and peeping Portuguese in the most detached manner, as though they were minutiae which had filled the nights of someone else, not herself. She walked down an icy, wet, snowbound street in a pair of pale alligator French-heeled shoes to knock at our door, wearing a tiny hat, draped with a dotted veil, which tilted up with expensive art to emphasize the charming line of her retroussé nose, and a thin jacket of faded fur.

Lottie was always poor, in fact at times quite starving; once Gene and I had gone to her room near the Brevoort to find her cooking a hot dog in a small frying pan over a can of Sterno, although some friend or other had left not long before and there was still the disorder of love in the room. We had gone there trying to find the Harold de Polos, and although Gene had known her for perhaps a couple of winters, it was through Harold that I met her one afternoon at the Brevoort. I had not been able to make her out at first, and remember Gene had smiled rather ironically at my questions, but one afternoon I happened to run into her in Washington Square, and she calmly told me a story of her attempts to live in this (to her) somehow alien world that surprised me and touched me with pity. At that time she had been infatuated with Harold de Polo, seeing in him perhaps something she had never seen in anyone before— and even, as Harold's wife told me later—moving in with them when she was broke. . . .

But she seemed to have some money with her when she came to Provincetown, and she brought us an elaborate box of chocolates tied with a wide lavender ribbon with a flat bow. "Aggie," she said. "You can use that for your hair." She told us she had paid twenty-five dollars for the saucy tricorn hat at Tappe's— and then didn't have enough left to get a coat. She liked to talk about clothes, but not inordinately; she was always willing to stop and listen when anyone else talked, which I think Gene liked about her, because so many people thought when he paused or hesitated that he had come to the end of a sentence, and would go on with their own talk.

Lottie had a certain special feeling about Gene, caused by the fact that her name too was O'Neill, which in her mind seemed to almost make them members of the same family, brother and sister even, or at least bound together in some special way: for she had no family of her own, not a soul in the world that she knew of, though at one time she sentimentally invented an old

Irish mother—for Gene's benefit—and a truck-driving father. But these were transient phantoms and soon disappeared into the spaceless opalescence of her mind. I think Lottie was born of a young witch under a toadstool one night (who knows where) and grew up evading leprechauns and watching the fairies dance in a ring, so that her own head was filled with moonlight which never quite left her.

I think that it was Lottie who took the picture of me and Gene outside our door. She approved very much of our being together, but taking me aside one afternoon while Gene was working, she gave me some advice—which she seemed to think very necessary. I should brush my hair up, not down: take better care of my fingernails even if I *did* use the typewriter, because my hands *were* pretty and men loved nice hands, but *most* important (she had watched me and looked at me very carefully, even when I was in New York, and especially that night when we came looking for Harold), I had a habit of keeping my mouth partly open—my lips parted—and I must get over *that*. It gave me, she said, a sort of *look*— just what sort of look I'm not sure, but probably foolish or too absent-minded, or too expectant: I think that was what she was trying to imply, or get across to me without going too far.

I was astonished, but very grateful for this advice, for there was no doubt she was very earnest and had my interest at heart. I examined myself carefully in the mirror at the first opportunity, side-face as well as front, and came to the conclusion that she was right, and from then on I remembered this. . . .

Lottie left as quickly as she had come, because she said the bugs and the towels and the Portuguese were too much for her. But I believe it was the icebergs and the wind and the lonely street at night. We took her to the station and put her on the train, looking so slender and young and immaculate, with her soft pointed mouth and skin without a blemish or a line—and very little make-up, for she always liked to look a little pale, because it made her more interesting. . . .

I cannot get over the shock I had when one night later that

same year I went in to see her at the Lafayette Hotel, where she had, temporarily, a small room and she asked me how old I thought she was. She told me that she was forty. I thought of Lottie being in her early twenties. I couldn't believe her and stared in amazement, for forty seemed very old to me then—I think in those years, too, it was a more advanced age than it is now.

8

I must go back to our marriage—the ceremony and what led up to it. Dear little Alice Ullman, with her gay, pretty face and quick mind, had, as I said before, become interested in this matter, and although Lottie O'Neill's visit had kept us from seeing much of her for a while, it was she who helped us over whatever difficulties there were. There was a little Presbyterian minister whose home was not far from hers. If it was more convenient for us—and this meant Gene—he would perform the ceremony in the evening at his house, at nine o'clock. But we would have to let him know several days in advance. Then someone else had to be consulted (it must have been in regard to the license) and this was the genial, white-haired owner of the town's important drugstore—Mr. Darrell. Gene and I knew Mr. Darrell well—he always greeted us with genuine kindness when we came in to make small purchases. But it was Alice who consulted him about this solemn matter, and, to avoid embarrassing us with a conversation in the drugstore, she asked him to come over and see us, telling him that Gene's morning working hours were over by one or two o'clock. It turned out to be more embarrassing—particularly for Mr. Darrell—than if we had discussed the matter and given the necessary information to him in the drugstore.

Gene was in a particularly affectionate mood that day after lunch. Spring had come, the sun was hot on the shingles outside, little birds were singing and hopping along the branches of the elms, making love and looking for a place for their nests. We had the door open while we ate lunch, letting in all this warmth, and then Gene pushed it closed, stripped off his clothes—he never had any feeling about being naked—and splashed himself all over with water, rubbing himself hard and vigorously with the towel to dry off. He then grabbed me, despite some mild protests, and pulled me down on the narrow couch under the back window.

We lay there a while, talking, and then went to sleep, Gene deeply and I probably only half asleep. We were not aware at this time that Alice Ullman had already arranged with Mr. Darrell to come and see us. I probably did not hear the first knock on the door. Gene's arms were twined tightly about my head—and *he* certainly did not. (Mr. Darrell said he knocked two or three times.) I did hear a knock though, and decided not to open the door just then, feeling very comfortable where I was. Mr. Darrell, however, thought Gene was upstairs on the balcony and could not hear him, and as he wanted to get the matter over with—he was a very busy man—he pushed the door wide open and stepped inside, saying in a booming voice, "I've come to see about you getting that marriage license, Mr. O'Neill!"

That awoke Gene and he sprang to his feet, still stark naked, while I, I'm afraid, cowered abjectly on the couch, unable to make a move, but watching the tableau of the two astonished men, frozen into immobility, facing each other across the room. I don't think Gene knew just what had happened, but Mr. Darrell, backing politely toward the door, said to him, "Ah! I'm afraid I've come too early. But Mrs. Ullman said you would be through work by two o'clock. *Suppose we make it at half-past four?*"

Alice Woods wanted us to have dinner with her the night of the wedding and then go over to the minister's house, but Gene refused. So we walked alone through that soft, misty night of spring, through the town, beneath the dripping, still-leafless elms, as silent ourselves as the town was; hearing the waves moving against the wharves and anchored boats. A nebulous moon made a small circle of herself somewhere above the mist;

there was no light but the dimmed and silent lights of houses as we walked along hand in hand. The minister's house was brightly lighted as we came up and Gene looked around nervously, afraid for a moment that the gregarious Alice might have arranged something. . . .

We knocked, the door was opened by the minister's wife; Gene greeted Alice, who was in a small room waiting for us, with a grateful smile when he saw she was alone. Then there was some whispering and low talk, and, as I recall it, a sort of rehearsal—Gene and I being made to walk toward a closed door (behind which was the minister), after which Alice was to come in through another door. Anyhow, there was some sort of a ritual that had to be followed, and to my astonishment I saw that Gene was very patient and amused by it—it was I who was beginning to get nervous. I don't remember what I wore, but I guessed to myself that I didn't look much like a bride. I was so proud of Gene; he looked happy and handsome and seemed quite at ease. At last after some maneuvering the doors were opened. We went in and were greeted by a nice dark little minister holding a book. He rose from behind a table and asked us some questions, read some prayers—and so we were married.

Mr. Johnson—I think that was his name—congratulated us, and his kind wife offered us some cake.

Alice was delighted about it all and begged us to come to her house for a while; but Gene shook his head and said no, he had to be getting back now. I was pleased, as we walked back together, that this was his decision. The moon had broken through the mist, and there was a silvery and mysterious light mingling with the fog and dripping trees. We were strangely happy and secure and sure of ourselves, and everything else. . . . Though it had seemed, before it happened, only a ceremony that was to be gone through and got done with, we now felt that it had made a difference—that we had come into a new estate. I felt it in the proud way Gene held my arm. We were awed and deeply happy. For me it was perhaps a confirmation and for Gene it was a new and peaceful freedom—freedom to live, to become, to create. . . .

He told me all that and more the next day. He told me how proud he was of his father and mother; and how he wanted to make up to them for the many things he had done in the past, to make them proud and happy about him—*we* would do that, he and I. He talked of his love of the sea, and his hatred of drink, not as drink itself, but because of what it could do to his brain. He gave me a physical description of this, which I could see, as he explained it, actually terrified him. The brain was a texture like a raw white of egg, but enough alcohol toughened it like a cooked white of egg. "I will never," he said, "or never have written anything good when I am drinking, or even when the miasma of drink is left. That's why I didn't want to go to Alice's—she would, of course, have opened a bottle of sherry to celebrate our wedding. I might have been ashamed to refuse—might have thought it looked weak. Oh, love of my life, we need nothing, you and I, but ourselves. I have found my work, my peace, my joy. No—let me say it this way—I have found *myself!* I will not say to you, my love, as a poet once said, that I will pluck the stars of heaven to hang them in your hair— I say to you there *are* no stars in heaven, unless I *can* hang them in your hair. . . ."

. . . And, soon after that, he said, "Now that you are Mrs. O'Neill, I want to put our bank account in your name. You make out the checks and take care of all that—then I won't be bothered." He had opened an account in a Provincetown bank when the royalties from *In the Zone* began coming in. I didn't like the idea, but he insisted. Then he wrote to his family, telling them about his marriage to me; and once again what a wonderful person he had married. He had very nearly finished *Beyond the Horizon*, and for the first time he spoke of money in connection with it. He felt pretty sure now that he would get a five-hundred-dollar advance on it. He read all he had written of it aloud to me one afternoon. It is a great play, a *really great play*, I thought, silent and shaken with happiness. *Our* play, he said; and was going to even then start on the last act; but changed his mind. *Let's walk up to Francis' flats—we should move up there, darling, as soon as the weather is a little warmer. . . .*

I was living in the present, happy, expanded, transformed. The world was a golden haze, no longer alien, but an ally: nature, too, was sharing in my love, and was more than ever beloved. There was no sense of effort or strain to anything; there was no attempt to become anything, no goal of fame or money or living differently or better. There was no feeling at any time that there was something that *had* to be done, no guilt at things undone, for the past and the future did not exist as states of being, only as calendar marks of man's necessary measured time. And in that time there was rhythm that in itself was a delight. It came into being through the harmony of our life—night and day, morning and afternoon. We got up and ate breakfast and went to work, and in the afternoon took walks, and in the evening we talked or read. Gene was living in the creation of his characters, knowing their thoughts and what they felt, and it all came out in tiny inked words, beautiful in themselves, as he sat on the bed on the balcony with the drawing board on his lap or against his propped knees, his dark eyes absorbed, seeing something that was beyond the room. If I had spoken to him at those times he would not have heard me.

I, too, shared the lives of these people, of Robert and Ruth, old Mrs. Atkins, and the others. As he read aloud what he had written that day, we talked about the farm where they lived, and I told him again something of the farm I knew so well. Behind the people, and the farm, growing barren, was the feeling about life that he wanted to express—*that* illumined and shaped the plays (like a God standing behind him), coming out almost unconsciously through the people and the scenes. And, along with that, and an exciting part of it, too, it must have been, was the structure, the form of the play; and the theater itself, into which it was all going. He was happy in that, and sure of it too—very sure. He wrote the descriptions of the scenes as he came to them with as much creative absorption as when he wrote the dialogue: and as he read to me that the road was "*winding like a pale ribbon between the low-rolling hills; their freshly-plowed fields . . . The old, gnarled apple tree just budding into leaf*"; and of the field, "*from the dark earth of which myriad bright-green blades of full-sown rye are sprouting*," I never dreamed of how this would look in the painted props of the theater, and of the shock it would be when just two years later I first saw it, sitting alone without Gene in the theater.

9

Then one day a letter came from New York for Gene—from Louise Bryant. Gene gave it to me to read. When I had finished it I was trembling.

"What are you going to do?" I asked him.

Louise wrote that she must see him—and at once. She had left Jack Reed in Russia and crossed three thousand miles of frozen steppes to come back to him—her lover. Page after page of passionate declaration of their love—of hers, which would never change; of his, which she knew also would never change. She would, and had, forgiven him. What if he had picked up some girl in the Village and become involved? There was no use writing letters—*she had to see him!* It was all a misunderstanding and *her* fault for leaving him, for going to Russia with Jack. . . .

I was afraid—deeply afraid—for I saw some sort of uncertainty in Gene's face.

"I'll have to see her—to explain. I can't let her suffer like this. I can't do this to her . . . now!"

"*See her——*"

"I should go to New York, I suppose. After all, she made a trip of three thousand miles . . ."

"Three thousand miles of frozen steppes—yes! She knew

that phrase would get you!" Already this woman was invested, in my mind, with all the wiles of the serpent. I had read in her letter such assurance, such surety of her hold over this man. I had already begun to suspect that he liked to suffer. He was beginning to suffer already before my eyes, looking away from me, looking deep into himself. I could see him remembering all the dark passionate travail of their love. . . .

"She loves John Reed. She is his wife. She chose to go with him—not to stay with you!"

"You don't understand. She's not"—he hesitated—"there has never been any physical relationship between them."

"Oh, you fool—you *fool!*"

Why hadn't I told him *that* when he had related to me one evening the start of his love affair with Louise? Why had I listened quietly and understandingly, though privately I had immediately put her down as a very artful woman? Perhaps it was because I had wanted to protect him, not to destroy his belief in anything—even a rival woman. But at that time she was a figure in the past, a nonentity so far as Gene and I were concerned. Now she was a threat, living and possessive—ready to claim her own. Her pride had been hurt. She would stop at nothing. I recalled his story of that summer when he had arrived in Provincetown with Terry and a suitcase full of plays. . . .

She and Jack had a house here then. She was one of the group who read the plays and acted in them. Gene admired her—her Irish beauty, her charm, and her work. He admired Jack too, he had told me, almost loved him. He and Terry borrowed books, saw them at their house and at the meetings.

Then one day Louise had to go to New York. The night before her departure she came to the door with Gene and Terry as they were leaving her house and gave him a book, saying, "You will like these poems!" He did. But he found a note slipped into a page halfway through the book. It was in her handwriting! *Dark eyes. What do you mean?* He was astonished—and unnerved. Terry got a quart of applejack and they drank it together. Jack was his friend—who trusted him. And yet——

When Louise returned she knew he had found the note and that he was unhappy about it. She wanted him very much. He had for her that curious fascination that he had for many women. But she wanted Jack too. Gene watched her and Jack together—torturing himself; feeling now that he had loved her from the first. She tried to see him alone, although he was avoiding her. He was afraid. He had not been in love since the days of Beatrice, the unattainable beauty of his dreams. He would not betray Jack, his friend. . . .

But Louise sent a note to him by Terry.

I must see you alone. I have to explain something, for my sake and Jack's. You have to understand.

She saw him alone. He was told the secret no one must know: she and Jack lived as brother and sister. Jack was ill—he had put sex entirely out of his mind. He would understand and not blame Gene for this strange passionate love that she so needed. . . .

So it began. . . . Gene pitied her as well as admired her, and she became to him a great woman, something out of the old Irish legends, betrayed by life. Jack appeared to understand. He did not seem to mind. It probably never occurred to Gene to wonder what Louise had told Jack—or if she had told him anything.

On and on this had gone; that summer; that winter; another summer—Louise sharing herself, never willing to give up one for the other, confused herself perhaps, but always the pivotal person, beautiful, passionate and strange. . . .

10

I was remembering this story and watching Gene to see if I could get any clue to his feeling and what he was going to do about the letter from Louise when there was a knock on the door. I opened it, wondering who this could be. . . . It was the postman. He had another letter—special delivery this time. I handed it to Gene, recognizing the handwriting and afraid— very afraid now. He looked at it with some irritation and put it aside.

"I don't want to read it—*she's crazy!*"

But he did read it, and I could see that this letter upset him more than the first. He looked very gloomy and thoughtful.

"I guess I'll have to go down and see her," he said. "She'll never understand otherwise that it's all over."

"Gene, you can't! And I can't understand *you!* She calls— and you go! How will it seem to everyone? She comes back from Russia and you immediately appear on the scene. She just wants to show everyone she can get you back——"

"I don't give a damn how it looks! She's badly hurt—I can't explain what happened without seeing her. I can't make her believe——"

I began to weep.

"What's the matter," he said, with sudden surprised tenderness. "You're not afraid I'll go back to her—it's impossible you could think such a thing!"

"But you *are* going back if you go down there now. And your work, what about that?"

He looked serious. "I won't drink—is that what you're afraid of?"

I won't—— So he was already planning to go. I was too miserable to say any more. Now his mood changed. I saw that he was looking at *me* with irritation. Suddenly I knew I had made a mistake—and a serious one. This was not love and understanding that I was giving him. . . .

Gene was right about one thing. I wasn't really afraid of his leaving me; going back to her. What was it I felt—pride? An unseen contest between this woman and me, in which I didn't even want her to have the satisfaction of winning the first round by summoning him to her side? Some of that perhaps—one's motives are so mixed sometimes. . . .

But more than anything else it was something between Gene

and myself that hurt me so badly. How could he, for some motive which I couldn't understand, leave me, his work, expose himself to the temptations of the city, which he might not be able to withstand? How could he, who had held me in his arms so tenderly night after night, decide, without taking me into the workings of his mind, and immediately, as if it were the only thing to do, to take that long, boring, and uncomfortable trip to explain to this woman that he loved me and no longer loved her?

I saw very soon that what had happened to him was that he considered it a sort of obligation—very seriously too. That night, after reading her second letter and showing it to me, he spent several hours over a letter to her.

I sat by in a sort of furious misery, pretending not to care but, I suppose, jealous and chaotic, veering from one attitude to another. I felt scornful as I saw him cross out words, recompose sentences (even using other slips of paper when the final draft was under way in his neat firm handwriting and he didn't want to have to do it all over again): spending twenty minutes or more on paragraphs which, when read, would sound as if they had been torn from his heart and from the depth of his soul. I wondered in my scorn what she, the fair Louise, would think, could she see him doing this.

When it was finished he handed it to me to read. I hesitated—didn't think I should read it. But he insisted. He wanted me, also, to understand what he *had* felt, and felt now.

The letter was all I had expected—and more. It began with a review of their love and their torture—a searing memory of the past but bringing a great beauty to it, too, so that here and there I seemed to catch a cadence of Irish words, a memory of the Aran Islands, and, of course, the sound of the sea. I read this with my lips suddenly dry, for I thought that only to me had he brought this wild longing and restless desire. I could now see this girl, this menacing and determined hussy, of whom my main impression was from a photograph Gene had showed me of her, in which, with legs in tight riding breeches spread apart, hands dug in the pockets of a smart jacket, she leaned against a shingled, weather-beaten wall, a gamin cap rakishly on her head, a provocative smile on her lips, as a half-mythical symbol of the great old and mystic Irish legends.

From there on, his letter went to betrayal, secrecy, and more torture—particularly for Jack. A few bitter gibes at Louise were thrown in; hints of deceit and of playing with him as a cat plays with a mouse, and then he told Louise what had happened to him. I read this with trembling lips and a humble heart—a description of myself and of my meaning to his life that, somewhat as in the letter he had written to his parents, gave me a curious wonder as to why, if I was really like this, I hadn't known it before. . . .

Gene ended the letter by saying he did want to see her, but now, in the process of finishing a long play, it might be fatal for him to leave. Why, then, couldn't she come up to Provincetown?

This was a blow to me, of course, for I didn't want her to come. But I accepted it as being better than his going to New York. Perhaps I sensed that she would not make the trip—for she, I felt, wanted him to go to her, and not be running after him; and the next morning Gene was back at work, serene about it all.

(But it seemed to me that he waited rather impatiently for the arrival of the mailman.)

The day after that, another letter arrived, and he read it and laughed rather ruefully, again perplexed and disturbed. Louise was adamant. She must see him, in New York—and alone. There were also messages from Jack. Her last words were that she knew all about his marriage. And about me—that I looked very much like her. She understood the marriage—it was both escape and revenge! But she would forgive that. There were more, much more important things in the world now than marriage. . . .

Gene went back to his work without too much comment. The situation was thus left suspended. He took a long walk alone that afternoon. I could see when he came back that he was quite miserable and we ate our supper in silence. Afterward he took the script of *Beyond* and began working on that. I immediately felt sure that this working on the play in the evening (which he never did) was to get it finished so he could go to New York, and I brooded in silence, feeling that my dilemma was becoming worse and worse. What was I to do— what should I do? I thought suspiciously about his wanting to finish the play; but I know now he did it because it was the only way he could get his mind off the problem; and probably, also, off my brooding and miserable face.

Before he went to bed he came over and put his arms about me and pulled my head down on his shoulder. He looked so miserable, with such a longing to be helped, to be once again calm and peaceful, that I, holding tight too, was especially happy and relieved, and determined that in some way I would help.

11

This was difficult (as one can see looking back on it), for there were his feelings to consider; what he thought he should do; what he wanted to do. I must, in order to see his point of view and thus be able to help him, look with more kindly eyes and a better understanding at the absent Louise.

I might if I were in his place insist that I must see my past love once again if only to not have to face during the coming years the feeling that not seeing her was all a mistake which a meeting would have cleared up; for one thing that haunted Gene then was that, after all, there had never really been a break with Louise. They both expected that when she returned from Russia there would be a renewal of their relationship.

It now turned out, not only from Louise's letters, which began arriving once and sometimes twice a day, but from my own questioning of Gene, that leaving him that last time and seeing him rebellious and sullen she had promised that while in Russia she would talk to Jack, explain once again that she loved Gene as well as loving him, but that Gene had a more desperate need of her; she must now reverse the roles and live with Gene while still remaining Jack's companion and friend. (I think it is possible that she *did* talk this over with Jack—he must have told her that he and the Russian revolution needed her more than the crazy young playwright did!)

She repeated in her letters that this was what she must see him about—and hinted broadly that Jack for love of her had agreed. *Had she not left him and was she not here?* Had she not crossed alone those three thousand miles of frozen steppes?

But the more I thought of it the more complicated and un-solvable it all became. Are problems ever solved by thinking? One may get to see the other person's point of view, know more about it, but—— Through desperation, through intuition, I saw what I must do: reject the *me I was* and become what I *wasn't*—a firm and determined female who was taking matters in her own hands. I was frightened inside of me of this role, I am sure of that now, nor have I ever attempted it since. But when I saw the look of curiosity, then relief, and the admiring and almost wicked smile on Gene's face when I told him my decision and that I *meant* it, because it was fair to everybody—I was immensely relieved myself.

I would not consent to his going down to New York! He must write her that. But, understanding the circumstances and wishing to be fair to them, I *would* consent to Gene going to Fall River (alone of course) and meeting and talking to her there. She could leave New York for Fall River on the night boat: he would leave Provincetown and meet her there on her arrival. I in Provincetown would await the consequences . . . and I looked firmly at Gene.

"You mean it?"

"I certainly do!"

He thought it over, decided to write her, and, with a little amused smile appearing at times on his lips, he wrote the letter. I think it struck him as funny—and as an original idea. It put

Louise, to use one of his pet expressions, "on the mat." It eliminated the long train trip to New York. It meant only a day or so away from his work—and no danger of drinking, for Louise never drank in those days. It also made me out to be a fair person—and it relieved him of making a decision he did not want to make.

It seems that before Louise's reply came we both began to look on it as rather a joke. I think we both knew in our hearts what *she* would say to this eminently fair scheme. Gene in his letter had been kind, but very firm. She could not dismiss it as an idea to be discarded until something else could be arranged—even a longer wait for him in New York than she had anticipated.

Her reply was quick and impetuous—a vibrant assault upon and belittlement of me; and a denunciation of Gene for his weakness and lack of understanding. She made it clear that he had fallen greatly in stature in her eyes; and also that there were other and greater concerns on her mind than going to Fall River. She implied that as she was a clever journalist and writer there was a greater orbit in which she circled—of world happenings and important events—than that to which Gene in his Provincetown flight had relegated himself. She broke off abruptly as if she, then at least, could say no more. . . .

I suppose Gene replied to her letter: this he would have done; but what he said I don't remember. There was another letter or so from her saying that Jack was coming back from Russia. . . .

So she revolved back into her orbit of exciting events, of glamour and journalism and many admirers. . . .

I had no animosity toward her and at times even admired her brilliant escapades and journalistic prowess. But much later I heard from persons intimate with her how she had told of having broken Gene's heart—how, after her return from Russia she had to turn him out of her apartment—and how she found him morning after morning drunk on her doorstep. I knew then what had been her idea in having him come to New York—her pride. The story of Gene drinking and following her around only to be ignored by her became quite a legend, though it seems to be forgotten now; Gene more than once had to indignantly deny it, puzzled at how she had changed. Then the story came to him that *she* was drinking, and that, at first, he didn't believe, for she had been rabid against drink when he knew her—her father, it seems, having died of it. But there were other tales, too, as her journalistic fame increased. Jack Reed is buried in the Kremlin; and after the failure of another and brilliant marriage, Louise Bryant died lost, alone, and penniless in a sordid Paris room.

After *Beyond the Horizon* was typed, Gene sent the script to the editors of the *Smart Set*. They praised it highly, and Mr. Nathan gave it to the producer John D. Williams. Gene did not feel like starting work immediately on another long play and we thought vaguely of going to New York again, to see the production of *The Rope*—a short play of New England which he had written at the studio that spring. It was to go on at Provincetown Players on April 26th. Then something wonderful happened, and we decided to go down to New York at once and stay for two weeks. John D. Williams wanted *Beyond the Horizon*, and sent Gene a check for an option for six months.

The Past Comes Back to Francis' Flats

I

I will never forget that first morning when I stood at the window of our flat over John Francis' store in Province-town and saw the dawn breaking over the harbor. From behind an open partition came the sound of vioces, speaking at longer intervals. Gene and his brother Jamie had been talking all night, Jamie stretched out on a cot, Gene in a chair beside him— and a bottle on the bureau. I had gone to bed at midnight, leaving the two of them alone. It had seemed to me whenever I woke that Jamie was doing most of the talking, and it was his strong voice telling a story and laughing that had awakened me again at dawn. . . .

During the night there had been the noisy lapping of waves as they broke against the pilings and small boats below. Now there was only silence from the harbor, pierced by the excited cries of sea gulls in the distance, and I had gone to the window, wondering what had happened. I had forgotten about the great rise and fall of the tide at Provincetown. The harbor and outer sea were spread before me. Since my childhood, the sea, the tidal rivers and bays, the sledgy outposts of Barnegat had been part of my life, but never before had I seen anything like this. Below stretched the whole muddy bottom of the harbor, brown and glistening in the early morning: far out, the turbulent sea was rushing back into the harbor, whitecapped, becoming a gentle streak of pale blue water as it came inside. Half a mile or more out a man was digging in the mud, putting something in a basket.

Jamie laughed again; then I heard Gene's voice, low and monotonous, going on where his brother left off. . . . There was a long silence. Gene appeared at the end of the partition, his hair ruffled, his eyes flaring with that faraway look, a half-empty bottle in his hand. He wore his bathrobe, tied with a cord around his waist, and his feet were bare.

"I'm going to get some sleep!" he said. "What are you doing up?"

"The tide—I'm watching it come in. Look, Gene!"

He leaned over me, his hand on the window sill, steadying himself as he looked out over the muddy flats to the distant whitecaps. Then he straightened, took a long swallow and went over to the bed. It creaked as he sat down, putting the bottle on the floor beside him. "Get me a glass, dear, will you?" he said, and rolled over on his back, his arm covering his eyes. I put a glass beside the bottle, then, looking around, saw the couch cover and quietly hung it on two nails conveniently placed in the frame of the window next to the bed, darkening that part of the room. After a moment he took his arm from his face and rolled over on his side. He was silent—then he began to breathe heavily. After looking once more at the harbor, on which the sunlight now glittered, making flakes and pools of gold, I lay down beside him. *Thank God it was all over!* I would get some sleep and wake later in the morning, feeling refreshed, and do all the things I wanted to do around the place.

2

We had stayed in New York a week longer than we had expected, and the last week, or it may have been ten days, had been an extraordinary time and, when it was going on, a pretty awful time! But afterward it seemed funny, and Gene himself grinned over it, and told it as quite a joke—particularly on me. We had gone down for the rehearsals of *The Rope*, which the Provincetown Players had decided to produce at the end of April. We stayed at the Garden Hotel, on Twenty-seventh Street across from Madison Square Garden, where, in an apartment above, Stanford White had entertained beautiful Evelyn Thaw. The Garden Hotel was small, rather dingy and dark, and all I remember of the entrance floor was a small lobby and to the right a bar. There was no elevator—one climbed narrow stairs to the rooms above. We had one of the larger rooms—a double bed, and possibly a bath. Jamie for a year or more had occupied a hall bedroom on the same floor, going from there every day to see his parents at the Prince George Hotel nearby. They had left a few weeks previously and Jamie spent most of his time with us.

Everything had gone very well: Gene attended rehearsals; saw the opening of *The Rope* and several people he had to see, and took the finished script of *Beyond the Horizon* to George Tyler (I believe it was), a great friend of his father's, who wanted to read it. I had gone down to New Jersey to see my father, who was staying alone at the house there and had fortunately managed to rent the house to a summer tenant. We decided to let the creaky old windmill stay as it was but to put in electric lights and a new bathtub, and I went back to the Garden Hotel to find Gene still sober (not having taken one drink since he arrived in New York) and terribly glad to see me. He told me that I must not leave him again—not even for two days—but when I explained that we were going to get three hundred dollars for the summer rental, he had agreed that it was a good trip.

We had planned to leave for Provincetown the next day, and Jamie was coming with us. I went up to Grand Central Station, bought the tickets and made reservations for the next night, for we had decided to take the train to Boston and change there for the Cape. The next morning everything was packed; we had lunch at a small restaurant; Jamie had a couple of high-balls and didn't eat much; Gene seemed happy enough—but I noticed that he was more nervous then usual. He hardly spoke to me at all. We went back to the hotel and sat in our room—Jamie had left us in the lobby, "*what-hoing*" his way into the bar for one more "hooker," as he called them. Gene looked handsome, I thought, more suave than usual, his hair brushed back, a new suit of gray gabardine—and, yes, a tie, a dark red, conservative tie. He sat looking out the window, smoothing a gray hat which he and Jamie had picked out the day before. I never liked Gene in a hat: it shaded his expressive eyes, hid his soft hair, and made his face look too small—emphasizing his mouth, which for some reason looked sullen whenever he wore a hat. But I could see that he cherished the new hat—and that made me happy. I wondered if I looked as well as he did. I had bought myself a new suit (navy blue pongee), a pair of blue shoes, a new bag and white gloves. Gene, watching the entrance to Madison Square Garden across the street, made a glum remark about wishing that the six-day bike races were on now—he'd stay down and see them with Jamie. *He and Jamie* . . . Rather depressed, I said something vaguely about our coming trip—it should be much more comfortable going on the train, we could sleep all night, have breakfast in Boston, and the train trip down the Cape was much better than that from Fall River. Then—how wonderful to get back there at last!

Only the night before, we had been talking about it. Gene had written John Francis to move our things from the studio to the same flat above the store that he had occupied the previous summer, to put in an order of groceries—and to be sure that the kerosene stove was full! I remembered how meticulous he had been writing the letter.

But my remarks only seemed to deepen the gloom in Gene's face. Was it because he had not heard anything definite from Williams about the production of *Beyond the Horizon*, I wondered? I didn't have a chance to ask him about this because Jamie entered, having had not one "hooker" but four or five, I imagined, from the deepened color in his face and his cheery, leering eye. He produced two pints of Old Taylor and announced with sarcasm that one of them was a gift for Gene— "on the house!" The hotel didn't want to lose the patronage of the promising young playwright and his sweet little wife, *that* was the reason for the gift! He opened one bottle and took a drink and asked Gene to put the other in his suitcase. Gene did this, still gloomy, without a word, and Jamie, seeing the situation, went off to his own room to take a nap. He told me to be sure and wake him in time for the train. . . .

Gene thought he'd lie down too, and I watched him carefully arrange his head on the pillow so as not to disturb his hair or rumple his shirt. We had three hours before the train left. I began to think it was foolish to have packed so early in the day and have this period of bored waiting—but Gene had insisted on doing it that way. He had started packing and getting ready even before we had breakfast. Now he asked me if I would do him a favor—hand him *The Saturday Evening Post?* I did, and then suggested that I better go and get the last copy, and a couple more magazines from the drugstore. I had meant to get aspirin too—I'd forgotten that. Also, there were a couple of telephone calls I should make—I couldn't phone there, as we had no telephone in the room, and I didn't like going into the bar.

Gene thought this a good idea and, putting down the *Post*, asked me if I would call Fitzie for him at the Provincetown Players. He wanted me to deliver a message about giving someone some tickets. . . . I left with trepidation, never giving a thought to the subject of drinking but wondering if I had done something to offend him—or didn't he like the way I looked in my suit? Gene was quite critical about my appearance, particularly when other people were around—and Jamie, of course, thought I should dress in a much more dashing style. I wondered about Jamie as I went downstairs, and said a little prayer that he would sleep now until we were ready to leave—*sleep it off*, was the expression I had learned to apply to such times.

I bought the aspirin, the magazines, and some candy, made my two calls, and then called Eleanor Fitzgerald at the Provincetown Players. Fitzie was a warm and generous person and talked to me for a longer time than I expected, telling me how good I was for Gene, what a change there was in him since he was married. She also told me that Louise had been in the night before—not to tell Gene this, but she had been rather peevish when she found that he was not there. She was *most* dramatic-looking, Fitzie said, laughing over the phone. She wore some sort of a red, embroidered Russian jacket and high black boots. "But she doesn't hold a candle to *you*," Fitzie added warmly, "and Gene knows it. . . ."

I decided to tell Gene about it anyway when I got back to the hotel. I knew it didn't make any difference to him any more, and it would be something to talk about. Then I suddenly remembered that I had not answered my father's telegram received the day before. He had telegraphed me that he could get the house wired for electricity and a new bathtub for the sum of one hundred and thirty dollars—a hundred for the wiring with outlets and thirty for installing the tub. I should send a telegram now, telling him to go ahead before it was too late. This took up some time. . . . But I did not hurry—it would be easier for Gene to take a nap while I was out. . . .

After I got back to the hotel and climbed the three flights of stairs, holding my packages and the magazines, I paused at the top step, getting my breath. Down the hall I saw that the door of our room was ajar. I could hear someone talking—it was not Jamie, but Gene, and as I came nearer the door, my spirits sank. I recognized the tone of that voice and knew what it meant. . . . He was going on firmly, slowly and with a sarcastic undertone, about something. I stood outside of the door a moment, listening. He was talking about trouping and trips, and *his* experiences when he was traveling as assistant stage manager with the *White Sister* company. I had heard these stories before. Then Jamie laughed. There was a silence inside—and I heard the gurgling of liquor being poured from a bottle. . . .

We didn't leave that day, so I went up to Grand Central and

changed the tickets to the next night. Although the two of them sat up and drank and discussed the past until three o'clock in the morning, Gene did go to bed then, dismissing Jamie and telling me that he'd be all right tomorrow. There was no liquor left, and, feeling quite good, he firmly declined Jamie's offer to get a bottle from the night porter for a pickup the next day.

The next morning, still packed, with Gene's suit only slightly mussed, his new hat on the table and his leather portfolio on the table beside it, we woke up around noon. Jamie had not yet knocked at our door, and Gene lay in bed, staring gloomily through the dusty lace curtains. Among other unpleasant things, he was thinking of the long wait we would have in the Boston station before the train pulled out for the Cape, for he mentioned it to me almost as if it were a personal imposition upon him and his work—a dirty trick of the damned railroads! He got up, brushed his teeth, and, looking at himself in the mirror over the washbasin, picked up the safety razor. His hand was shaking badly.

"I'll *have* to shave. . . . Listen angel-face, you go down to the bar and get them to mix me a milk shake with a *shot of brandy*."

I hesitated a moment. I had never been in the bar below, and going alone into a bar seemed something I could not face. I saw him watching me, waiting for my decision. Obviously he shouldn't go down himself—he wasn't dressed and he looked bad.

"I'll *have* to have something before I can shave. . . ."

I went down, stood inside and saw men silhouetted against the light from the front window as they sat at the bar. What should I do? The barkeeper was at the far end, talking to someone. I moved to the bar and stood waiting, rather panic-stricken. At least if I did not sit down, these men wouldn't think I'd come in to be picked up, have someone buy me a drink. Several of them did stare at me—and I felt that in a moment some remark would be made, when the barkeeper saw me. "Hello, Mrs. O'Neill!" he said pleasantly. "Anything I can do for you?" I tried to pull myself together, and as I assumed a nonchalant voice to make my request, his pock-marked Irish face softened and he gave me an understanding smile.

"Please—a milk shake with brandy—and charge it to Mr. O'Neill."

"Milk shake and brandy for Gene, eh?" he said. "What's wrong with him this morning—getting to be a sissy? How's Jim?" And after he put the milk shake on a small tray he added, "Leaving today, I hear—sorry to see you go, Mrs. O'Neill!"

I carried the tray upstairs, wondering how he had recognized me; but I learned later that everyone in that hotel knew everything that was going on. . . . Gene drank the milk shake gratefully, shaved, felt better and began to wonder how Jamie was feeling. And at his request I knocked at Jamie's door but he was asleep.

Gene sat on the bed, his arm around me, and talked about how wonderful it was going to be that summer at Francis' Flats. He had an idea now for a new long play—he would tell me about it later. We put back the few things we had taken out of the bag and locked it so we would be ready, even though there were several hours before the train left.

Gene became silent. He looked over the papers in his portfolio vaguely, and I suggested that we go across the street for breakfast. He picked up *The Saturday Evening Post*, looked through it and said if I did not mind going down again and bringing him up another milk shake he'd feel better and *then* we'd go out and eat. . . .

"Don't wake Jamie," he said. "He'll get potted immediately. He better sleep it off—we'll get him later." Then he stopped, and I waited. "Bring me an eggnog this time—two eggs and a double shot of brandy, dear."

A double shot of brandy! *But* with two eggs. That would make it all right. He would be getting some nourishment. I went down and got what he wanted—he was right, he knew what he was doing. . . .

He *did* know. He just didn't have the courage to ask me to

get a milk shake with double brandy. I'm sure he didn't want the eggs at all.

I really thought that he would be all right that day. It never occurred to me that we would again not make the train. I knew how nervous he must be from what happened the night before. I was happy with what seemed to be his firm resolve to get back to Provincetown. He had looked over his script. He was thinking of work. . . .

Was it in my hands to stop him—could I have helped him? A few years later he would sometimes turn on me and say with desperate resentment—*why didn't I help him?* Could I have helped him then and not carried double brandy eggnogs up three flights of stairs when I knew his weakness? I felt that he *did* need what he asked for; that he would eat afterward and that night we would take the trip that he dreaded and yet must take in order to get back to that which was most important to him—his work. What I did not know then was that after one drink the cycle must be fulfilled. I *did* help him at last, many years later—but in a way that he or I would never have thought possible.

Before Gene had finished the eggnog Jamie arrived, bringing with him a bottle of Old Taylor, much amused that he had been able to get it on credit downstairs by saying that his brother would pay for it.

I went across the street and had coffee alone. Gene refused to go with me; when I left the room they were talking and starting to feel happy. Gene had not taken a drink from Jamie's bottle but he was certainly feeling very amiable. . . . I returned and found Gene laughing and gazing at himself in the mirror over the mantel. I looked at the table—there were two glasses next to the bottle. . . .

From then on, my anxiety and bewilderment increased, because Gene wasn't thinking about leaving for Provincetown at all. When I spoke about it he didn't seem to know just what I was talking about, or didn't appear to hear me. The afternoon went by and I suggested that we take a taxi—even a bottle if necessary—and at least get to the station and sit in the waiting room; or go to the bar at Grand Central. He paused, looked at me with his eyes vacantly amused and said: "Don't get so worried—there's lots of time! Tomorrow's another day! What are you worrying about?" Jamie said nothing—he was leaving everything in the lap of the gods.

So again I went up and changed the tickets—of course we'd make it tomorrow! But we didn't. Gene didn't even ask for a milk shake the next day. Jamie had left a partly filled bottle in the room. . . .

This went on for over a week. There was some variety to it, to be sure—after the fifth trip to Grand Central I said that we should not get tickets until we were sure of going. . . . Then Gene pulled himself together at once and said—we'd get the train next day.

Gene did not leave the room at all, but Jamie would wander out and sometimes not return for quite a while. He ate in the restaurant down the street: but if I could get Gene to eat even the one meal a day which I had the waiter bring up from the restaurant, I was lucky. At last he refused anything but soup. By this time he was so nervous and shaken in the morning that it didn't seem possible he would get through the day. But after managing to keep down one drink, and then several more, he would be doing an imitation of his father in King Lear, or ribaldly going back to his sailor days.

I had soon realized that my anxiety and fear were not going to help anything—in fact were making things worse, even my relationship with Gene. So I made the best of things, even to the point of making private bets with myself as to how long this would go on. I got over feeling ashamed when I faced the man at the ticket office and had to tell him once again that I wanted to change the tickets for the next day.

My husband did not want anyone at the Provincetown Playhouse to know that he was still in New York. They thought that we had left. But he managed to contact, through Jamie, an old circus friend, Jack Croak, who came over from Times Square, where he had a job luring the public to buy tickets on the sight-seeing bus that went down to Chinatown. He had been a famous barker in the freak shows at one time. I listened to fantastic tales of circus lore, of bird men and women, of hermaphrodites and women who either weighed five hundred pounds or were almost small enough to put in a man's pocket. . . . One night a little colored man came up—shabbily dressed, but with great dignity. Joe, I think his name was, but I'm not sure; he was boss of a Negro underworld near the Village, and he told Gene much about people he already knew. *His* tales were startling—but Jamie was bored and went to visit a friend of his own while Gene and I listened.

"Spanish Willy," a fascinatingly quiet bootlegger friend of Gene's from downtown, came up with two very polite lady friends, bringing liquor that cost less and was better than what was to be had at the hotel. But most of the time we were alone—the three of us—and I would lie on the bed, sometimes going off to sleep but more often listening to the tales that the two brothers told. . . .

Gene finally got fed up, as he put it. He was "fed up and had to get out!" The eggnog diet this time solved the problem: for Gene by now was not able to keep anything else on his stomach. For two days I took up not one or two milk shakes or eggnogs but one every two or three hours—and one for the first thing in the morning: Gene now resolved to get to Provincetown at all costs—said he would not drink any liquor unless it was diluted with milk.

The morning before we left, he tried to shave—he had a four days' beard. But he was unable to hold the razor firmly enough to pass it over his face and gave up, trembling with annoyance. Jamie ventured an idea. I should shave him; or, he added, Gene should take two big straight shots and then he could make it.

Gene was firm—he wasn't going to do that. I had an inspiration. Without their noticing, I ran downstairs and asked the barkeeper (who by now was a good friend and seemed to sympathize with and get much amusement from the farce that had been going on upstairs) if we could possibly get a barber to come up to our room and give Gene a haircut and shave. He went to the telephone and told me a good man would be over in half an hour.

I said nothing when I went back, but began picking up the contents of our bags, which by this time were hanging in the closet or pretty much scattered over the place. When there was a knock on the door and I let in the barber Gene looked frightened—but (with a wicked glance at me) allowed himself to be shaved. The haircut, however, he bluntly refused—he had changed his mind about that, he mumbled to the barber, handing him the price of both haircut and shave—along with a big tip. He didn't need a haircut, that was true: but I'd been afraid the barber wouldn't come just for a shave. I had started something—for after this, Gene, who hated barbershops, always had a barber come in to cut his hair. I think he got to enjoy it being done this way—and if he felt he couldn't afford it he'd let his hair grow until he could.

At last we got into a taxi and up to Grand Central Station, Gene quiet and very self-conscious, Jamie full of the spirit of fun. While we waited for the train to be announced he disappeared. Gene and I were going to leave without him when he suddenly appeared, drunker than ever, at the train gate.

When we got on the train the porter was making up the berths. Gene sat nervously, trying to read a newspaper, while I for the first time was able to relax—pleased at the thought of a good night's sleep. . . .

Everything was quiet, the lights were down and the train was rushing through the darkness when suddenly a stentorian and familiar voice boomed through the sleeping car. Jamie, staggering from side to side, came down the aisle, clearing his throat with leering relish and announcing that he was looking for a big blonde with a bad breath. . . .

A porter stopped him—or tried to. But the truth about Jamie was that there was some quality about him or his ribald humor that never annoyed people. The porter grinned in sympathy as he tried to lead him away and Jamie's remarks were so funny and uttered in such a droll and peculiar voice that soon most of the green curtains were pulled aside, and before long all the occupants of the berths were laughing or smiling.

This happened three or four times during the night. Even the passengers began to get irritated: when we at last got off the train in the Boston station Jamie was still looking for a big blonde. . . .

By this time Gene was in a bad state of nerves and very sore at everything and everyone—particularly at the railroad for not making better connections. When Jamie went to get a *Morning Telegraph* at the newsstand Gene told him stubbornly he must come back right away. I was completely exhausted, trying to hang on without collapsing, but now followed a nerve-racking two hours, waiting for Jamie, looking for him, going into the street and into nearby bars and restaurants and even thinking of calling up the police—for Jamie did not have his ticket, and no money as far as we knew. Five minutes before train time he appeared, strolling slowly toward us, leading a weak flea-bitten white dog on a string, and with a loud "what-ho comrades" announced that he was taking the dog to Provincetown.

This was too much. . . . Gene scowled angrily, but he was never one to raise his voice in public, which was the only way Jamie might have listened to him, for he seemed even more under the influence of liquor than when he left us. Where he got it, or the dog, we never really knew.

We started to get on the train, Gene first, with me following, when Jamie was stopped by the conductor, who asked what he was doing with that dog. An argument then followed, Jamie giving all sorts of reasons why he should take the dog. He and the conductor were still arguing outside, and a couple of minutes later the train slowly began to move. Again no Jamie . . . the conductor said nothing as he punched our tickets, merely glared at us. Half an hour later, when we were well out of

Boston, Jamie appeared at the other end of the car and strolled up to our seats. He seemed very pleased with himself.

"Bowser is in the baggage car," he informed us, swaying back and forth as he held to the back of our seats. "And the boys from Brooklyn are coming over the bridge!" That phrase was a favorite expression of the two brothers. It meant the heebie-jeebies, or, as they say nowadays, pink elephants—in other words, what happened and what they saw when liquor was gone and the d.t.s seemed just around the corner.

"The boys from Brooklyn will be coming over the bridge before the night's over!" Gene muttered, looking pale and sick. But Jamie only laughed. "What d'you know, kid? I got me a bottle—from a big blonde with a bad breath!"

3

I had a long time to think of all this, as Gene and Jamie both slept until two in the afternoon. Jamie woke first and came around the partition, an old bathrobe pulled tightly over his plump stomach. His eyelids were granulated and watery and he needed a shave, but he seemed sure of himself and rather pleased at being where he was. He needed a drink and he got it from the bottle at the side of Gene's bed—a good half tumblerful, which he diluted with tap water and sipped as he looked out over the bay. I saw nothing at all of the jovial Jamie of our trip, looking for the big blonde, only a quiet middle-aged man, contemplating something—what, I did not know.

I cooked eggs and coffee for him over the small kerosene stove, and he gave me the impression, without saying it, that he was very pleased and grateful. I had never before seen him until he'd had a fair start on the days' drinking and I was rather touched. He had another drink after breakfast, took a shower and dressed, coming from behind the partition this time with his thinning hair parted, wearing a clean shirt open at the neck and new khaki trousers.

Was there anything he could do to help, he asked? I had

decided not to do anything until after Gene woke up. So Jamie said he was going to take a look around, and after opening his frayed wallet, which appeared to be empty, he went off down the wooden steps. Half an hour later I happened to look out of the window and saw him out in the harbor at the edge of the incoming tide, his khaki pants rolled up above his knees, leaning over to look at something in the muddy sand. . . .

There came an interval of quiet, broken only by the flapping of the shades as the breeze from the sea blew through the rooms. There was nothing to do now but wait for Gene to wake up. I sat there, relaxed, looking at words that he had painted in red and black on the rafters; *Before the eye can see it must know blindness. Before the ear can hear it must be deaf to the noise of the world: before the heart can learn to love it must have known the agony of emptiness.* . . .

I had read them before but I did not know where. . . . The Upanishads? No, that was not it. I tried hard to remember where the quotation came from, thinking that I would tell Gene that I remembered it. *My lover!* . . . I looked at the words again and felt that I understood them.

Sitting there, rather lonely and sad, I thought of the past and my very young girlhood. My maternal grandmother, a tall and commanding old lady, had had a rather irregular religious life. Brought up in the faith of the Church of England, one day after her marriage she found a Catholic missal, left behind by a departed Irish servant. Grannie, who, in almost everything except her religious emotions, was a most conventional woman, felt this was an act of God, meant especially for her: she read the book, called on a Jesuit priest, and became a convert. It must have been some time after her marriage, for my mother was then seventeen, and she too became a devout Catholic. Somehow, probably because of the instruction and study considered necessary for their baptism in the Church, they became friends with a group of brilliant Jesuit priests, who visited the house and of whom my mother became very fond.

After many years, and various interesting and startling vicissitudes, Grannie (over sixty by then) was living in London in a club composed of intellectuals and free souls when she discovered Mr. Sinnet's theosophic writings and began to read Mme. Blavatsky. She wrote long letters to my mother in New Jersey, telling of her experiences (mostly mental), among others how she had found the real answer to the mystery of Easter Island and its gigantic statues. She became an ardent theosophist and told my mother about a place in Washington, D.C., where she too, could get books on the subject. . . .

My mother had been interested (though with a more critical mind than dear Grannie, who to her last days read with enthusiasm the novels of Ethel M. Dell) and every month books arrived from the Oriental Esoteric Society, a circulating library in Washington. The only charge being that my mother pay the postage one way. These volumes included everything from the Upanishads to Meyer's *Survival of the Human Personality after Death*. I believe mother veered off a bit in favor of the survival-after-death idea and what happened then: but I was reading all the books as they came along, including a yoga series which started with *Hatha-Yoga, the Science of Health*, which she bought and gave me so I could learn how to take care of myself; and by the time I was thirteen I had firmly, and with great feeling, decided I was going to become an Adept.

That summer, after deciding that my destiny was to be an Adept, I went through a discipline which I worked out by myself; for I felt that an important part of all this was that no one must know what was happening. *A young girl in a middy blouse and blue serge skirt—that's what we wore in those summer days long ago—took care of the babies, sat in the hammock and watched the yellow jackets building a nest in the eaves of the porch, braided her long hair because it was hot weather, but no one knew the truth.* I don't believe that I thought of it much during the daytime—though I do remember that when my aunt Margery came over from Paris with her two children and wore a strange Indian-style garment called a jibbah around the house

I felt that a jibbah would be more appropriate for my dedicated life than a middy blouse. . . .

How I thought up this schedule of mine I don't know—but a shabby volume of the *Critique of Pure Reason*, which I still have, brings much of it back to me. . . . There was a Baptist minister in the village, with a keen and surprising mind—I believe he afterward left the Church. My father sometimes visited him and they would spend the evening talking; the minister was interested in water-color painting and my father, who was doing landscapes at the time, helped him with that. I sometimes went along on these visits and listened to Mr. Clark and his wife, a plain little woman but even more brilliant than her husband, discuss philosophy—a favorite subject of theirs. One night he and Mrs. Clark talked about Kant at great length. I sat there, amazed and enchanted, and, when we left, shyly but with determination (feeling I *must* read all Kant had to say), I asked if I might borrow the book from which he had read a passage or so.

I could remember my hurt indignation when Mr. and Mrs. Clark both laughed at me, very amused, telling me I could never understand it. How I appeared to them and to my silent father, I don't know, but Mrs. Clark abruptly went into her bedroom and came back with another copy, explaining that she had kept it from her college days and I could keep it as long as I wished. She was sure, she added gently, that it would take me all summer to read.

I started immediately on getting home—up in my bedroom. Alas, I was stunned! But I was hopeful. If only I could take it slowly, and get that *a priori* fixed firmly in my mind. . . .

This baffling book played a large part in my schedule for becoming an Adept. Perhaps I unconsciously wanted to kill two birds with one stone; read and understand the book—and become an Adept too. . . . Every morning for three months I woke myself at three o'clock in the morning, at first with a tiny battered alarm clock, but after two or three days this was not necessary. I put on a bathrobe, and, sitting at a table by the window, read Emanuel Kant with great concentration. This took an hour, but as the print was very small, and the kerosene lamp gave a poor light, I may have shortened the hour at times and gone on to my next step: this was to practice yoga breathing, during which time my mind was concentrated on my breath. After that I sat at the back window, looked at the stars or dark sky whichever it was that morning, and meditated. I had read a great deal about meditation. Then, two hours having passed, again I read and studied—*Light on the Path*, one of the yoga books, if I felt sleepy; or Mr. Sinnet's *Esoteric Buddhism*. I seemed quite easily to understand it all—except Mr. Kant.

By now I was happy and illumined by my secret ritual; allowed myself another period of meditation and prayer. None of us got up very early at the house, so I slept after this, or went for a walk in the garden. Nobody noticed anything, except that I was going to bed early every night—although I sometimes saw my mother look at me rather strangely.

That spring our funny fat fox terrier, Minnie-Mouse-in-the-Hole, had given birth to several puppies. I had become deeply attached to one brown fuzzy little thing who seemed to adore me too. As the fall approached, my puppy caught some infection and became sick. We did everything for the little dog, but he got weaker every day, looking at me so pathetically that I felt my heart breaking at my own helplessness.

At last one night we saw that the puppy was dying—he could no longer walk, or even move, and was barely breathing. My mother told me to stop brooding—to leave him alone to die. I sneaked him upstairs in an old coat and laid him on the floor in my closet. . . .

Before I turned out the lamp I leaned over and touched the puppy. His poor little nose was cold, and he felt lifeless and inert under my hand, and going off to sleep I wished ardently that I *was* an Adept, instead of just learning to be one. I would then quite easily be able to bring my puppy back to life. . . .

I woke at three o'clock, and as there was no sound from beneath the old coat in the closet I refrained from looking and tried to think of my puppy frisking on the astral plane. Kant seemed unusually difficult, and, though I tried hard to concentrate, instead of the printed words all I could see was the old German, very ugly and quite unhappy as he was pictured on the frontispiece, and I wondered why he had gone to all this trouble when it had not made him look more happy. The windmill was wailing like an uneasy banshee in the wind when I went to sit by the window for my meditation, and I was conscious only of sadness and emptiness. All I could think of was the puppy—how he would give that puppy bark and pretend to be a big dog when, on a windy afternoon, the windmill would start turning like mad and begin pumping water up to the tank.

The chapter from *Esoteric Buddhism* helped me realize that my puppy was making the rounds of the worlds in some cyclic fashion and next time would be higher in the great spiral. But by the time I was finished with Mr. Sinnet I had weepily convinced myself that my pup should have finished his cycle here first and then gone on. I spent my last period in the sort of prayer that does not petition but sees things as they should be—as they *are!* I saw my puppy strong and playful; I stroked his head and patted him as he leaped up joyously. . . .

This vision faded after I had held onto it as long as I could; pictures in color of people and places began to float before my eyes, the usual sign that I was going to sleep. Then something made me open my eyes—I heard a sound. I looked—terror and amazement went through me, for there was my pup, out of the closet, not leaping (as in the prayer) but very wobbly. He gazed at me, and I was sure that I saw gratitude in his eyes. He even managed to slowly wag his tail. . . . Why I did not continue my training after this experience, I do not know. Memory is a strange thing, and I do not even remember continuing my morning ritual after this. Perhaps I was afraid of the results.

I hate to say that one other thing came back to me; this is that as the puppy had grown weaker in his illness his fleas had become more numerous and the night before, wrapping him in the old coat, I had sprinkled his head and his poor little overrun stomach with yellow powder that my father kept to get rid of chicken lice, for I wanted him to die in peace. The next morning after taking him to the kitchen and seeing him lap up some milk I announced to the family, in a sort of glorified stupor, that I had brought him back from death by prayer. . . .

My sister Barbara, who had made up her mind to become a lawyer at that time and was reading a book called *Ramm on Facts* and was accordingly very strong on facts, announced cynically that it was flea powder, not prayer, that had brought him back—she had seen me putting it on the night before! I will have to leave the decision to the veterinarians. . . .

4

I was thinking about this and that I would tell Gene about it someday—it might amuse him—when the bed—*our* bed—creaked and I turned my head to where Gene lay. But he was motionless. I wished he'd wake up—there was so much to do! *So much to talk about*. . . . The bed creaked again and this time Gene was sitting up, his feet on the floor. He leaned over and there was the sound of liquor being poured into a glass. He held it in his hand a moment, then his head went back as he drank it. I waited with tense pity. This was the critical moment. Would he rush out and make for the sink, or would it stay down? I waited, not saying a word. Then—he lay back, his head on the pillow, staring at the rafters in the ceiling.

The room was quiet—the cries of sea gulls in the distance, a dog barking monotonously somewhere on Commercial Street, were the only sounds that came through the open windows. . . . Time was held in suspense. At last he sat up again, put his feet on the floor, reached for his bathrobe.

"Aggie?"

"Yes—here I am."

He walked toward me and looked out of the window. His mouth and chin sagged.

"Where's Jim?"

"He went out. He seemed pretty good."

"How do you feel?"

"I feel all right, dear. A little tired, maybe."

"Did Francis leave us some ice?"

"Don't you remember"—I laughed, going over to the icebox—"me trying to get you and Jamie to mix your drinks with ice water last night?"

He smiled ruefully as I lifted the lid of the square box and looked down at the hunk of ice already beginning to melt. With an ice pick I began chipping some loose.

"It would have been a goddamn sight better if we had! That's how the mad don keeps on his feet!"

I put the ice in a glass, and he filled it from the tap (we didn't know about orange juice in those days and he wouldn't have taken it anyway).

He was thinking of the mad don, one of his affectionate terms for Harold de Polo, who had been through many lurid and amusing escapades with him in the past, and he drank the water with a slight reminiscent grin on his face—thinking perhaps that it would be fine if the gay don were here. I could tell that his thoughts at the moment were not absolutely on getting sober, and I was right. He poured another drink, a big one this time, and put the bottle on the table.

"Not much left, eh?"

He felt better now. "No eggs for me yet!" he said. "Did you eat?" I had; he was pleased. He went over and looked at the groceries that John Francis had arranged on the shelf over the sink. It was mostly staples, though there was a jar of bacon and two cans of beans.

"What about a nice fish chowder for tonight—*Your* kind?"

He was thinking of food, at least. "Wonderful! I'll need salt pork, and—you want to go out and catch the fish?"

"If I get as far as downstairs I'll be doing good. Wonder where Jamie went?"

We had not long to wait. Almost immediately we heard someone on the stairs—and a sound of something being dragged.

I went to the hall and saw Jamie, his neat parted hair disarranged and his face flushed, pulling a reluctant dog behind him. He came in, still dragging the animal. Gene's face took on a malicious grin, and he began cursing the dog and Jamie in foul and amusing sailor language.

"You bleedin' bastard! You bring that crummy, decrepit, muck-eating animal into my nice clean flat. Where's he been—the lousy mutt? I don't even remember you gettin' him out of the baggage car!"

Gene didn't remember because after the bottle that he and Jamie drank on the trip down from Boston—well, they weren't remembering anything when they arrived. But I did—and told Gene that dear Mr. Francis, seeing what the situation was when we arrived at his store in a taxi, had offered to tie the dog in his store for the night.

"He caught me just now, coming up here," Jamie explained. "Said he couldn't keep it there any longer. Too full of fleas."

"Too full of fleas" was correct. They could be seen—long black ones crawling across the pinkish skin of the poor animal under his thin white hairs. Gene looked at them, fascinated. Otherwise the dog couldn't have caused John Francis much trouble. He was too weak to walk, his tail hung down like a Spanish whip, he tottered on his weak legs, and there was a look of abject resignation in his eyes. He was mangy, his eyes were watery, and his toenails made long scratches on the wooden floor.

"*Holy God!*" Gene said. He reached for the bottle. "Here—give him a drink!"

" 'His Master's Voice'!" said Jamie—and I saw what he meant. The dog was the type of terrier that was once widely photographed in a phonograph advertisement looking into a horn with his ears cocked—a picture once as famous as the Rheingold Girls are now.

"Two well-known relics of the past—Bowser and I! *What ho!* A drink, Bowser! To the good old days when women were tarts and men had hair on their chests! You know what I mean?"

said Jamie slyly. He took a bowl, put in plenty of milk, and poured in a large dose of whisky, while Gene looked on grinning. He gave it to the dog, who, without a moment's hesitation, lapped the bowl clean while we watched expectantly. He looked up at us, sneezed, and was able to sit firmly on his haunches. There was a quiet moment—evidently he was wondering what was going on inside him. Then, one ear suddenly cocked just like the dog in the picture, he looked at Jamie and gave a weak staccato bark and, walking on very firm legs now, the rope dragging behind him, went over and lay down at his feet.

"We'll have to have one on *that!*" exclaimed Jamie, and, drawing his feet fastidiously away from the animal, at the same time pulled a pint bottle from his pocket. "Got this down the line—borrowed a dollar from Francis. He told me where I could get it. Had to go to a bootlegger. I didn't know this town was dry."

We all had a drink this time, and then it was decided to put Bowser in an empty flat across the hall. Jamie urged him to take another drink, but Bowser turned his nose away—he wanted to relax—so Jamie picked him up and carried him in, with a bowl of spiked milk in his other hand.

"I put him on the bed," he explained. "The milk shake's on the floor. He'll be able to get a pickup as soon as he's slept it off!"

They had a good time then, he and Gene, talking about the last days at the Garden and the trip up to Provincetown. "You and your blonde!" Gene laughed. "Hell, those dames peeking out were all hopeful——!" But he hadn't thought it funny when it happened.

I had a nice time too; I went down to John Francis' store, bought more milk, salt pork, potatoes and onions and a bottle of cream. Mr. Francis told me he'd send them upstairs to the flat, so I walked down Commercial Street to a wharf where a boat had just come in. It was wonderful being back in Provincetown again. It was May; the air was brilliant and warm and made me feel like dancing or going for a swim. I glanced at Susan Glaspell's house as I went by, but the doors were closed—Susan was probably upstairs working.

I walked across the cracked oystershell and down to the wharf where an old man was selling fish, and, having to choose between codfish and haddock, bought a four-pound haddock, fresh from the water, the eyes shiny, the flesh cold and wet.

That afternoon while Jamie and Gene laughed and talked I cut fat salt pork into dice and very slowly tried it out, so that after half an hour or so the little pieces were a deep, delicate cream color. Meanwhile I cut up the fish, simmering the bones and head in a little water; tying the firm white flesh into a cheesecloth, I put it in the icebox. Two onions were sliced thinly into the pork fat, after I had removed the diced bits, and allowed to brown to a color that matched the fat. When the fishbones and head had simmered down to a savory, seasoned broth I drained it, added the diced pork and the onions, and a cup or so of diced potatoes. Later, when we were ready, I would take the fish from the icebox and finish my chowder. . . .

5

Gene had put on a clean white undershirt and bathing trunks, and, with his uncombed wavy hair, his broad shoulders and narrow hips, looked very romantic as he began opening up the suitcases. He looked happy too, smiling and laughing as he worked, although his eyes had that abnormally alive look that I know too well. Jamie sat next to the table, near the bottle. . . . Whenever Gene needed it (to keep up to normal, as he said) he would go over and pour himself a drink.

It was a happy day—Gene had not started "tapering off," as he called it, but he had something to do and he was deeply pleased and gay at being once more back in his old flat and in Provincetown.

He arranged his books on a shelf which he had put up the

summer before, after sending Jamie down for a hammer to open the box which John Francis had kept for him. He put his underwear and shirts into the rickety bureau drawers, teasing me because I wanted him to wait until I'd put white paper there, coming over to kiss me and look into the pot where I had the chowder. He hung up his suit, carefully creasing the edges of the trousers into the trouser hanger. And *that* brought on a story which he had to sit down and recall to Jamie, who listened with silent pleasure, though he knew it all too well. . . . Something about how when they were once touring with his father's show, Gene had spent the night with a blonde, left in a cab the next morning to go back to the hotel and, angrily self-conscious anyhow, was irritated when people stared at him as he went through the lobby, only to find, when he started to undress in his room, that he had left his pants behind. Then Jamie told another—how he and Gene had two girls up in their room, and how a contraption that he had carefully rigged up outside over the window to make it look as though it were raining so the girls wouldn't leave failed to work when Jamie pulled the string. I can't remember what happened after that, I was more interested in the contraption.

Gene was going through a locker built under the front window and I noticed that he brought out about fifteen old copies of *The Saturday Evening Post* and put them under our bed. Then he brought out a tarpaulin; a faded pair of swimming trunks crusted with salt; a small pair of iron dumbbells; some worn-out odd sneakers; an elastic exerciser, which he attached to a bar on the wall; a musty cotton quilt; and then a white quart bottle, etched opaque from the beating of the sand on the dunes where he had found it, as Gene told me later. It had been wrapped in the quilt at the bottom of the locker, beneath the other things.

Gene shook it, then took out the glass-topped cork.

"*Tiger Piss!*" he cried exultantly. "What ho! Jamie—try some of this!"

"*This*" was a white, highly potent beverage with a taste so disgusting one had to swallow it quickly with closed eyes. It had to be taken straight, Gene explained, because mixed with anything the taste was so unpalatable, the odor so strange and upsetting, that as one raised the glass to drink, one had to put it down. It was made somewhere in Truro, I think, of what I don't know—potatoes or corn perhaps, although it might have been made of octopus tentacles from its flavor. Whatever it was it was liberally diluted with raw alcohol and must have been kept, before being sold, in kegs which had once held tar.

Jamie sputtered and swore after taking a drink but soon had another, saying the effect was unlike anything he had ever known and that he expected that he would soon be able to growl like a tiger—as well as roar like a lion. One of Jamie's great stunts, as I have mentioned before, was really roaring like a lion. He had a full, deep chest and although in conversation his voice was slightly nasal it had great power and a volume of ferocious sound would come forth that made the air vibrate. . . .

"Tiger Piss" made Gene smolder. He lost some of his gaiety and I saw his lips begin to press together in a cruel line as some dark idea began to gather in the back of his mind. I was forgotten. The chowder (which was delicious, Gene had said when he had tasted it after I had added the fish and cooked it some ten minutes longer) remained in the pot ready to be eaten. I put in the milk and some cream and asked him if he wanted some now. He did not bother to reply. He gazed at the lines on the rafters with a bitter and sardonic eye and then going to the window stood there by himself, looking out at the harbor already paling in the evening light.

It was not the harbor, the distant sea, the now translucent beauty of the passing day to him; it was the backdrop of a drama that went on in his soul—a convenience of God to prove his point.

"I will tear down the curtain of Eternity that God has hung in the sky!" he said somberly. "*Vomit all my poison up—on the bread and on the wine!*"

He turned back, regarding with malevolence something that we could not see—something in a dark corner of the room where his gaze had concentrated.

"Swallow your poison instead, kid!" Jamie jeered. "The curtain of Eternity has been there a long time and I don't think that you're the one to tear it down. I tried it once—it shattered to pieces like broken glass in my hands."

He picked up the bottle that had been etched by the sands and poured himself a drink.

"The answer is that there is nothing behind the curtain when you do tear it down," Gene said, raising his eyes from the dark corner and gazing with brooding intensity into space. *"Life is a farce played by a baboon who feels in his invertebrate bones a vision that, being an ape, he cannot understand. He scratches his fleas absently, with melancholy eyes, and then hangs upside down on the nearest branch and plays with his testicles."*

"My trouble is that there is nobody who wants to play with *mine!"* Jamie said in a nasal whisper.

"But I will find the answer!" Gene drew in a long, deep breath. Jamie, watching him sardonically, hiccuped and poured another drink.

"You'll *invent* the answer, kid—you'll never find it. You think the answer's in that goddamn play of yours? You got a line that the audience likes, that's all—'*Beyond the Horizon*'*!* It don't mean nothin'. There ain't no horizon in the first place— it's an illusion that happens in your eyeball. If it happened in your *balls* it would be allright—then you could do something about it."

"Let's cut out this talk in front of Agnes!"

"Sorry, kid! Thought Agnes had been around! Remember, my young brother, that I graduated from Fordham University, that great edifice of learning. I was reading Aristotle, my boy, under compulsion necessarily, when you were playing marbles with yourself. You were in the beyond-the-horizon stage then and you're still stuck there. Where'd the beyond-the-horizon idea come from? *Think back, kid!* I heard it every week when

Mama used to drag me to Mass. '*Be a good little boy! Be nice to everybody!*'—that's what it all boiled down to, didn't it? So your Robert gets kicked around and never goes to them thar far-distant places, but it's all there waitin' for him—beyond the horizon! 'There'll be pie in the sky by and by'—for your Robert —when he's dead!"

Jamie, I thought indignantly, *had* read the script of the play when we were at the Garden Hotel—but he didn't know what his brother meant! I put out two plates of chowder and set them on the table. I didn't feel like eating. Gene walked over to the bookcase without answering Jamie. He picked out a book and after looking at a page put it back. He came back to the table and took another drink. " 'May wild jackasses desecrate the grave of your grandmother,' " he quoted, apparently apropos of nothing; though I was to know later the next morning where it fitted in. . . . He had lettered it on a sign, with the words "if you disturb me" added, which he had used the year before to hang on his door when he was working.

Jamie's eyes were beginning to glaze and he leaned back in his chair. " 'Life's a tragedy—hurrah!' " he quoted mockingly. "That's what you're always saying, ain't it? But you're wrong— life's no tragedy if you got GOLD. Filthy lucre, the spondulics, the old ace in the hole, the stuff that glitters! I've seen through all the glittering that ever went on, and the only real glitter is the glitter of gold. *Women?*—I've got them doped out! *Fame*—what has it done for Papa? *Education*—what's it done for me? Mama gives me twenty-five cents every morning after breakfast for spending money!"

"*Gold?*" Gene was looking not at but through Jamie. The last drink seemed to have relaxed him somewhat, and though his face still brooded darkly and with a fierce intensity, there was a sort of bitter pleasure in his smile. He was still in some world of his own, but it was focusing into something more tangible.

"You're right—I'd like to have a pile of money—rich like Rockefeller! No damn piddling business . . . I would like to be possessed of an inexhaustible sum of money!" He paused;

Jamie and I watched and listened. Again he drew in a deep breath; he went on to draw an imaginary picture of an existence which astonished, and I think almost horrified me because it was so unlike anything that I had thought of him . . .

I cannot use his own words because they have gone from me, as things go that you cannot, for some emotional reason, perhaps, keep in your mind; but the image remains and I have wondered about it, particularly as some years later he said the same thing when he was very sober and in an imaginative and self-revealing mood, perhaps a mood of self-confession. . . . There is a place, an estate, as it were, of great extent (and this must be entirely in *my* mind, for I am sure if he described it at all, he described it as being of great beauty but I see it, this estate, as being dark, with somber trees). It contained within it everything necessary for his happiness and his comfort, and it was enclosed all around with a great fence, through which no one could enter; and the gates were barred and guarded. But the thing which even now I don't quite understand was that within this province and outside of it too, as though he possessed or dominated the world, he was the wielder of immense and unlimited power: over ideas; over things; over people and their ways of life, not only of his own life, but of all those with whom he came in contact in any way. And all this was a thing of *this* world; a domain on *this* earth, where it was he did not say, but not in any foreign or distant country, and not an empire of the spirit. . . . It depended on material things—cars and service and luxury and personal power—some of this he described. I don't remember any specific mention of human beings to whom he was related in this place—a woman, or women, lovers or friends—although there were people there, all of whom must have been in an unusual relationship to him, for over them (and this was very clear) this power of his was complete.

Jamie was gazing into space, getting restless waiting for Gene to finish so that he could get started on some idea of his own. It was evident that he regarded Gene's words as fantasy—not connected with reality. I was silent when Gene finished, watching the fish chowder in the plates wrinkling into a white skin as it grew cold: I got up from where I was sitting, and emptied the plates back into the chowder pot. . . .

Outside, it had grown dark and once again my husband stood at the open window looking out over the flats. He stood there a long time and I wondered what he was thinking about. Jamie groaned and, getting up heavily, went in and lay down on his cot. Gene turned back to the room and spoke to me:

"Get your sweater on . . ."

He went to the closet and took out a white T shirt, pulling it over his head. He held out his hand to me and I took it and we went together down the wooden stairs. We stood silently on the edge of the sand; the wooden pilings were dark shadows near us, the rowboats motionless shapes in the darkness.

"Leave your sneakers here—they'll be all right!"

The wet sand was cool and soft against my feet, between my toes. We went out into the flat, muddy expanse of the harbor, Gene holding my hand and walking a little ahead of me, still silent. He stopped and rolled up his trousers. There was a faint movement of the air, cool and damp against our faces and bare legs. Behind were the lights of the town, and above us we could see the faint light of the stars, swarming on in motionless peace in their great unknown cycle. As we trod the bottom of the harbor it became more soft and oozy, and beneath our feet we felt wet tangled seaweed and little sharp or round things. . . . We stopped, standing there silently, and then we heard an almost noiseless movement going on, a tiny sound of life moving on the emptied floor of the harbor.

"Fiddler crabs!" Gene said. "Don't be afraid—their bite is just a pinch that you can hardly feel."

He put his arm around my shoulder, pulling me close. "*My own! Beautiful, adorable, lovely wife of mine!*" I laid my head against his chest, full of a strange and deep gratitude. "The fiddler crabs come out of their shells, looking for food—not at the stars! You have never seen the flats in summer, little wife.

That's why I wanted to bring you here now. The little crabs—listen!" He paused. "Hear them scuffling. Can you?" His low voice went on as if he were speaking a poem that was deeply felt and without affectation; and to me, close to him, held by his encircling arm, he *was* the poem, the Word. . . . "They are vulnerable; their soft and unprotected bodies are an easy target for the enemies that God has lined up against them: but they live . . . they, too, are life."

His arm tightened around me.

"Do you know what they do? They find a shell for protection. They insert their tender bodies backward into an empty cockleshell and there they are secure. In the daylight you will see hundreds of the little cockleshells with one fierce little claw emerging. Some of them will be moving, for the fiddlers carry their houses around on their backs, and only when they feel safe, perhaps at night, as now, do they emerge entirely. . . ."

We were alone, small dark figures above the flat expanse which extended around us into nothingness. . . .

"Come on!" he said.

We ran, like birds flying across the flats, hand in hand, toward the distant outside sea. Now water touched our feet, splashed about us as we ran. Gene was laughing. When we stopped, the moving water was above our ankles. The air had more movement, it lifted my hair as he again held me close to him. I could feel his heart pounding hard, like a tired engine. Looking shoreward we could see the light in the windows of our flat. . . .

Jamie was at the table, sprawled out, and on the floor at his feet the white dog was sprawled out too, an empty saucer beside him.

"He's passed out again!" Jamie looked up at us and mumbled as we came in. Gene picked up the poor animal and carried him back to the bed in the next flat. When he returned I could see beads of sweat on his pale face.

"Come on—you get into bed!" he said gently to Jamie, taking

him by the arm and leading him behind the partition to the cot. A little later, as we lay motionless side by side in bed, we heard the bedsprings creaking, then his shoes drop to the floor. We heard him throw his clothes across to a chair, and the bed creaking again as he lay down.

In the middle of the night I woke up, wondering what was wrong. Gene lay breathing heavily, his arm under my head. My hair was damp. I was cold, with a strange chill, and lifting the sheet that covered us I could feel that it was wet. The bed beneath us was wet also with a sudden release of the sweat that had come from Gene's body. . . .

6

This is the first time I had the experience of helping Gene go through the process of recovery from a bout of drinking. When we came up to Provincetown that first time he had been physically low for a few days, "tapering off" on a regulated amount of liquor, but it was not the same thing: he had been "off the wagon," as he called it, for several months then, but he had been going out every day, eating at least one good meal, and there were times during that period when he drank more or drank less. He was going to rehearsals of his plays, seeing people, moving about. Outside of a few occasions (like the party at Christine's, the death of Louis Holliday), he never appeared, at least to me, to be very much under the influence of alcohol, nor did his return to his usual complete abstinence involve too much distress.

During the years that we were married, except for some sudden and rather dreadful outbursts of violence, and others of bitter nastiness and malevolence, I do not remember him as being affected by liquor in the usual way. He never raised his voice, he never staggered or walked into things, never "passed out." He never seemed to be what is called *drunk*, nor did I think of it that way or use that term to myself about him except on the occasions that I have mentioned, and then he appeared more like a madman than anything else—a strange being who was not the real Gene at all.

Rather he seemed to have entered another world where he greatly enjoyed himself for quite a while—until physical sickness and despair at last overcame him. His appearance changed after two or three drinks, his movements were slower than usual, but in some way he became intensified physically—or can I say more physically aware of himself?—thus giving the impression of a dark and increased vitality, and this vitality included a sardonic (and sometimes boyish) sense of humor.

Most often, with him, a period of drinking would start with what seemed to be an inability to face people *as he was:* after a few drinks he could face them (or a situation) as a somehow different person. But it seemed that in the country, at Peaked Hill, in Bermuda, or at Brook Farm near Ridgefield, Connecticut, where we lived for three or four years, it was never necessary for him to take a drink when people came to see us or even after they arrived. What I am speaking of seems connected with visits to the city, staying at hotels, going on trips from one place to another. He would never go to the desk and sign the register, but stood unobserved while I attended to it and to getting the rooms; and he would put off taking trips on a train or go about it in some unusual manner. Perhaps in the country, in a house of our own, he was like the fiddler crab, secure within its shell. . . .

Sometimes he did drink in the country but almost always because of people coming there whom he associated with drinking, and who themselves liked to drink—Hart Crane, Louis Wolheim (who later stopped drinking when he fell in love with a fine woman), perhaps Jimmy Light or Harold de Polo—and this would almost always be when he had come to a stopping point in his work, for the two, for him, never went together.

But vice and love are not static; even the physical body goes through psychological changes reacting to environment, or emotion, to food, to cigarettes or drink. As these things occur

I will tell about them. Alcoholism is properly considered a sickness now and it is true that Gene's drinking seemed to follow the pattern of a definite type of that sickness. There is much emphasis now on the *escape* angle or idea. Many people undoubtedly do drink to escape and it becomes a habit that they are not able to overcome—possibly because what they are escaping from is not worth a battle.

But there is another thing to consider, which is that the nervous system in people like Gene (I am speaking of when he was perfectly sober) seems to fail to come up to certain situations—does not, as it were, sufficiently stimulate the personality or the physical being itself. These situations are in the present—a funeral to be attended; a change of environment which will be boring when, instead, it should be enjoyed; the necessity of making a certain impression one way or the other—even the confusion of noise and movement of people, of traffic and crowds, which a less sensitive person would block out. Gene *wanted* to meet these situations, but there was no adequate response and he felt that a drink or so would give him response. Is that escape? I know that he wanted to meet the situation, not escape from it. It would work, but after the first day, or a certain number of drinks, that same nervous system behaved in such a way that his body became helplessly tortured and unstable without *more* drink—a sort of shaken, jelly-like protoplasm which stiffened into activity after a hair of the dog that bit it.

So alcohol, most of the time, seemed a needed prop to meet the situation, rather than an escape from it. He felt fine after the first drink. He talked for hours, laughed, and was gay if it was people or a party. If it was a boring trip, he enjoyed putting it off; or, if he took it, having the whole thing take on such a bizarre appearance that he enjoyed that too—if he had a drink. In more important things, alcohol enabled him to do what he wanted to do—*not* what was expected of him, or was the conventional thing to do.

It occurs to me *now*, as I write this, that in that empire of his that Gene talked about, where he had power over people and events and things, no situation would ever arise where he would be faced with the need of an adequate response to anything—for all would be under his control. There would never be any need of stimulating his personality or physical being because he would move everything around, himself, like checkers on a board and a situation could never arise that he was not fully organized to meet. . . .

I do not really know the meaning of this personal world vision of his—it may seem later on to be something quite different but it does seem now that this may be a partly adequate explanation.

7

I slept late myself the next morning and it was Gene, moving restlessly beside me, who woke me up. I lay there for a moment or so, remembering yesterday, and where I was, and last night. The sheets were still wet, no longer cold but tepid with the warmth from our bodies. I reached over and put my hand over my husband's, but there was only a listless response. He was lying on his back, his eyes closed, his cheeks sunken, his face a mask over which stern despair had cast its pallid shadow. His jaws were rigid, and his mouth, set in that heavy holding-back or keeping-in, looked as if it could never be kind or gay again. "Gene!" I said, but he did not answer me.

I moved from my side of the bed and got into my clothes. It was after eleven o'clock and very quiet in the room. I looked behind the partition—Jamie was gone.

Gene got up after a few minutes and without a word to me pulled on his trousers, then the T shirt. He took a comb from his pocket and combed his hair, wetting it first. This somehow upset me because the flat, severe hair lying flat against his skull made him look even more severe—older.

"Do you want some coffee?" I asked, feeling that it was somehow a stupid remark. He shook his head, and I realized then the physical battle that was going on inside him. A spasm twisted his mouth, and he swallowed hard, as if he might be going to be sick.

"Do you know where Jamie put the bottle?"

I had put what was left of the pint of whisky behind the books on the shelf and I went and got it. The "Tiger Piss," thank God, was gone. I shook the bottle that was on Jamie's bureau and found it was empty.

"I put this away, Gene—so there'd be something left."

He took it and held it against the light. It was over a third full. Then he asked me for a glass and carefully measured out a good-sized drink, then looked again at what was left, measuring it with spaced forefinger and thumb. He looked at the clock. He hesitated, then after a moment went to the sink and added a small amount of water to the whisky.

His hand was trembling so badly that I was afraid that he could not get the liquor to his lips without spilling it, and, feeling that I should not be watching him, I went over to the bed which he had just left and stood there, wondering what to do. I could smell, almost feel, the damp sweaty odor of the sheets.

"I wish you'd take those sheets off and fix up the bed, Aggie. I'll lie down and read," Gene said in a low, almost mumbling voice, which sounded as if he were asking for help. I turned back and saw that he was sitting at the table, the glass of whisky and water before him, and quickly, with a sort of half prayer, I pulled the sheets off, only to find that the mattress also was wet. I was baffled; I couldn't turn the mattress myself. I couldn't ask him to help. Probably it was wet right through. I made up my mind, went to the locker and took out the old cotton quilt. I was taking it back to the bed when Gene stopped me.

"Sit down a minute!"

I sat down and he swallowed hard again once or twice and then put out his hand for the drink before him, giving me a trembling smile.

"Everything's going to be all right now. You know that, don't you?"

I nodded. Of course I knew it. I only wished I could do something to help—to make him less shaken and miserable.

"I can't drink any coffee but . . . later maybe some *soup?*"

"A milk shake—how about that later?"

He hesitated, scowled and picked up the glass. He swallowed the drink, holding himself very still and tense for a moment afterward. I could see his mouth set against the struggle to keep it down.

"No milk shakes—sick of them." He reached out for a cigarette. "You fix up the bed. . . ."

I doubled the quilt and laid it on the mattress and put our worn brown army blankets over that. Two clean pillow cases . . . Gene asked for the other blanket and then he lay down, propping himself up on the pillows. He had taken the pile of *Saturday Evening Posts* from under the bed and put them on a chair beside him. "I'll read for a while." He put the magazine down for a moment. "Put the bottle out of sight, dear—where Jamie can't get at it."

He hadn't asked where Jamie had gone, nor did I know. He began reading just where he opened the magazine, not bothering to find any particular story. . . .

Later, much later, Jamie came back badly sunburned. He'd been out on the flats again and he lay down on his cot, groaning. . . . Later on, I heard the dog scratching at the door of the other flat and I let him out to go downstairs.

Gene lay in bed reading, looking sick, not wanting to be noticed. Someone came to the door and asked me if the flat next door was for rent and I said I didn't know. I made soup, and Gene said he'd have it later. The sun shifted from the south window and slanted in from the west, across the bed. Gene slept, and after a while I got up and inspected my clothes, and found that unexciting, and I then unpacked the carton of MSS. and letters which I had left at the studio, and wondered where

I would keep them. . . . I went down to Francis' store and bought two thick, unlined copybooks, and Mr. Francis told me that there was a bureau in the other flat that I could use if I needed it. When I got back the dog was sitting at the head of the stairs and I opened the door of the other flat and he jumped up on the bed right away.

Gene woke up and read for a while, and then said he'd like the soup, but another drink first. He finished one *Saturday Evening Post* and began another, and about four o'clock he had another drink and more soup, and read again.

I lay down beside him for a while and read over his shoulder, but it was something about a man selling machinery and I closed my eyes. I could hear the pages turning as Gene smoked a cigarette, and stubbed it out, then took up another. I wanted to be *doing something*, but I did not know what. . . . There was an emptiness, something was gone. We heard someone coming up the stairs and Gene got panic-stricken. *"Say I'm working!"* But I did better than that—I didn't want to see anyone either, so I tiptoed to the door and slipped the hook noiselessly into the catch and didn't answer the knocking and after a moment whoever it was went away.

Jamie was sleeping in his pajamas because of the sunburn. At four o'clock I took the bumpy, wide bus and rode up Commercial Street to the doctors and got a prescription for a pint of whisky. Gene didn't sleep that night, sweating again but not so badly, reading the *Post*, and taking about four drinks and more soup. He fell asleep just after it got light, and I got up about nine o'clock and opened one of the notebooks and began writing down some ideas I'd had for a story.

8

I was thinking of the sea; in that room in Provincetown there was silence and peace, and I was aware of that sea near which I had lived so long—the sea that was so much a part of my life that I never thought of it when I was away, never longed for it, because it seemed to me to be always there. . . .

I pick up a pencil and words come from somewhere and are put down on the white paper of the copybook; there is joy in doing it.

Old Captain Curtis. . . ? (No, it's not him, it's another sea captain.) *He cannot let go, in spite of his age, his uselessness. The sight and sound of the sea awake in him a passionate longing for something more tangible. His lost ship on which his thoughts dwell becomes the symbol of all this. . . .*

I go on, and then nothing more comes to put down on the paper. Three fishing boats are going out of the harbor, silhouetted against the pale background of water and sky. His boat would have been a whaler, like those that used to sail out of here. Not a coastwise schooner like my old captain's boat. His boat—what will I call her?—has been missing for over a year.

He's so used to his watch that he wakes up every morning at four o'clock and can't sleep. After prowling for a while through the silent house he always winds up by going up to the walk and keeping watch there for the boat that does not return. The lookout room on top of so many of the old houses here in Provincetown that gave me the idea last winter when I saw them. "The Captain's Walk." That's what I'd call my story. . . .

Gene slept all day, and toward evening I saw that he was awake, just lying there with his eyes open. He told me he'd been awake a long time but I didn't quite believe him. He was very morose and sad; it was as if the world had come to an end for him and he saw it stretching off into emptiness. There was a gloom so thick it was almost tangible; I could even feel it settling on my own physical being, like fog. I felt thin and lifeless sitting on the side of the bed, wondering what I could do for him.

"Do you want a drink now, dear?"

He reached out and took my hand. "I want to suffer, I

guess. How long *did* I sleep?" I told him and his eyes showed the beginning of interest. "I didn't even dream. Must have been good for me!"

He looked at his hands, spread out open before him, long, thin, spatulate, with tiny black hairs on the skin of his wrists. I could see that he was sinking again into some acrid yellow fog-part of his brain. He didn't speak for a while.

"I've got to put on more weight this summer. . . ."

I think it made him come together, grow firmer in his flesh, this thought; for he soon said that he'd better try and eat something, but he'd better have a drink first, which he did. While I was fixing something he had one more, enough to enable him to make some calculations on the amount of liquor left. I took him a bowl of chicken soup with an egg beaten up in it, and he asked me what day it was—Wednesday?

"Yes—I think so."

"What time is it now?"

"About five, dear."

He thought about this while he drank his soup. "Where's Jamie?" he said at last.

"He's been very queer all day, awfully quiet. He didn't want to wake you up, either. Glum. Guess he thinks this is an awful place and wonders why we live here."

"Mean he stayed in bed?"

"No, down on the beach most of the time. He took the dog up Commercial Street and had to carry him back!"

"Goddamn dog!" said Gene sourly. "Can you go up to the doc's again? Get a new *Post*, too, if it's out."

He showed me the bottle. There wasn't much left.

"If I can get through the night with a couple of drinks maybe I can get down on the beach myself tomorrow." He added glumly that it would take two weeks to get the last trace of alcohol out of his system—a doctor told him that. "I'll feel all right, of course, but—you know what I mean. . . ."

He asked if I'd find Jamie and ask him to sit and talk with

him while I was gone; and so I left them together, Gene smiling sheepishly at his brother. . . .

On the way uptown in the bus I wondered about Jamie—he must be having as bad or worse a time. I had found him downstairs, sitting on a barrel on the narrow strip of board porch that edged our building, while two steps down, her bare feet in the damp sand, a pleasant, plump, freckled girl of eighteen in a bathing suit was conversing with him about something while Jamie just listened—never a word! I knew that he had no money now, nor any way of getting a drink; he had seemed relieved when I asked him to go up and see Gene. . . .

9

Gene read again that night, almost until dawn. The doctor had told me to give him a sleeping pill but Gene said wryly that the *Saturday Evening Post* was his narcotic. I slept beside him, off and on, but I was awake when, about four o'clock, he turned the light off and tried to sleep—and did. I was very tired. I couldn't go to sleep. Not really thinking—but an old rhythm kept going round and round in my mind, an accompaniment to emptiness. No meaning to it that was connected to anything now. . . .

> *It's raining, wets the garden sod,*
> *Wets the long path where the gangrils trod,*
> *A maist unseemly thing o' God*
> *In mid-July . . .*

I listened to it going on; it stopped, and I went to sleep. . . .

10

Gene ate a little breakfast the next morning and then wanted to go down and sit on the sand, but he wouldn't because there were some people there who might talk to him. He lay down again but couldn't read the *Post* any more. He asked me what

I did yesterday, why I hadn't gone for a swim even if he couldn't? I said I hadn't wanted to, I was trying to write something—that was the greatest way to make the time pass. I suddenly got excited—*You'd like it, I think!* I got the copybook and he looked at the first page, saw the title, read the few lines, looked puzzled. . . .

" 'The Captain's Walk,' you know, where they watch for their boats to come back. This old man, he wants . . . he . . ." I hesitated, not quite knowing how to go on.

"Sounds all right." He closed the book gently. "Listen, little wife . . . I can't think of much now. Will you go over to Susan's and ask her for the *Times?* If she's working, get the maid to give it to you—she leaves them in the front room."

Gene read the newspaper (which the little Portuguese maid handed to me obligingly) and then started talking about the war news. It surprised me because he hadn't seemed particularly interested before. Provincetown was going to be different this summer, he said gloomily, and for the first time I found out from him that it was now a naval war base. I must have seen a lot of sailors uptown, he said—was I so stupid that I saw them and didn't know what it meant? I explained that I saw them, but I wasn't thinking about them or why they were there, and he laughed and said he guessed that was what he liked about me.

He didn't go down to the beach that day, even after the people left, because by then he was feeling pretty low again, wanting to be quiet and not talk. The false energy of that first spurt of unpacking and arranging could have come back to him only through alcohol, but he would rather suffer now, lie bored and melancholy. . . . He exchanged a few pessimistic words with Jamie, who, stoically quiet, also wanted to be alone.

So nothing much was done around the flat: I didn't want to ask him how he wanted to arrange that rather empty, wooden, interesting place. The long day and longer evening and night passed somehow—one of those empty spaces in time when everything is static. I wasn't thinking about anything that day,

I was just being there, though I did manage to go into the water when the tide was in and also got a bottle of mange cure from Francis' store and put it on the dog, tying him to a piling below. I opened my copybook and wrote a few more sentences, but the old sea-captain friend of my childhood didn't fit into that lonely lookout on top of so many Provincetown houses; I couldn't make them come together yet, and I was as foggy about it all as Gene was about his *Posts* (to which he had again resorted), and had to let it go, though one thing was now sure: what went on in the lookout—or even that structure itself—was the story; not the little old blue-eyed sea-captain friend of my childhood.

II

Gene did not start writing for several days. He slept late; had insomnia; was shaky and depressed for a day or so, and his main interest seemed to be to get back to his swimming. He was a fine swimmer and the first day he went in and I saw him do the crawl I was amazed. He figured out how many strokes he'd swum, did an equal number of the backstroke and said tomorrow he'd show me the racing breast stroke. Then he went back upstairs and exercised with the dumbbells. Jamie took this with some amusement. *His* form of relaxation and "getting back on the wagon" was eating more than usual and working up some sort of a mild interest in the young girl with whom I had seen him talking. Or rather, let's say, watching with some amazement *her* working up an interest in *him*. She came over to the beach every morning and made straight for Jamie, who would be sitting there waiting to see what was going to happen and half-expecting that she wouldn't arrive. . . .

Gene managed to avoid encounters with people. I remember someone came to see us, and Gene, after a cursory greeting, sat with us, reading and never saying a word the entire time. But one morning he got up feeling very much better and after some exercise and eating breakfast he began to do some arranging of the small amount of furniture in our flat. There was a long wooden table, used for typing the summer before, on the side of the partition where Jamie slept. I had been working the last day or so at the table where we ate, putting my writing material into a bureau drawer when I was finished. . . . Jamie was down below on the beach. Somebody came to the door and knocked— then went away. Gene stood there rigid, his hand on his lips, until he heard whoever it was go; then he relaxed and again looked at the table.

I had been trying to work on my sea-captain story when he decided to get the place arranged, expecting that after he'd finished with his dumbbells he'd go down on the beach and join Jamie. He stopped staring at the long table, which seemed to puzzle him, and unpacked a carton from the studio. Papers, MSS., books . . . I watched him, aware of his dilemma, perhaps feeling some irritation myself, wondering again how we *would* arrange where to put things—where *he* would work. I was even more aware of the situation because Jamie that morning on greeting us had said jovially, "What ho, kids! For a newly married couple you rattle the bedsprings not at all! I can hear every time you turn over in bed, but that's all!" Well did I know——! And I am sure that somewhere in the back of my mind was a long talk Gene and I had had before our marriage— *his* very firm ideas and my agreement with them. Now Gene himself, my genius Gene, was wondering how we'd manage. . . .

"Can I help, Gene?" I asked rather aimlessly, because I did not see that there was anything that I could as yet.

"No—go ahead with what you are doing."

I had closed the copybook and put it aside. I didn't want to write now. I saw him take the carbon copy of *Beyond* from the carton and lay it out in an orderly fashion on the table, after removing some of the things that Jamie had left there. Then he pulled the table out into the room, but the light wasn't good—it was too far from the window.

Somehow I rather resented his not taking me into his confidence about all this. Why didn't he say "How will we manage dear?" or, "Have you any ideas"? (I wonder now why I didn't say something myself.)

Just at this moment we heard the mailman below and Gene went down to see what he had left in the box. When he came back I could see that there had been nothing for him—only a letter for me from the farm. He handed it to me silently, then went and lay down sullenly on the bed. There was a book on the chair next to the bed and he picked it up and opened it. I sat there at the table a moment before opening my letter—I could see that he was not reading.

I went through the letter carefully, and my depression increased. It was not good news. My father wasn't well after coming up from New Jersey and doing all that work on the house there. He wasn't able to get around to his painting. My child had a bad cold and was in bed. William Jones was up to something about the damn note—my mother couldn't figure just what. Did I send him the last payment? I sat there, holding the letter in my hand. Poor darling Teddy! (We had always called my father by his first name.) Why had I asked him to do so much? My poor little kid! *And that damned note* . . .

I was thinking of all this when Gene put the book (I noticed that he had not turned a page) down angrily, came out and looked at me sitting there.

"Another of those letters from your family? *Why don't they leave you alone?*"

"Why don't I leave you alone?" I repeated, in a daze and rather vaguely.

"*You know what our agreement was—as well as I do!*"

I stared at him.

"These letters get you so that you don't even know what you are saying!" he said, with a cruel and antagonistic tightening of his mouth. I still looked at him without saying anything. I didn't believe he even knew what I was thinking about. . . .

"I thought you were going to start making those cuts on Act One today, Gene!"

"I was!"

He glared sourly at me, then at the letter, which I was still holding in my hand, and went over to the table where the script was so neatly laid out. . . .

I put the letter in my copybook and got up. Gene took a chair from the table, and without speaking to me placed it next to the long table and sat down. He began spreading out the script. There were two copies—one bound in brown, the other a typed script from which he had made the final draft to send to Mencken. I went out, down the stairs, and sat staring out at the harbor. No one was in sight—not even Jamie and the dog were around. I was glad. I don't think I could have faced anyone then.

Was this our first quarrel? I didn't even know if it *was* a quarrel. The long talk Gene and I had about our marriage came back to me. It wasn't exactly *one* long talk—or, rather, it was a sort of recapitulation, made, or put together, one evening quite seriously (before our marriage) from other talks; from ideas, feeling, wondering about things, about ourselves.

12

But sitting there alone gazing at the distant edge of the harbor and not seeing it or anything else, I was concerned only with the words that Gene had just thrown at me with such angry emphasis when he spoke of "*our agreement*." He had spoken in that way because I had received a letter from my mother. I had noticed this attitude of his before—a sort of sullenness when I received letters from anyone in my family, or even from friends . . . as if he were jealous of anyone except himself claiming any part of my interest. But he had never said anything before. I was sure that he said what he did this time, not because of the letter or my apparent depression over it, but because he himself was frustrated—the result, really, of his own breaking of the agreement that he had mentioned.

I suppose I was resentful—the worst of all possible states to be in—because I thought he was being unfair; and along with that there was an even deeper feeling of unhappiness over his being upset about where to work, how to get started, and so on; so, to justify my resentment, which I didn't like at all, I recalled in detail the meaning of the agreement to which he had referred. . . .

It was a rather basic thing about our families and our way of life, and his very definite wish that we could be alone in whatever house or place we should live—except if we sallied forth, as it were, for occasional talks or visits with friends. It was already understood that we were to spend this summer in Provincetown in John Francis' flats; then another summer we would find a shack with kerosene heat and a couple of rooms further out of town, toward Truro, for the "studio," contented as he had been there for the time, was too near civilization to really suit him.

His parents we would see when we went to New York; they were a devoted pair who knew by now that they should not interfere with him: they lived in a hotel in New York in the winter and went to New London in the summertime. About Jamie he just didn't think, so firmly was his brother committed to his own established way of life, his fifteen-dollar-a-week allowance and his constant companionship with the older O'Neills, with whom for a long time it had been understood that he would spend at least a good part of every day. . . .

I had told Gene about the farm and about our old house in Jersey, which I had taken over and which had been more or less empty for a year or so—except for the summer rental. I believe he was pleased at the idea that either one place or the other might be a refuge to which we could retire if necessary. But he was only vaguely interested in my family—they too, should be kept at a distance—for it must be *he and I*, in a world of our own. As for my little girl, he was sure she was happy with my mother. I knew this was true; and so great was my feeling for Gene, and so preposterous would have been the idea of my poet-genius with a child around that I don't think the idea ever occurred to me. That didn't mean that I didn't think of her; the sonnet that I spoke of writing, one night after walking along the snowy street of Provincetown the winter before, was written to her. . . .

As for having any children of our own, I'm sure we never thought of it. A strange attitude, perhaps, for people getting married, but then Gene was an unusual person, and so perhaps, at that time, was I. . . . No—to be alone with me—that was what he wanted; we had everything—work, love and companionship. Never, *never* let anything interfere with work or love!

And now (really because of Jamie's being with us, and then only because of space, or room problems) something was stirring up between us, something for which, after his remarks about the letter, the blame was being put on *me*.

To be truthful it had seemed to be so expedient, so necessary for Jamie's sake that he come to Provincetown with us that I had never given it another thought. If it was what Gene wanted, and satisfied him, it was quite all right with me. I hadn't remembered what the flat was like, although I knew he'd lived and worked there with Terry Carlin. Once on a cold windy day last winter Gene got the key from Mr. Francis and took me up there; but the thought of where to work, keep our things, or even of privacy hadn't bothered me; thinking that Gene would have that (as he used to say) "doped out," I knew that his work—and where to work—was the most important thing. Now, wondering about it, I didn't know just how he'd thought it *would* work out—maybe that Jamie wouldn't like Provincetown and wouldn't stay. . . .

I walked at last around the Francis' store—about all I could do about anything was to get something for lunch. Gene would probably work out his problem better by being alone for a while. I had two things on my mind—not related, but having some bearing on each other; not only Gene, his writing and so on, but my own problem as outlined in the letter from my mother. I was confused about William Jones and his note, and

I realized now that Gene *was* right in what he had said: this letter and some previous ones had depressed me. What a mix-up . . . what tangled threads there already were!

13

John Francis, benevolent and Buddha-like, simple and kind, silently wrapped the groceries and vegetables that I needed. He seemed to be pondering about something. His intuition, when he did speak, startled me—as it was to do many times in our Provincetown years. He said that it must be very uncomfortable having the three of us in one flat—he didn't see how Gene could work. . . .

The solution, he went on without waiting for a reply, was to take the other flat now before someone else wanted it. He would be willing to wait for the rent, and he would make it less rent, because then we would be taking the whole floor.

I asked him eagerly if I could tell Gene that, and he nodded—he and Gene could talk it over later.

My husband was at the table working on his script when I came up. I put the groceries on the shelf and told him what Mr. Francis said. His aspect, which was still gloomy when I came in, changed at once—he had thought that the price would be too high to even consider! But now——! He finished what he was doing, went downstairs, came back and began moving Jamie's things across to the other flat. He wiped away the dust himself and swept the floor, feeling unexpectedly vigorous—even singing a sea chantey. When Jamie came for lunch he, too, was pleased, and slyly announced that now he could invite his girl friend up for a visit.

I wonder if Gene, wherever he is now, remembers that summer in Francis' flat at all: or if he ever thought of it again after it was over. . . . For some reason it comes less clearly to my mind than other times that we lived together. Perhaps because it was a hiatus between what Gene once called "the old mad studio days" and those wonderful, peaceful creative days at Peaked Hill Bar: or maybe it was because that summer was spent in the town, which was crowded with activities; with something always going on; new or old friends appearing first on the street and then coming up to see us; discussions and arguments centering around the Provincetown Player group; people having trouble with Portuguese maids, or girls getting into trouble with sailors (this would reach us in a roundabout way). There *is* one image that comes back, almost entirely a visual one, and so unconnected with anything that it's hard to place in time—but I don't think it was that summer. . . . There's a small shack, dark, with pots and pans and rubbish; a man there, young, unshaved; a gallon jug of liquor; my going there, walking through brambles and darkness to see what I could do, for Gene was there; it seems he wanted to leave and either he sent for me, or someone else (possibly Terry) came to get me to go there. We didn't seem to leave, and it comes to me that we stayed all night, talking and wandering in and out to a seaweedy beach, and I, too, drank out of the potent jug that time and tried to glimpse something of the world that the others were seeing.

I find, in looking over certain notes and diaries of mine, that some disturbing, if not exactly dramatic, talks occurred during our occupation of Francis' flat; and I have put them down because, if not significant at the time, they contained the tiny seeds of that change which comes into the lives of everyone. Talks that we had, things Gene told me, attitudes toward life and people, seem important because they are threads woven into the web and woof that later became the tragic pattern of Gene's life.

It was a long summer—longer than I thought at first; in going through old letters I find that we did not leave Provincetown until November of that year. There seems to be a small output of work for that number of months; and knowing how he did work—for that could always be counted on—I've gone back over it, keeping in mind that there were (even as officially recorded) only two one-act plays finished. However, after a week or so in New York that fall when we went down to the old house in Ocean County, he had already done a great deal of writing and hard work on *The Straw*, and on *The Old Devil*, or *Chris*, as he called the play that much later was to become *Anna Christie*.

That summer he was also looking forward to the coming production of *Beyond the Horizon*, which was going to be done as soon as possible, in an uptown theater, by John D. Williams, and with that knowledge he had a certain sense of accomplishment and pride . . . so, in one way or another, he was more outgoing with people; more concerned with the practical aspect of the theater; and also becoming more involved in the managerial goings on of the Provincetown Players—with Susan and Jig right across the street, and many other members of the group in Provincetown.

Perhaps it was this preoccupation with outside things, with people and events outside of his writing, my own attempts at adjustment with other affairs and my family during this first summer of our married life, and the fact that we were less alone together than during most of our marriage that make it, (except so far as he and I were concerned) less clear to me in some ways.

14

It was less than a week after Jamie moved to the other flat that Gene decided to do a short story. He had finished revising *Beyond the Horizon* and wasn't quite ready to start another long play. In April 1917 he had sold a short story to the *Seven Arts* magazine, receiving a remarkably fine letter of praise and criticism from Waldo Frank, who was editor of the magazine at that time. After making a few changes that Mr. Frank suggested, he had received a check for fifty dollars, and later sold them *In the Zone* for the same amount of money.

Now he wanted to write the story of a young Negro gangster, and as he talked to me about the boy who sneaked back to see his old grandmother on her deathbed Gene felt sure that he could better emphasize in short-story form the psychological split in the young Negro.

But the Provincetown Players were anxious for a one-act play to start their season in the fall. And as Gene talked, something else in him began to overcome the psychological aspect of the story. I could see his eyes darken, then become intense; he began to pace the floor as the dramatist in him took over. I have sometimes wondered how Gene's talent would have developed had he not been born, as it were, in the theater.

He got the idea for *The Dreamy Kid* during a conversation with dark, pock-marked Joe Smith, his old friend at the Hell Hole. I think that was it—as unimportant a thing as Joe merely mentioning someone of that name. *Dreamy!* I remember Gene speaking that name almost lovingly and then laughing. Negro gangster named Dreamy—so Joe had spoken of him. *Why Dreamy?*

He did a page or so of the short story, then put it aside—decided it should be a one-act play—and then he began writing the words: CHARACTERS: *Mammy Saunders; Abe, her grandson, "The Dreamy Kid . . ."*

So now he was working, everything was at last as it should be: the rhythm and creative happiness of our days in the studio were back again. . . .

I woke at dawn the day after he started work and lay there for a while. Gene slept more soundly than usual beside me. His face had repose and strength—today he would start writing *The Dreamy Kid*, he had talked about it again last night. . . .

I sat up, put my feet on the floor, and bending over kissed him on the forehead, softly so as not to waken him. *My love, My sensitive, strange darling! What made you what you are, what were the hidden stigmata that had wounded you, and at times bled with drops of bitterness?* But what I saw was the haloed nimbus, not yet really visible, of a great poet, of the creative man.

I picked up my clothes from the chair and went out to where the dawn came with thin streaks of bright gold past the edge of the drawn shade. He would sleep another hour or so, and quietly I got into my clothes and went down the wooden stairs.

It is not easy to describe the ecstasy and joy that just being alive on certain days brings—the effect of light and sun and air, of distance, and of small things nearby. . . . I saw gulls flying and it was as if I had never really known before what a sea gull was. I smelled the odor of pilings, damp from the night, and the odor of the sand over which people had walked and left footprints. I saw the harbor, the distant sea, and there seemed to be a silence behind the glittering water and sky. At my feet little objects caught my eye—tiny shells, bits of wood polished by water; mussels; tangled seaweed. There is a poem by Emily Dickinson that brings back that walk in the early morning:

> *I taste a liquor never brewed*
> *From tankards scooped in pearl,*
> *Nor all the vats upon the Rhine*
> *Yield such an alcohol!*
> *Inebriate of air am I,*
> *And debauchee of dew.*
> *Reeling through endless summer days,*
> *From inns of molten blue.*
>
> *When landlords turn the drunken bee*
> *Out of the foxglove's door,*
> *When butterflies renounce their dreams*
> *I shall but drink the more!*
> *Till seraphs swing their snowy hats,*
> *And saints to windows run,*
> *To see the little tippler*
> *Leaning against the sun!*

I came back from a solitary and enchanted wandering along the edge of the harbor, past the old wharf building where Gene's plays had first been produced two summers ago—*Bound East for Cardiff, Thirst.* I thought of how he had come here, a young man with a suitcase full of plays. *Thirst*—that was the one he played in—he as a half-naked sailor and Louise Bryant as the beautiful dancer dying of thirst on a raft in mid-ocean. *Louise* . . . I remembered the dilemma of the studio days. Louise had already passed like a ghost into a nonexistent past (though probably some part of me was wondering if I'd ever see her, and if she *did* look like me!). "Let the dead past bury its dead!" Where, I wondered, did that quotation so often used by Gene, come from?

He was still asleep when I came back to the flat. I pulled up the front window shades and then went and stood for a moment or so looking down at him. . . . We had come through again; we were in Provincetown; we were safe. . . . Without even putting it into words I knew that he had not meant what had happened to happen; he had not wanted it; he had not wanted to drink; and he could not (and it seemed to me then, never could) be blamed.

15

Gene got up every morning about eight o'clock, ate breakfast, started to work. I cleared off the table, sat down again and began to write too. . . . After Gene was finished working he went across the street to Jig Cook's house, read the headlines, talked to Susan Glaspell, who would be through her work by this time, and brought back the previous day's *Times.* He'd look at this for a while and then go down to the beach for a swim; sometimes I went with him, sometimes I stayed upstairs and got lunch ready. Jamie was in and out—it was nice having him there.

After lunch Gene would lie down and take a short nap, then go over what he had written that morning, or do some typing—

but he did not spend as much time on this as usual, for that summer there was a great deal of excitement going on; navy vessels came in and out of the harbor—submarines were supposed to be off the coast; people came to the beach in the afternoon and talked about the war and all that was going on in the town; as a rule before three or four o'clock we were down there too, walking out over the flats for another swim if the tide was out, lying in the sun. . . . In the evening after supper we read or talked, or sometimes went to see the Cooks or the Hapgoods or some other friends. If Gene was interested in the conversation he talked, or if it bored him he picked up a convenient book or magazine and sat there reading. No one seemed to mind—but I'm ashamed to say I didn't like it, nor did I like it when he did the same thing when people came to see us. It seems to me now that it was a sensible enough thing for him to do.

One other thing I didn't like—and I realize now also how foolish and young-wifeish I was about that. For some reason I got quite upset at his going over to Susan's as soon as he had finished his work and staying there, often much longer than I thought he should, talking to her. . . . I suppose I was jealous, which was absurd—but also it made me feel very much *out* of things. I believe that these two feelings on my part went up and down like weights on a scale whenever I was really concerned about this matter—which was usually when I was waiting for him to come back! Susan was very attractive, but she was older than Gene and really very much in love with her husband, Jig Cook, which gave her considerable to think about. She was not too strong physically and Jig had built for her, in that little Cape Cod cottage, an elevator with ropes so she would not have to climb the stairs to her room. She talked and thought about her health with some concern—but to women, not to the many men who found her conversation stimulating and helpful. She was a slight and girlish woman who looked attractive even when she was not feeling well; she had a sort of feminine inner spirit, a fire, a sensitiveness that showed in her fine brown eyes and in the way that she used her hands and spoke. She seemed to me an ethereal being, detached and yet passionate. She was so far beyond me in her knowledge and understanding of everything that was going on in the world—economics, the rights of mankind, the theater, writing, people—and she was able to talk of them when necessary with charm and interest, while I, it seemed to me, only managed to stutter mentally when I tried to put anything into words. . . .

But I *was* jealous of Susan—which I'm sure would surprise her if she were alive today. I was grumpy and quiet when Gene came back with the newspaper after having stayed in that quiet restful house for too long. At last he asked me what was the matter. So I told him and he laughed; grabbed me and lifted me up in the air, hugged me tightly against his chest, and told me I was a plain little damn fool. . . . After that (being a darling then!), we went swimming together as soon as he had finished working, or if he did go over to Susan's he didn't stay so long.

16

We went over to Jig and Susan's house the evening *The Dreamy Kid* was finished and he read it aloud. There was enthusiasm for the play; but a little later there seemed to be some doubt about it—whether they did not think it as good as his other short plays, or if there was some difficulty in regard to the Negro cast, I don't remember. I do know that they definitely wanted *another* play from him with which to open their season on Macdougal Street in the fall.

After that evening Gene took a few days off from work. There were letters to write; typing to be done; notes and ideas about *Chris* to go over. He and I took long swims and lay longer in the sand in the hot sun. Gene became as dark as a Hawaiian, and I got very tanned too—only, my hair was bleaching out in strange streaks. Sometimes, after a long swim, doing the crawl or the lazy backstroke, we would sit, dripping with salt water, on the sand, and Gene would talk of the South Sea

Islands and how we would go there some day and go up the Amazon—he had a yen to go up the Amazon. . . .

Sometimes Jamie sat with us, the dog beside him; or, more often we would see him out on the flats with the same quiet girl, and the dog, looking for fiddler crabs. Someone gave us two tiny kittens, and we kept them upstairs in the flat, with a box of sand in the corner for their toilet. Bowser, when he accompanied Jamie from the other flat was most considerate toward the kittens—it was as if, after being rescued from his sordid canine youth in Boston, he must be kindly toward everything. . . .

After lunch, which we took down to the beach and ate with pleasurable greed from paper plates, we would lie drying ourselves in the hot sun for a while and then Gene and I would go back upstairs to our flat, pull down the shades, and in our half-dry suits, grains of sand here and there on our skin, we would lie down on the bed in the warm darkness. . . .

One afternoon we walked eastward from Francis' store and turned off down a sandy road through scrubby trees and tangled undergrowth to where the sand dunes started, gently rounded under the stretch of low, clinging vegetation from which emerged stumps and crooked dead branches of fallen trees. Gene was taking me to the coast-guard station which Mabel Dodge had discovered and made livable, spending a summer there with her friends. . . . He had spoken about it often, and now we were going to see it. As we walked, holding hands, the dunes appeared to change and move, some long and gentle, others steep and grass-crowned; they existed in a world of their own, quiet, peaceful and detached from everything; we no longer saw the trees and vegetation that edged them on the Provincetown side, nor could we yet hear the sound of the ocean on the outer shore; there was only air and sky, and here and there the long eelgrass which traced circles in the sand about its roots as it was blown restlessly by the wind.

We climbed the last long dune and stood there and saw the old coast-guard station beneath us—the long gray roof with its lookout; two or three other buildings near it; and everywhere sand, piled and blown against the buildings to the very edge of the roofs. We went sliding down the dune, and then walked up the roof of the house to the railed lookout: Gene, laughing, sat down on the wide bench and pulled me down beside him.

"This is the house you and I should have!" he said, looking at the ocean, which stretched out beyond a beach of white sand and seaweed in a great circle to the horizon. "We would live here like sea gulls, two sea gulls coming home at night to our home. . . ." And we slid down the roof to the sand and ran up the beach together, tiny sandpipers scattering in flocks before us and settling down again in the wet sand after we passed. We found a place, dry and hot, behind a dune that was close to the ocean, and undressed, ran down, plunged and splashed through the low breakers, and swam a while beyond them; and then, returning, wet and salty with dripping hair, embraced in ecstasy on the hot sand, beneath the silent sky. . . .

One night, lying in bed with his arm under my head, he told me a secret that had bothered him—a secret fear of impotence. "It has happened at times," he told me, "and I don't know why. I had a fear of it somehow, coming back to this flat. It has nothing to do with physical feeling, but sometimes when that feeling is most intense, I think of that fear, it comes and then it might happen, I don't know why." I did not know why either, for it had never happened that way. What was he afraid of; it was always rather a mystery to me, his saying this; but he did say it, and was worried then for a while. . . .

Then, one morning, there was the sound of gunfire, and after that, panic; for a German submarine was seen in the harbor, or just outside of it, emerging and then disappearing. No one knew where it was going or what it was going to do. There was a panic in the town, a mingled hush and expectancy. Strangely enough, I do not remember our taking it too seriously. Gene did not seem worried or afraid—mainly, it gave him an opportunity to write a long letter to his parents describing the dangers of war.

He seemed, about this time, to be in a reminiscing mood—to want to bring into some sort of focus other things that had occurred in his past that might be of use to him. No longer did he sit at night with Jamie and talk of their lurid days; nor did he seem to be thinking too much of his sailor days; or of old Chris, who lived on a barge with his woman Marty. He had been writing that down and seemed to have come to some sort of block with it; it didn't yet take the form of the play he wanted, and he had put it aside for a while and didn't want to talk about it.

We continued our long walks in the afternoon or early evening. One day, going out to Race Point, not along the road but crossing through little paths and small sandy cliffs, he began telling me of the time he spent in New London working on a newspaper; sitting down on an abandoned rowboat half buried in the sand, he spoke about a girl with whom he had been in love at that time—a beautiful girl and with great charm. . . . It was a real love affair, perhaps his first—and his most orthodox (if that is the word) feeling about a girl. He had wanted to marry her, and as he talked, it seemed to me that he almost thought for a while that he could live and be happy (at least with her) in a conventional life. But she was too frightened of her father, her social position, the future. . . . There had been a crisis of some sort—a demanding on his part, a demanding in return on hers—a misunderstanding; or, more likely, an understanding, for they parted, both of them perhaps hoping that this parting was not permanent. But it had been the ending for them in spite of his seeing her again, and letters between them even after he went to Baker's class in Harvard; and she remained in his memory, beautiful and once deeply cherished, but a symbol of a woman who would not give up all for love. . . .

He showed me her picture when we came back that evening, and some poems he had written to her—some written with romantic feeling, others amusing. He told me about that Christmas when he left his family to go to the tubercular sanatorium. And after supper he began talking about the sanatorium. . . .

We sat near the open window, hearing the waves moving against the pilings below, expecting perhaps to hear gunshots off shore that meant the German submarine had been found; my own mind was half dreamily preoccupied with the face of the girl whose photograph he had just shown me, but he talked in his low, slow voice of the "San," as he called it, intent on recalling it again and sharing it with me. . . . He paused only to get up and bring out some more photographs—which I'd seen before, but without particular interest.

The next morning, after sitting a while at the typewriter copying some notes that he had made, he told me that he had been thinking about the "San" before he went to sleep the night before, and that even while he was at the typewriter it had been in his mind—particularly a girl there whom he had almost forgotten. . . . His face became compassionate—he said it was the goddamnedest thing, what happened when patients had been there a while. People came to see them, the family and friends; then, pretty soon nobody comes, there's very little mail—in fact, he said, they are forgotten. . . .

He had spoken, the night before, of himself at the sanatorium; what he had thought about, what he had read there, and how gradually the conviction had come to him that he wanted to write plays. But now this was put aside—he was thinking only of the girl. . . .

After our swim he was very silent for a while and then he began talking about her again, and even while I was getting something together for lunch and setting the table, he went on talking about her and about his feeling of pity for her. . . . It was this girl who later became one of the leading characters in one of Gene's plays.

17

I was having my own troubles and keeping quiet about them, for I did not want to worry Gene. He noticed that I was finding excuses to get out of my more or less regular hours of work;

the kittens' box had to be filled: I was planning something special for dinner and had to go out to buy what I wanted; or I was just tired and wanted to go down early to the beach and lie in the sun. . . .

He asked me, one morning when after he had finished his work he saw that I had been engaged, not in writing, but in assembling together equal amounts of sea bass, codfish, lobster claws, two eels, a small grouper, and a piece of haddock, all of which I had cleaned or washed and put on one end of the table; on the other end I had already laid out a small jar of olive oil, onions, leaks, parsley, tomatoes, garlic and some herbs, including a piece of fennel from the fields—he asked me, after looking at all this with interest, why I was cooking at this time of day?

"I thought you'd like a bouillabaisse!" I said. "It takes time getting the things, *not* the cooking. I even got some saffron at the drugstore."

"Sounds fine! Had some once in New Orleans. But don't pass the buck, baby, why don't you do all this in the *afternoon?*"

"I want to be with you then."

"Well—this'll hit the spot! But what about that novelette you were going to write? You got a letter the other day, didn't you, from *Young's*, or *Snappy Stories* asking for one?"

My inertia turned to complete emptiness inside me. *He* had hit the spot—the very sore spot. I didn't want to write the novelette. . . . Bouillabaisse was an excuse—everything was an excuse.

"You know you told me that you thought I should go ahead with the better stuff——" I said, trying to be firm.

Gene grinned with tender malice. "So bouillabaisse is better stuff? You're not doing any writing. Seriously, Aggie, you're getting thin! Hutch Hapgood told me someone was saying that *you* had tuberculosis. Just gossip, of course, among our envious friends! What have you got on your mind?"

"I don't see any reason why I can't do a *good* story and get money for it—say, from *Harper's!*"

He picked up a towel. "I'm going down for a swim. I'm stumped on *Chris* myself right now—been doing the outline this afternoon but it doesn't come right, not yet. I'll go over what you've done on your story, and if you have anything else on your mind, let's hear about that, too!"

I went on fixing the bouillabaisse (which was really a fish stew) after Gene went downstairs; but whereas I'd been absorbed in this before, my mind was now distracted by our talk. Most of the work was done: now all that was left to do was to arrange everything in a large pot, with the piscatory pieces that took the longest to cook on the bottom; add the oil and vegetables and not too large an amount of water and let it stew very gently for a short time. I did it all, except putting it on the stove; I could have gone down to the beach for a while and come up later to start it cooking. . . .

Instead I sat down looking blankly at the table, from which the assortment of fish and food was now removed, and tried (glum as Gene himself could be at times but I'm sure more confused than he ever could be) to arrange in sections (as I had the fish) and tackle separately *what was* wrong. . . .

Well, what *was?* How to separate it anyway? Maybe it was all one problem, not several! *Let's see . . . that empty feeling about "The Captain's Walk . . ."*

That was not quite true; when I was working on it I felt wonderful, though there were, of course, problems about this and that in the story; but even *that* was fun—so why the empty feeling? *Because you know it's not going to sell.* . . . No magazine that would be interested in this story uses novelettes. It's almost that already. . . .

What makes the empty feeling is money then, isn't it? Or, damn it, having to *think* about money! But I did have to think about it—something was always coming up. The taxes, the mortgage interest on the Old House in New Jersey; nasty letters from the tenant, the screens had rotted, mosquitoes were killing them, he had ordered new screens for the entire house, and that used the balance of the rent. I knew perfectly well that at the most all he needed were three or four new screens instead of twenty-seven! A small doctor's bill from Dawn Hill; some mix-up about a telephone there—but on top of all that, and adding up to a complete and baffling confusion in my mind, those goddamn letters about the note for the cows!

(I was getting to swear, in my thoughts at least, like my husband, whose vocabulary was frequently emphasized by the greatest collection of oaths and swear words that I've heard before or since.)

I pulled out the drawer of the table and looked at the collection of envelopes, in more or less illiterate handwriting, that I had hidden away out of sight. I closed the drawer quickly—it was too much! It was a good thing that *I* had been going for the mail lately. Then I pulled it out again. There was no use evading them. Also there were three letters from my mother which I had put there, but those I didn't bother with now.

The letters about the notes for the cows had been arriving at intervals; I took them out, looked them over again and still could not make any sense out of them. . . .

Buying the cows had seemed a good idea at the time. There were a hundred or more acres of pasture on the farm, and another hundred acres were in hay. The idea was this: one bought some stock—or dry heifers; in the summer they were put out to pasture; in the winter they ate the hay. So the farm itself supported them; there was no milking and very little work connected with it, as the hay was cut on shares and half of it put in the barn—which was three times the size of the house. At the proper time, usually when they were two years old, the heifers were bred to a neighboring bull and when, as they said up there, they "freshened," then one sold them to a neighboring farmer for a good price.

But in the meantime, one had bought them either for cash

or on a note—most of the farmers did the latter, and William Jones, cattle dealer par excellence, always kept a number of half-grown heifers for just such transactions; or, if he didn't have them, went out and bought them overnight, driving miles to get them from some run-down farm in the mountains and offering ready cash. . . .

I knew that I'd made the last payment . . . I *thought* I had made the one before that. But in the moving around Gene and I had done, the receipt could have been lost. Anyhow, now it seemed I owed fifty dollars—and from some of the letters it appeared I owed the entire note, not only to Mr Jones, but to several other people!

It was at this moment that Gene came up, wet and smiling after his swim. He saw me sitting there disconsolately and, leaning over me, looked at the pile of letters which now I did not try to conceal. . . .

"Can you make these out?" I said, looking at him desperately. I added what I thought was the proper businesslike phrase: "*I don't know where I stand!*"

He sat down beside me and I saw that he really wanted to help me. I handed him the letters, which were clipped together. He removed the clip and looked through them.

"I can't make head or tail of this," he said at last. "What's it all about? You've been making payments on the note—I know that. Where," he added belligerently, "are the cows?"

"That has nothing to do with it, Gene," I said, rather curtly. "It's the notes—not the cows."

"I should think it had a lot to do with it! Can't you sell the bloody damn cows? And what do you mean—*notes?* I thought it was *a* note. How do you handle this thing, anyway?"

"Every month I pay something on my note—what I can; usually twenty-five dollars and interest. Then I make a new note, for the balance, whatever it is, and send that back. Last month I only sent ten dollars, but Mr. Jones said it would be all right to send what I could if I was short." I picked up the first of the letters. Gene read it aloud slowly. I could see he was bored:

Mrs. Agnes Burton O'Neill
Provincetown, Mass.

Dear Madam: Enclosed find some Blank Notes, and please send renewal as soon as possible, I wish you could get the new note back here by the 20th, but date it the 21st, as I want to try and use it in the bank and you know they don't want any past due paper. Try and make the payment as large as possible as I am very hard up for money. I am just haying, the crops are fair. I see by your letter you are married and wish you many happy days.

Yours truly,
William Jones

P.S. The old note is $167.50

"Now," I added hopefully, feeling that I could interest him: "I'll read *this!* It came from Fred Baker, Grocer, New Milford."

Miss Agnes B. Burton

Dear Madam:
    Mr. William Jones is holding a note against you for $185.50. This note is past due. Mr. Jones is in a bad way and has put this note in my hands for collection and security. If not convenient to pay the whole note, kindly send me a hundred on the principal and you can make a short term note for the balance.

Respectfully yours,

"Now wait a minute! Here's another from Henry Ashlord, Real Estate.

Dear Madam:
    I hold a note against you for $157.00. I also hold one for $135.60, signed Ageness O'Neill. Mr. Jones has made an

assignment of his personal property to me . . . I do not just understand the notes, and ask you to write me just what you owe him. He has left the country and I am going to try and settle up his estate, kindly advise if one note is a renewal of the other or if you own them both. Estate of William Jones.

"Now," I said, really trembling as I saw the look of blankness in Gene's eyes: "I wrote Mr. Jones. Here is his reply:

Dear Madam: In reply to your letter I must say the reason i left note with Mr. Baker is that I got mixed up in a wood job this spring and come near loosing everything I had so i had to go crowding everyone that owed me. But you must still send renewal and payment of note to me, as i have to indorse it and make it as large a payment as you can and I will see that Mr. Baker doesn't crowd us. I am sorry I had to make you this trouble but I couldn't help it, but my crops are good this year so as soon as I can turn them I expect to be on a good footing again, hoping you are getting along fine, yours truly William Jones.

Gene took the letter and looked it over: "I thought he'd disappeared? Where's Brookville? Wait a minute—he's got this one dated *1819* . . . he's as crazy as you are!"

"I did what he said," I went on, ignoring this. "Then came this one—you read it!"

Agnes Burton O'Neill Madam: In the matter of the note given by yourself to William Jones and now held by Compton of East Bridge, will you please let me hear from you at once what you intend to do?

"Who the hell is *Compton?*" Gene yelled, putting the letter down. Then his expression changed: "*Where are the old notes— the ones he returned to you?*"

"He hasn't returned them, not all of them, not for quite a while anyway. I don't know why he doesn't—he just doesn't."

"NO—he handed them out to his creditors, that's it!" Gene said. "Well he can't get anything from *me!* God damn it—let them take the cows and stop bothering you."

"They can't, or they would."

"Why not?"

"The cows broke through the fence into a tobacco lot on the next farm and ruined all the leaf tobacco. The farmer put them into his tobacco barn and sold them for damages before mother even knew about it . . . !"

"Well," Gene said at last, "just don't do anything about it. *See what happens!*"

I think the truth was that he didn't know anything more about it than I did, and, somewhat relieved, I decided to follow his advice. So, for the present at least, that was off my mind. However, *his* mind was now made up—he was going to get me straightened out about my work also, and I was only too glad to talk to him about this.

18

He read what I had done on "The Captain's Walk" with absorbed interest—then told me it was great, but not dramatic enough. It wasn't dramatic dialogue! He didn't seem to hear me when I told him I saw it as a character story, a story of atmosphere and obsession; and without listening to me he began, after we had eaten the bouillabaisse, to visualize it in his own terms of drama. I listened to him eagerly, but it didn't seem to help—it became something else than what I'd intended as he began to elaborate it.

"Do you think I can sell it to one of the magazines?"

"No, it's too long. Why don't you put it aside for a while?" He regarded me thoughtfully. "Or let me work out the action? Why not go ahead with a novelette?"

So I started a novelette—thinking of the money I needed for the note, the farm and other things. But my former attitude toward the girl who wanted this or wanted that wasn't amusing any more. It dragged, and it dragged me down into the depths of inertia with it. Gene noticed this and a couple of days later came in to where I was sitting listlessly before the copybook and handed me a rather frayed, blue-covered manuscript.

"Why don't you do this? Here's a copy of *Now I Ask You*—something I did quite a while back. It's not my sort of stuff, but it's a damn good idea for a popular success. Take it and use it if you can—it needs something done to it, and you might be able to fix it up. Either a novel, or even a better play than it is now—why not try, anyhow? I've been thinking out an idea for "The Captain's Walk"—only I want to change the title. It would make a damn good short play. . . . What do you think of *Where the Cross Is Made?*"

I could not get interested at that time in doing anything with *Now I Ask You*. It should remain a play, of that I felt sure, and Gene agreed. But all this gave me a new impetus—probably in order to escape from both *Now I Ask You* and "The Captain's Walk"! So I turned to writing about two sisters, one of whom went wrong and one who went right, and the naughty girl got the man they were both after. That was one of the virtues of the pulp magazines—sin sometimes did pay! And I got paid too—two hundred dollars—which made me feel quite rich and quite defiant about that old William and his note. . . .

I was excited about what Gene was doing with my sea captain. He brought in the idea of treasure, of gold, and a map that marked where the treasure was buried, and called it *Where the Cross Is Made*. Much later on, this short play was elaborated into *Gold*, which was produced in the summer of 1921 by Mr. Williams. We were in Provincetown then and he was working on another play, and for some reason he wanted me to go down to New York and take his place at rehearsals. What took place then, and the strange (to me at least) goings on prior to this fatal production, made me curse the idea that I had ever handed him my poor little manuscript, that summer of 1918. . . .

As for Jones, from whom I was now waiting to hear—nothing

happened. Nor did I hear more from the auctioneer, the to-bacco man or Mr. Compton's lawyer—not alas, until much later. At the time, I decided that Gene's advice had after all been quite right. . . .

19

One stormy afternoon in August, with the wind blowing from the east and the water a blur of spray, Gene stood at the window and gazed out at the rain-swept harbor. Then he picked up a book he had started, and tried to read. After a few moments he put the book down and restlessly went over to the other window and stood there, looking down Commercial Street. I felt his restlessness and it disturbed me and made me restless too, for there was nothing I could do about it. Jamie was in his flat, reading—he had been in a rather taciturn mood for a day or so.

When Gene was bored or frustrated his face changed and sank into a mask of fixed gloom. The very shape of his face would change, his cheeks sagged and his mouth grew heavy and lifeless, and his skin, as if vitality had completely left him, assumed a flaccid and lifeless look. He was bored and frustrated now—this was the second day he had not been able to swim—and when I suggested that we go for a walk in spite of the squally wind, he did not want to consider it.

"In the old days I would get happily blotto on an afternoon like this! Even last summer—but now you are my guilty conscience. Terry understood me, he was always the same. If I was bored it didn't affect him, he didn't get bored and unhappy too. If I felt like a few drinks, he felt like a few drinks too."

"Why do you tell me you don't want to drink then? That you want me to help you not to drink? Get a bottle—I don't care if you have to have it." Gene was silent. "Why don't you go up the street and see Harold de Polo. He'd be only too glad to see you—there's always a drink there," I said angrily.

"No. I don't want to see the don—not now. The kids in the

house—even with Harold it's not like the old days." He went to the closet, took out a sweater and pulled it over his head, lit a cigarette and stood again at the window. "I don't want to go anywhere—that's the trouble, I just want to escape from myself."

He came back, picked up the sheets of paper on which he had been working that morning, then put them back on the table. He pulled out a drawer, looked through some scripts and took out an envelope that held some photographs, and sat looking at them in silence.

"How do you like me without a mustache?" he said, with a sudden grin, "Maybe that's what I should do—shave off my mustache this afternoon!"

I stood behind him, my hand on his shoulder, looking at the pictures. "No, I like you better *with* the mustache!"

He reached out and put his arm around me. "Look at this. That's the burro I had to ride going up the Terla River."

"Maybe you wish you were in Honduras again—is that it?"

"No! That I *don't* wish! I didn't enjoy myself—it was hell. I was never so bitten up in my life—flies, fleas and mosquitoes— and that was only part of it. Lucky thing I got malaria and had to come home. How about a cup of coffee?"

As I was making it, he roamed around again, then picked up the book. I heard the wicker chair creak as he settled down. But he couldn't get interested, and as he stirred his coffee I saw his eyes get a reminiscent look.

"You've never said much about that trip—it sounds exciting, going for gold, the jungle, all that. What happened, that you you don't even talk about it? The only thing you ever told me about it was the story of that horse—remember?"

"I wasn't keen about going in the first place. . . ." He paused, looking back into the past. "Maybe after I got started I *did* expect something . . . but I'd sooner look for gold on Broadway than in Honduras! What stinking vile food we had! Everything cooked in grease. And *tortillas*—you'd fill up on them—sort of a soggy, heavy pancake, made of ground corn—

no bread of course. I had cramps from the lousy food—that and the damn bugs. . . ."

He took up his cup and rinsed the coffee around in his mouth before he swallowed.

"There were some pretty Spanish towns, the boys and girls walking around in circles in the plaza in the evening, the band playing . . . but we didn't stay there long. As for the natives, they were the lowest, laziest, most ignorant bunch of brainless bipeds that ever polluted a land!"

I saw his wry grimace with some amazement. "I would have thought—— I remember reading *The Conquest of Peru* up in the attic when I was a kid."

"Hooey! I saw them! Someday Fate will get tired of watching those human maggots groping in the dark, and exterminate them!"

I watched him take another sip of coffee and it seemed to me he looked peevish rather than scornful. His words came slowly, with careful emphasis, when he spoke again. "Until God shakes those human lice from its side, Honduras hasn't a chance—it's the Siberia of the tropics!"

He paused, smiling at his phrases, and then went on:

"Only a fellow used to sleeping in a pigpen and eating out of a trough could live there any length of time. Nobody will stay there as long as the yearly revolutions keep up, either."

"Were you in a revolution?" I asked hopefully, remembering the night he had led an imaginary revolution in Sherman Square.

"No. From what I've heard, these South American revolutions are a good example of comic opera. Everybody has a good time, and they go home and sleep it off! So, I've had my little say about the well-known country of Honduras. I felt that way then, and I haven't changed my mind!"

"And *no* gold?" I said vaguely—in order to say something.

"No gold! There *was* gold there, but I didn't find any!"

He was looking through the pictures again, a strange and rather brooding expression on his face. I was aware of something—I didn't know what—and this made me ask him a question rather pointedly. I remembered something he had said at the beginning of the conversation.

"Just *why* did you ever go there, Gene?"

20

He had been living at the Prince George Hotel with his parents, he told me, going out every night drinking with another fellow. He'd met this girl through his friend Frank— a damn nice girl, very proper and well brought up. She was a friend of the girl that Frank was going around with at the time, and she'd brought Kathleen along with her one night. After that the four of them started going around together. "Frank was quite serious about his girl, and it all seemed pretty mild to me at first. . . ." Gene went on. "I was used to the kind of gals that got lit and involved in crazy adventures. I don't know what *she* thought of me . . . but she began telling me about her background, which was pretty conventional and which she didn't seem to like particularly. And I began by feeling sorry for her and ended up by falling for her."

Gene paused. There was a faint smile on his lips. "She must have fallen for me too, for after a month or so of going around together—always the four of us—Frank and I suggested we all go over to Jersey City and she and I get married. She agreed, so we got married! It was going to be kept a secret from everybody for a while—which suited me. I knew damn well what the old man would say if *he* heard of it. She thought her parents wouldn't like it either; they were all ready to marry her off to some young stockbrocker who was being very persistent, and I think now one of her reasons for marrying me was to get rid of *him*."

Gene looked at me, then paused to light a cigarette. "I was scared to death when I realized what I had done. Her parents were away at the time, and after the wedding we all went over to her apartment and celebrated. After Frank and his girl left,

I stayed a couple of days—her folks wouldn't be home for a week. It was fun—of course I was nipping away at her father's liquor, and she cooked and tried to get me to eat. We had a great time trying to disguise every evidence of our honeymoon before I left. . . ."

Gene laughed to himself and then went on: "She wanted to ride down to the Prince George with me on the subway and say good-by there before I saw my folks. But I was afraid I might run into them. So I left her at the apartment, and she did put her arms around me at the door and say she hoped we'd have a place of our own soon. I remember it gave me a sort of a chill—I went and got good and drunk before I went back to the Prince George."

"It was a crazy thing to do—we didn't have any money or any plans. I couldn't go to her apartment again; for one thing I was afraid of running into her parents. She didn't want to tell them about the marriage until I was ready to take her out of there. I'd never met them and she thought they wouldn't approve of me. They were a bit on the snobbish side—that was evident!"

Gene paused and gave a rather sheepish smile.

"I probably thought with that big apartment—and it seemed to me that they had plenty of money—that she could just as well stay on there! The truth was that after I'd been married a week or so I practically forgot I *was* married to her. It seemed a joke, a lark. Frank looked at it that way too—it even seemed to me that was *her* attitude. She was trying to be a good sport, I suppose. Anyway, when the four of us would all go out together it was just about the same as before."

"Then, I don't know how, her parents got wind of it. I was living at the Prince George with the folks, of course. I came back there late one afternoon after spending the night with Frank at his place—and was Papa in a rage! He'd been waiting for me to come in—pacing the floor! Mama was furious too, mad and upset. I'd never seen them in such a state before. She just sat there and didn't say a word, while Papa did the talking, but I could see how mad she was. . . ."

"Of course they were sore as hell about me getting married without telling them about it. That was one thing they never worried about—*me* getting married! But it turned out that the ones they were really sore at were her parents. It seemed that when Kathleen was faced with some real evidence she broke down and told them the whole story. And then, without telling her, they went down and paid Papa and Mama an unannounced visit, stating that their daughter was married to their son, and they wanted something done about it right away. If said son had no job and no money, it was up to Papa to get an apartment and support the young couple until said son *did* get a job! They took the attitude that my old man was a millionaire. Also, that he should be pleased that his son had managed to marry into such a good family as theirs—it seemed that her grandfather was one of the founders of the New York Stock Exchange—a big hit all this made with Papa! It wound up by their telling him that they were going to bring her to the Prince George and leave her with her new husband—*they* were closing the apartment and leaving on a trip."

Gene paused and gave an impish grin.

"*'You're the one that's going on a trip—and right away!'* the old man yelled at me. 'That'll solve everything. And meanwhile you're not going to see that slick adventuress—understand?'

"Papa was all wrong about her of course—there was never a nicer girl than Kathleen. But nothing could convince him that the whole thing was not something cooked up by the parents and their daughter in order to get her off their hands. He wouldn't listen to me at all. Mama was quite as firm. . . . I managed to see Kathleen. She clung round my neck and was more upset than I was at what her parents had done. But she could see their point of view and tried to explain it to me; they felt that she had been badly treated and that things must be straightened out. I got drunk, she went home, and two weeks later I was on a boat to Honduras."

There was a pause. I felt a little dazed by all this, but knew I had to say something. I was going to ask him, not knowing what else to say, how his father managed to arrange the trip so quickly, when he began to explain it:

"I've told you all about Papa's mania for investing in cattle ranches, phony oil wells, gold mines, and so on. Well, it seems that this time Mama had put some of *her* money in a real deal— a guy named Stevens who'd found good prospects for gold in Honduras; later on it turned out to be quite a good deal for her. The expedition had been arranged, Stevens had gone down with his wife, and plans were being made to start into the jungle; the old man and Mama sent a joint wire to Stevens, and it was arranged that I should join them. And that, my angel, is *just* how I got to go gold hunting!"

I looked at him silently; he had never told me this about his marriage before. And now he told it so casually—as though it was nothing more than an episode leading up to his trip to Honduras. I laughed; I, too, would be casual if that was the way he wanted it.

"So you were shanghaied!"

"Not exactly—don't remember just how I did feel about it. I took a boat down to join the Stevenses soon after my birthday. I was just twenty-one, remember that! Once I knew that I was going I suppose I romanticized the whole thing—gold, the jungle, the unexplored land."

"What about the girl?"

"They insisted I shouldn't see Kathleen again, and I suppose by then she, too, was pretty much in the hands of her parents. It was already something in the past, to be forgotten. I was sure that neither she nor I knew what we were doing—it was just a youthful escapade that had turned out too seriously. As for the future—any consequences such as divorce, money or anything else—I never thought of it. I guess," he added thoughtfully, "that I just didn't consider myself a married man. I left everything to Papa. He was grim-lipped and said nothing about anything. . . ."

"But what *did* happen about all that?" I asked, rather faintly. Gene grinned and shook his head and was silent; his whole face was cast in that pensive look of oblivion that came over him whenever he thought of the past.

"Did I ever tell you *that* story—the time I tried to commit suicide?" he said at last.

21

"It was probably a year or so later," he said. "I only stayed in Honduras three or four months—I've told you how I got malaria and had to come back home. The old man had the *White Sister* company on the road and I joined as stage manager. They didn't want me to stay around New York, of course. Never heard a word from Kathleen. It was after that tour with the *White Sister* company that I shipped to Buenos Aires—eighty-five days at sea—without once sighting land. Maybe Honduras *had* planted the adventure bug in me after all. . . .

"Then after I shipped back to New York again I stayed at Jimmy the Priest's on the waterfront and, being flat broke, wrote the folks. They wouldn't do anything unless I went up to New London. They gave me the fare and I spent it on booze. . . . Guess they thought that I was crazy by this time."

Gene, although he had done so before, described to me again the atmosphere and the odd characters at Jimmy the Priest's. It was an obsession with him—this place and his memories of it; and often during the years that we were together he spoke of wanting to write a play about it and the men he knew there, but he never did. Perhaps there were too many characters to bring in, nothing that he wanted to leave out . . . until many years later when he wrote *The Iceman Cometh* and then (to the discomfort of those earlier audiences) leaving nothing and nobody out of the place as he knew it, besides introducing many new characters.

"I really was in bad shape at the time," he went on. "Under-weight, a bad cough, and of course blotto whenever I could be, which meant whenever one of the remittance derelicts got a check—we would immediately drink it up! It sure was lousy stuff that Jimmy served. So I again asked the folks for money, putting it so strong that I was sure this time they'd send a check —at least enough to get me to New London where they were going to spend the summer."

Gene shivered, got up and looked out the window at the wind-swept rainy bay, and then came back and suggested that we have some more coffee in a little while. "I didn't know it, but they'd gone away for a couple of weeks, taking Jamie with them. However, I did get a letter—it seemed that Kathleen wanted a divorce. I didn't answer; then I thought it over. I decided to take matters in my own hands. . . ."

A day or so later Gene found himself in a room with a sordid blonde who sat on the edge of the bed and smoked one cigarette after another, while he nervously paced the floor. She finally got up and casually removed most of her clothes—mean-time telling him the story of her life—so that by the time a detective came in Gene was as sorry for her as for himself. After that there was nothing for him to do but return to Jimmy the Priest's, feeling utterly sick, degraded and—without a drink. He had a desperate hope that the expected check would be there from his father, but it wasn't. Everyone was broke and sitting around with the jitters, just about as he described it later in a scene in *The Iceman Cometh*. Gene spent a nickel of the small amount he had left and made a collect call to New London—no answer! Jimmy refused any more drinks to any-one. He was in a bad mood that night and even hinted to Gene that he pay up his room rent or leave the next morning. Gene went up to his dusty dismal room, sat on the cot and brooded. Somehow this whole episode with the prostitute, the connection of all of it with the nice and really innocent Kathleen, whom he now for some reason recalled regretfully and who seemed like himself just another pawn of fate; the rejection of him by his parents (for of this he was sure now) and no Jamie there to talk things over with—all this threw him into a depth of despair from which he could not or did not want to emerge. He had enough change for another drink or so, but he knew from experience that a couple of drinks would not help him. Besides, could he drink in front of the others downstairs while they were suffering—they who had always shared with him?

So, determined to end it all, and no doubt somewhat comforted by the thought of the horrible effect on his parents when they found that their refusal to send more money had caused his death, and also, he said, because he couldn't stand his thoughts any longer, he went out, unseen by the others, and bought a lot of veronal tablets. At that time, according to newspaper stories, this was an often used way of ending one's life. Determined to make a good job of it and never again wake up, he took all the tablets, washed down by a glass of dirty water, put the hook on the inside of the door and passed out without even having time, first, to experience that glimpse of eternity or nothingness which he had expected and was waiting for. . . .

"I must have been there twenty-four hours, maybe longer," Gene told me. "I vaguely remembered coming to, hearing a knocking on the door, then silence. . . . This happened a number of times, but I paid no attention to it. It didn't occur to me that I was alive—after all those pills! At first I probably thought I was still on my way, not dead yet, but getting there. Perhaps I didn't think at all, just felt resentful that the veronal hadn't yet completely put me out and that I could hear the knocks. . . .

"Then a horrible thought came to me—I *was* dead, of course, *and death was nothing but a continuation of life as it had been when one left it!* A wheel that turned endlessly round and round back to the same old situation! This was what purgatory was—or was it hell itself? My body was dead, but *I* was there too. Frozen in a sort of motionless unbearable horror, I went into a stupor, hardly conscious—at least that was an escape from purgatory, or hell, whichever it was. . . . At last—how long I don't know—the knocking came again. This time there were loud bangs and oaths. Someone pushed hard against the door and then the flimsy hook loosened. I sat up. I knew then that I wasn't dead, for my old pals from below were all there, in the room, in the hall outside. They looked worried and excited and all badly in need of a drink and old ——, who came in first, held a letter which he waved at me—from my father. *He* opened it. There was a check for twenty-five dollars."

Gene paused a moment. . . .

"Jimmy deducted the room rent when he cashed it for me—and then drinks were on the house." He shook his head. "*Wow! What a celebration.*"

"But *you*—you mean you got right up and went down and drank?"

"No—I'm coming to that. I tried to stand up, couldn't make it. They propped me up on the bed and brought me a drink, but that didn't do any good. They told how they'd been trying to get to me for hours—every once in a while somebody'd come up and bang on the door. Then they decided maybe I was dead and they'd break in. Then the major saw the empty pill bottles and I had to tell them what had happened. That's how the celebration began—they celebrated my return to life! The Boer War colonel endorsed the check for me, and they went down to the bar and began to drink. But there was a brotherly love behind it—they had to get rid of their shakes in order to be able to take me to the hospital. Jimmy himself insisted on this. I think he still was afraid that I was going to die at his place. Every half hour or so he'd come up to see how I was feeling. Finally they got me downstairs. Jimmy called Bellevue and found out I'd live because I'd taken an overdose, but I should go over at once and let them look at me. . . . By this time I was feeling a little better, and so the gang had another round to celebrate *that!* I was able to keep down a drink myself.

"Anyway, to make a long story short, we didn't get going for a couple of hours or more. Jimmy would start to call a taxi, then put it off. At last we made it. The taxi got there, but Jimmy couldn't leave, and I was still rather weak and they thought I shouldn't go without them being along to take care of me. So five of them climbed into the taxi along with me. Jimmy Tomorrow brought a bottle along. We stopped on the way up twice, and the taxi driver had a couple of drinks—he didn't know what it was all about but he thought it was a good joke anyway. . . . Jimmy Tomorrow passed out on the way over, then the general, and when we got there I was the only one sober. Ole Olson and Pete were hardly able to get out of the cab and had to be dragged out forcibly by the taxi driver. It seems"—Gene laughed wickedly—"that he had taken us to the entrance of the alcoholic ward!

"First thing they did was to take away the bottle, which had a couple of drinks left in it. I was still in a sort of daze when I heard the intern telling me he'd take care of them—they'd get the works and be all right in a few days. I found myself alone at the desk. They'd all been taken away protesting incoherently, of course, and I was trying to explain without saying a word. 'Tough job you had!' the intern said politely. The taxi man was grinning; he evidently thought I'd had a tough job too. I got into the taxi and drove back to Jimmy the Priest's and managed to get potted to the gills. We all thought it was the biggest joke in the whole damn world. . . .

"Oh God—those old days. Nobody'd believe it. Nobody'd understand it. . . ."

22

The rain was beating against the windows, the east wind roaming around the building in gusts; then abating; then shaking the windows as if it wanted to get in. Gene walked around softly in his slippers, going to the window and looking out, trying to see what the harbor looked like, a sort of mournful and baffled nostalgia on his face. . . .

"*The sea gulls—where are they tonight?* I should have been a sea gull. . . ." He came and put his arms around me tenderly. "*Own little wife . . .*"

"Did you—take the pills because of the girl—wanting to get a divorce?" I asked him, after a few minutes.

"No! Good God! I thought *you'd* understand me. . . ."

"What about *her?* You've never explained to me. I mean—where is she now, for instance?"

"I understand that she's married again—that's why she wanted the divorce. I've been wiped completely off the slate—you needn't worry! Guess it turned out the same with her as it was with me—as if nothing had happened. Even the boy doesn't know about me. The lawyer told me that they were going to bring him up to think the man she was going to marry was his real father. No claims would ever be made on me."

"*The boy——?*" I said, in a faint voice. "You mean—she had a *child?*"

"Yes!" He grinned, rather shamefaced, but as if he had thought I too would consider it more or less of a joke. "Why not? He'll probably grow up to be a darned good stockbroker, don't worry. They'll never want him to know what a drunken wastrel his real father was. . . ."

23

Trying to explain to others a situation where a girl married several months to a man only just discovers, and then, as it were, casually, that he has had a child, I was puzzled. Particularly as we were then, and had been from the first, so very close, so intimate. I had told him about my first husband, or tried to, but he had been bored, not interested. He didn't want to hear anything about it. He had not so far talked about his own marriage. He didn't think of it, and most of the time didn't even remember that it had occurred. What he had just told me explains a great deal of it. It was just that Gene was *like* that. . . . Who, having seen *Long Day's Journey into Night*, would ever realize that Edmund, the younger son, had been married and divorced and was the father of a child nearly three years old on that August evening in 1912?

24

Sunday morning, after a late breakfast at which Jamie joined us, we sat around watching Bowser and the kittens playing together on the floor. Gene got a bright idea—the darned kittens were old enough to get out and see the world!—and holding one in each arm he went downstairs, Jamie and I following, and set them down in the sand, after stroking them gently. . . .

The tide was out; the sun was hot, there was no movement of the air, and the kittens, who had never yet been outside our rather dark flat, sat blinking their amber eyes, motionless. Bowser watched them eagerly. They walked gingerly on their toes in a small circle, saw the expanse of sand, and first one and then the other decided that this was a big toilet, and dug a hole. This was not necessary, as they had used their sandbox toilet upstairs, but sand was sand and had one purpose only. They sat a moment—nothing happened! They got up, neatly covered the spot with their paws, looked around, paying no attention to *us*, moved away a little—nothing but sand! So they dug another hole, went throught the same business again, and cleaned up neatly. Then they walked five or ten feet away from us—dug and covered up, this time not bothering to sit at all. They got tired, rolled over, chased one another—and then, suddenly realizing their responsibility, began digging holes and covering them, very methodically, in the most businesslike manner.

After that they washed their little faces and then went on a reckless hole-digging spree, frisking and digging holes, not covering them up but scattering each other with sand. And, believe it or not, Bowser, after watching them for a while and hearing our laughter, went and madly dug a couple of holes himself, barking and looking at us for approval, and then digging a few more with mad enthusiasm when we became breathless with laughter over *his* performance!

After that, Gene had great fun taking the kittens downstairs if anyone came to see us, and showing them how *our* kittens regarded the outside world as one great big toilet. . . . It was strange about Gene and cats. Like so many men, he always said he didn't like them but once they were there, he became very fond of them. One summer when we were staying at Peaked Hill Bar a hungry, wet and exhausted cat howled at our door, which was battened against a heavy storm. At first determined not to let her in, Gene looked out and saw that a huge barge had drifted up on our beach almost in front of the house—*she* was the only survivor! He was fascinated by this, named her "Anna Christie," and, in the end, after she had been our pet for a year or so, tried vainly to have her life saved in a New York cat hospital—at least to try and keep her alive until after the opening night of his play. . . .

Speaking of cats . . . it is one of those Strindbergian coincidences (to which he so often referred in his discussions of the Swedish dramatist) that the green bronze bust of Eugene O'Neill was done by the man after whom an old cat of ours in New Jersey was named. . . . My parents went to London after they were married and my mother insisted on taking along her pet cat, "*Quinny*." They rented a flat in Chelsea, on Cheyne Walk; and there, some nine months later, I was born, and Quinny (named after my father's great friend Edmond T. Quinn) had kittens on the same day. When I was six weeks old they brought Quinny and her kittens back with me to the States, and she became the ancestress of the many cats that roamed around the house in New Jersey when I was a child. . . .

After *Anna Christie* was a great success, Gene and I were living at Brook Farm in Ridgefield when he saw a photograph of the bust of Edgar Allan Poe executed by Edmond T. Quinn. He admired it greatly; and before long he had Ned Quinn and his wife Emily staying at the house, while Ned modeled a bust of him. Gene also wanted a bust done of me. The two heads were cast in green bronze, with marble bases; for a long time they stood on the mantelpiece at Ridgefield. Gene's bust is now at Yale; while mine is on the mantelpiece at the Old House, looking down at me serenely as I write this.

25

Jamie, oddly enough, did not grow restless that summer or appear to yearn for the fleshpots of New York. But the O'Neills had returned to the Prince George and they began to feel that Jamie should return too—that he had perhaps too long imposed on us. It was soon after hearing from them that Jamie went out and purchased somewhere a bottle of liquor. We knew nothing about it until he came in after supper, weaving a little and *what-hoing* loudly. Bowser followed, looking meek and dejected, and very carefully crawled under the table, watching Jamie with fond distrust. It seemed his master had again placed before him a bowl of spiked milk. But Bowser was a reformed animal—he had not only refused, he growled at Jamie, who, it appeared, had then tried to force his nose into the dish. . . .

Jamie was in the mood for talk—much talk—and Gene, after a reluctant moment or so, wanted, it seemed, to talk too, so he joined Jamie in a drink. He had finished *Where the Cross Is Made* by this time and that day had gone over the script of *Chris* rather aimlessly, not really wanting to start on it then. I don't think that he felt that a drink with Jamie, who so evidently needed a companion, was going to start him drinking again. He wanted to go ahead working on *Chris;* even though he had not done much with it that day. At first, I was a little upset when Jamie came in and I saw the bottle. But, even then, I never thought that Gene would decide to join him. Fortunately, perhaps because of the swimming, the good food, and his own desire to remain in that good physical shape he had reached that summer, he did not drink too much the next day, and the day after that not at all. . . . Also, there was at that particular time no strain of having to meet people, or any decisions to make.

He was gay and quite happy. And Jamie was very good about it all, too—he took only a couple of drinks the next day and seemed a little guilty about having brought in the bottle at all.

26

That night I was to hear some more of Jamie's story—at first just sitting with them and listening. Gene listened too, for evidently Jamie wanted to talk about himself. And later in bed, until four or five o'clock in the morning, I listened to more of it—things he would not have wanted to say in front of me.

Jamie was forty years old that year; there was some sort of a fixation, or vow, or something concerned with his fortieth birthday in his mind. This did not come out clearly at first. It *was* concerned with his sex life, however. That was obvious. Gene who was both understanding about it and slightly scoffing, seemed to know what it was.

The girl—the quiet, freckle-faced girl—had in a sense brought all this to a head. . . .

It was blowing again, chilly and suddenly cold. Gene had another drink and closed the windows. Jamie, his shirt collar open, his face beginning to take on a harder, redder look from the liquor, regarded me with a half-satanic leer.

"Ora pro nobis," he intoned in a priestlike chant. "*Such is life, little wife . . . What have you been doing all summer long . . . ? What have you been doing with my brother, little wife? Wash the dishes, wild Irish rose, dirty your hands in the soapy suds and then let us celebrate! Let us drink,*" he said, rising with a solemn and dramatic gesture, looking at Gene. "*Let us drink to the beautiful, the lost, the divine Pauline!*"

He poured a drink, swaying slightly.

"*Just for a handful of baubles he sold her. . . . Just for a ribbon to tie in her hair. Suddenly there came a tapping, as of someone gently rapping, rapping on my chamber door. . . . Last night, ah yesternight, between her lips and mine there fell thy shadow, Cynara . . .*"

Gene's eyes were pensive; and suddenly, without explanation, Jamie was silent. . . .

Gene had told me about Jamie's love for Pauline Fredricks, the dark beautiful star with the classic profile whose photograph in a silver frame he kept at intervals on his bureau. She, too, had been very much in love, and for a while they planned marriage. But from her point of view—and she grew more insistent about this as the years passed—this marriage must depend on the fact that he first give up liquor. He had given it up several times, but only for a while. At last, very firmly, she had given up the idea of marrying Jamie. . . .

"No, Mr. Jimmy. It's liquor or me. Not both—never!"

These words came from Jamie, in his slightly nasal voice, from somewhere in the past and he spoke them solemnly. He shook his head and the Punch expression came back to his face. "And, *what ho!* It was liquor!"

Gene was perhaps wondering what marriage would have meant to Jamie. He regarded his brother pensively for a moment. He had told me once that it would never have worked, even had Jamie stopped drinking long enough to convince her that he was through with drinking. She was a wonderful woman, a fine person, Gene said, but Jamie had the seed of self-destruction planted too deeply in his soul. They were fundamentally different—perhaps that was what had attracted them; perhaps, too, she saw in Jamie something that no one else had ever seen, for she waited a long time, always hoping. . . .

"Pauline is just an image that you fool around with in your sentimental moments," Gene said. "You convince yourself that if she'd married you, you wouldn't be hanging on to Mama, letting her secretly hand you out a quarter a day!"

"Mama—there's never been another like *her*, my little kid brother! She takes that bath every morning, all that sweet-smelling stuff in it—what for? The old man! The old bastard doesn't appreciate her even now. Sometimes I go into the bathroom and dip my hands into the water before it's all run out—umm!"

It was incongruous. I couldn't understand or even imagine Jamie doing this. He was sitting there, his eyes glazed. Gene watched him, absorbed in what he was saying—as if, through his brother, he was going back to the past that they had shared.

"*Ruffles and lace*—me, not Mama! *Louis the Thirteenth! . . . I was good, eh? Papa even thought I was good . . . Everyone thought I was damn good. When was that, eh? What a company! Edmund Breese, Maud Odell, Gertie Bennet . . . and James O'Neill, junior, as Louis the Thirteenth!*" Jamie hiccoughed and added: "*Now Louis the Thirteenth is at the end of his rope!*"

I moved the dishes away and sat down. A kitten crawled up Jamie's back and sat on his shoulder, closing and unclosing its amber eyes. Jamie closed his eyes too, and began quoting from *The Three Musketeers.*

Gene was silent, there was a certain sadness between them— nothing that they could joke about.

Jamie changed the subject and informed us that he had allowed himself to get into a mild and nostalgic state of pastoral love for the freckle-faced quiet girl. . . . For all her calmness, that girl was an enigma to Gene and myself. We had no clew from her what her ideas or intentions were, only that she spent all of her disengaged time with him: if she had revealed her feelings or state of mind to him, Jamie did not tell us. He had never felt this calm affection for a girl before, or even believed that it was possible. It seemed that he had a desire (though he poked fun at himself for it) to remain always at her side. It is possible that she may have consented, or even desired this too, for Jamie, even then, had a fascination for the female sex. Obviously marriage was out of the question, for unless, as Gene suggested, the girl supported him, what were they to live on?

But it didn't even go as far as this with Jamie—the great obstacle was his sex life; and what would he do about that? For his own prophecy about himself was true. At the age of forty he had always said that he would have to alter his sex life —or was it his sex? I was for a moment confused. Because at forty he would be impotent. He had gone too far, too long, too soon, to keep it up after that age. As he believed, so it was. It didn't seem to bother him much at the moment—except in regard to the girl. That affair, it seemed, had never gone beyond Jamie's holding her warm young hand as they dug scallops.

But his dilemma, as he discussed it that night with Gene, furnished material for much lewd speculation—various modes, manners and types of loving that deviated from the normal. . . . Stories of strange women with strange habits, of Lesbians and so on . . . of some old actress of seventy who, while the unsuspecting Jamie was talking to her, slowly inched her long black skirts up until Jamie, looking down, saw with a gasp her bony knees clad in thin black stockings and slightly opened out. . . . A male homosexual who had made advances to him—and that long horrible story ending with Jamie making him crawl out of the bedroom (which he had managed to enter by bribing the waiter to let him take in the tray of lobster mayonnaise and wine Jamie had ordered) on his hands and knees. It seems to me that Jamie did something with the mayonnaise too, but I can't remember what. He told Gene that he had been in a black mood that night because he had been stood up, not once but twice; first a girl that he had picked up, who didn't show up in his hotel room as he'd expected; on top of that, a luscious little actress in the company who had promised to visit him after the show and for whom Jamie (thinking he had at last made a conquest after many attempts) ordered the lobster and white wine, telephoned him at the last moment that she couldn't possibly come. . . . So Jamie took it all out on the poor infatuated young homosexual. I could hardly believe this as I heard him telling it to Gene, his voice coming through the thin curtain. I'm sure they both thought I was asleep. It was a revelation to me of the ways of men and of their moral values, for Jamie told this story with gusto and with a sadistic emphasis on just how brutal he had been at the end—evidently convinced that the little guy more than deserved it.

27

So Jamie purged himself that night of what was on his mind, as people so frequently do, and evidently felt the better for it, although after that he didn't see the girl as frequently as before. Several times she came looking for him and he wasn't there. He was his quiet, kindly self again, and when we put him on the train for New York he was robust and tanned and apparently sorry to leave us. But there was never any word on his part or any indication in any way that he was going to alter his old way of life after he got back to New York— neither did he seem to look forward to it. What was, *was*. The past was over and he could not change now and be that which he once was—or might have been. Gene too, seemed to take the same attitude. There was never any thought on his part that Jamie might now, after this healthy, happy summer, stop drinking or change his way of life. . . .

About his own life, and particularly about the drinking, he had a very different idea. He wanted *not* to drink—even then. He firmly resolved that when we got to New York that fall this would not happen—no more of those long drunken sprees which interfered with everything. His friend, Harold de Polo, had told him the secret, which was to take your liquor with lots of water—even ice was not necessary. That way you could drink all night and never have it bother you, and Gene said that if he had to take a few drinks, that was the way he would do it. . . .

28

There seemed no reason to return to New York, and we both wanted to stay. Provincetown was beautiful, with autumn not far away, and with Jamie gone it was almost like the old days in the studio. The harbor was a flat oval of glittering water, meeting the yellow sands almost without a ripple. The birches glittered along Commercial Street in the late afternoon sun as we looked from our front window, and sometimes in the early evening we walked up to a little restaurant and ate our dinner there, perhaps stopping in afterward to see Mary Vorse or Susan, if we felt like it. One of the reasons that we stayed so long in Provincetown that fall was that Gene was waiting to hear from John D. Williams when rehearsals would start on *Beyond the Horizon*. It was definitely decided that John and Lionel Barrymore would play the parts of the two brothers—but when?

When he wrote early in September that he wanted to open with the two Barrymores we were both in a state of happiness and exultation. It's hard to explain how much this meant to both of us. To Gene it was a confirmation of his belief in both Williams and the resources of the commercial theater—the uptown as contrasted to the downtown group. We went over the play together, Gene reading first Robert's part, then Andrew's —reading aloud in his low expressive voice, thinking of how John Barrymore would do it; then visualizing Lionel when he returned to find the farm a neglected waste. We had been told that the brothers were excited about doing it, but I sometimes wonder if they read the play at all! Anxiety—there was none of that feeling. Mr. Williams would arrange everything. We were like two trusting children who were sure that everything was going to turn out all right. . . .

Then we heard the bad news: John Barrymore was going to open in *Redemption* sometime in October. Susan, who had perhaps grown a little weary of hearing how the Barrymores were going to appear in Gene's play, saw a notice in the *Times* to that effect and brought it over. From Mr. Williams, not a word—he evidently did not consider it any obstacle to his designs for the play. We did not know until much later the rather complex personality of Mr. Williams, which included, among other things, a strange desire for secrecy and aloofness. There were periods when he seemed to disappear from the earth and, no matter how urgent the matter, was incommunicado. But this was all in the future, and in spite of Gene's disappointment and what he thought was his knowledge of the theater, he was sure that the delay would not be a long one. *Redemption*, he was sure, would never be a financial success. After it closed, John would be free. . . .

29

There was an ominous thing happening now in Provincetown, and everywhere else. The influenza epidemic that took so many people and swept like a plague over the country came to Provincetown. Gene and I walking up Commercial Street, shivering in the fog, saw the little church turned into a hospital, often saw mourners following a hearse into the graveyard. Gene got a letter from Jamie that their mother was ill—an attack of the influenza, but fortunately a light one. A couple of days later he wrote again saying that she was much better.

Among brief notes of something or other that I wished to remember, ideas for stories, a memoranda of some particular day which for some unknown reason I saw fit to put down, I find some letters to me in the delicate, slanting handwriting of Ella Quinlan O'Neill and I find also a letter to her in my handwriting:

Francis' Flats, Provincetown

Dear Mrs. O'Neill:

. . . Jamie sends the good news that you are better. Gene wrote you yesterday I know. He was awfully upset by your sickness. He's so cheerful at your being better and so anxious to see you again—not a bit more than I am, though. I've been looking forward to meeting you and Mr. O'Neill. Gene, you know, occasionally gets started about his wonderful mother and actually—well I never heard of a mother who got so many bouquets!—so I can imagine a little bit what you are like. Also I've had a good system of getting an imaginary portrait of you by asking Gene just how he and Jamie resembled you two. I'd say—"Are your mother's eyes like yours or Jamie's?"—and so on, until I think I'd know you anywhere. Of course I've seen some pictures of Mr. O'Neill and that helps some. Aren't you dying to see Gene? I suppose he would laugh if he saw that and make some teasing remark. He's an awful tease in some ways. He's looking fine and goes swimming every day, much to the admiration of the Portuguese fishermen. As for writing, well, I wish I could get as much done as he does.

Owing to the epidemic it's doubtful if we can get down until November. Still it's really lovely here, and quite mild. Tell Jamie that the two kittens now follow Terry all over the flats, getting soaking wet, thinking he'll give them some clams. . . .

30

The days were getting chilly and we borrowed a kerosene stove from Mr. Francis to keep warm. Gene wore his old brown bathrobe in the morning and sat propped up on the cot, working again on *Chris*. We expected in every mail to hear from Williams. There was a sense of uncertainty—not about money, for Gene had been getting the fifty dollars a week from *In the Zone*, and the advance from Williams had not been touched, as I remember. Our rent was absurdly small, and except for some sweaters and a pair of new slacks for Gene we had not bought any clothes. Our food did not cost much, and outside of an occasional magazine and items at the drugstore and stationery shop, we had no other expenses.

I had sold a novelette and a short story to my old markets during the summer. . . .

But we were wondering what our life would be like, where it would be spent during the winter that was ahead of us. We had thought at first of renting a little house in Provincetown where we would be warm and comfortable, and Gene could continue his work after rehearsals were over. But Gene wouldn't consider leaving me in Provincetown while the rehearsals were going on, even though this meant only a separation of possibly six weeks. He was determined not to stay in New York after the play was produced, no matter what the results of the production might be.

Gene knew about the Old House in New Jersey which had been rented for the summer. . . . When there was no word from Williams and *Redemption* opened with a fine production by Arthur Hopkins on October 3, Gene began asking me about the place: what was it like, how far was it from New York, and above all—would we be alone there?

I described it, and the more I told him about it the more he liked the idea. He teasingly told me that there was nothing like being married to a girl who owned a house or so. There would be no rent to pay, and certainly for the coming winter it would be a great convenience—or rather for part of the winter, for at that time we were sure that *Beyond* rehearsals would start soon after the new year. After that, Gene said, we would take a trip, he and I; and he talked of the South Seas and the long white beaches and of how wonderful it would be there. Later in the spring we would come back to Provincetown—not to Francis' Flats, but perhaps get a cottage in Truro. Once again he spoke of the old coast-guard station. *If only that were for sale!* By that time perhaps *Beyond the Horizon* would be making money and he could buy it. Once again we walked over the dunes and sat in the cupola and watched the sea, never dreaming of the years that we would spend on that stormy, isolated shore.

31

There was a sort of exuberance in our relationship in spite of everything that autumn. Gene was gay, joked about small things, teased me and made love to me and took more pleasure, if that is possible, in his bouts with the water, which was colder by now, his dashes up and down the beach, and more joy in his physical being; he seemed to expand, grow even more handsome. He wrote his mother, telling her what he could of our plans and, after hearing from someone that John Barrymore might consider leaving *Redemption* in order to create the role of Robert, he began going over the script again. Williams, he had heard, was a genius when it came to production; he would take care of the sets, cast, the other parts, find the perfect actress for the touching part of Ruth. . . .

I was so contented that I'm afraid I became lazy and, living in the present and thinking of the creative future as assured, neglected things I should have attended to—particularly writing letters. At times I thought of the house in New Jersey and about our being there. . . . I was hoping that Gene would like it there—hoping that the windmill wouldn't creak too much at night, that we could keep the house warm; wondering which room Gene would work in. It seemed to me that there was much he could enjoy there—books, records to hear, walks in the pine woods and above all the solitude that he desired—that *we* desired.

There were drawbacks, too, besides the creaking windmill; the stoves; seven coal stoves to be shaken down every day, ashes carried out, coal brought in the coal scuttle. *But* there were the two fireplaces. One smoked, but we would use the other, and sit before it in the evening watching the logs burn. . . .

So I put off writing to my family and telling them that Gene and I would probably go down to the Old House after a few days in New York. The truth was that Gene didn't really want to leave Provincetown, and although the Provincetown Players had successfully negotiated for a larger theater at 133 Macdougal Street and were planning to do *Where the Cross Is Made* on their first bill, Gene convinced himself that it wouldn't be necessary for him to attend these rehearsals. He was completely wrapped up in working out the outline of *Chris*—as he and I always called that play which at different times had different titles. He didn't want to have to stop work on it—at least not for anything less than the news that *Beyond* had gotten started. When we shivered and were uncomfortable because of a few days of cold weather he would tell me that we had better arrange to pack up and go. . . .

Perhaps this was another reason I put off writing to my mother. It all seemed too complicated to try and explain. I had not heard from her, as a matter of fact, for three or four weeks and I wonder now why this did not strike me as rather strange. There was a lull in my mail at that time anyhow, which pleased me, particularly as I no longer heard from William Jones, nor any further demands from the pulp magazines for more stories.

But Gene got a letter—an emphatic letter from Jig Cook. Jig insisted that Gene must be there for the casting and re-hearsals of *Where the Cross Is Made*. Already there was strong disagreement as to how it should be done, and Jig wanted Gene there to back him up.

Susan, who was staying alone in the house across the street and working on a play of her own, came over and urged that Gene go down at once, having had a letter from Jig the same day. She added that in her opinion we'd both be down with pneumonia if we stayed any longer in that chilly flat.

So Gene reluctantly decided that we had better leave. I wrote a letter to my mother, saying that we were going to New York in a couple of days and, if there was anything urgent, to write me care of the Provincetown Players at 133 Macdougal Street, as I wasn't sure where we were going to stay.

Gene was rather glum and irritated at having to leave. Jig was right, of course, he said, but he damn well didn't see why the Provincetown Players had to call on *him* again. I think he suspected that they wanted his assistance in not only moving into the new place but in some major matters of organization. Before we left he got into the mood of being rather aloof with them; they mustn't think that they could make unreasonable demands on his time and advice. We would go to a small hotel somewhere—not in the Village—and, listening to him, I realized that he thought we should be in every way very circumspect and businesslike. He would go to rehearsals—but by God they were going to do the play the way he wanted it done!

We packed rather sadly, gave the kittens to friends who promised to keep them until the spring, and had to leave Bowser with a young friend of John Francis' with whom the dog had been spending a lot of time since Jamie's departure. We got dressed before it was light outside; Gene wore his suit and velour hat and a smooth topcoat that he had bought in the village the day before; to me he suddenly seemed very grim and conservative. The taxi honked outside and we went down the wooden steps for the last time in the chilly empty dawn, carrying suitcases and parcels, to take the train that left for Fall River.

Waiting with the Little Clowns

———— •◆• ————

1

The little pines stood together, behind and next to each other, growing together, looking over one another's branches, as it were, from the other side of the road that ran behind the old house. . . . Little fantastic clownlike pine trees with spiked branches extending, always green, each one alone and yet a part of the others, always standing there waiting —for what?

I called them the little clowns, for that's what they seemed to become as I looked at them from the window of the kitchen in the Old House. Snow at times bent down the small boughs, or a sudden change of weather, mild and wet, left them glistening, the top branches alert, each individual, each alone, waiting. . . .

2

Gene may have seemed grim and determined when we left, decided, as it were, to embark on a new life altogether; but chaos surrounded us soon after we arrived in New York.

There was a day or so of seeing people that he knew; talks with Jig Cook and then a party at the Provincetown Theatre on Macdougal Street. This started off well enough—everyone was gay and happy and pleased that Gene was back; there was excitement and talk about the new season and about *Where the*

Cross Is Made, which was to be on the first bill, but the end of that evening was a shock to me. . . . We had gone to a Village restaurant to eat after leaving the party at the Provincetown Players. Teddy Ballantine and his wife and some others were with us, and I was sitting near one end of the long table, happy and enjoying myself at being back with people we knew and liked.

It had seemed to be in order that there should be a celebration for Gene—this home-coming party as a welcome back to the Village; and I had taken care to look as well as possible for Gene's sake as well as my own; a little lipstick to go with my tan; my hair (longer now) brushed loosely around my neck. Gene admired me when we left our small hotel room. "You look beautiful!" he said. "I'm proud of you!"

At the Provincetown Players on Macdougal Street everyone was wonderful to me, Christine greeted me with a big hug and exclamations of how well I looked and Gene (the real center of attention) seemed pleased that I should share it with him. Gene did not intend to take even one drink that night. We had not seen his parents, which we were to do the next day; and he had also made a list of people he had to see, copied it in his neat handwriting and put it beside the telephone—people he would have to be sober to see and talk with.

But he changed his mind, not because he needed it, for he was at ease, and really happy, but because he wanted to join with the others, who were drinking quite moderately, and because he felt he wouldn't drink much either. He was careful to follow Harold's advice, and he didn't seem to mind the teasing when they saw him drinking whisky diluted with a lot of water, instead of the old straight shots. I, too, thought that everything was all right, and when we left, Gene was smiling and perfectly sober. A group of us decided to stop at a small Italian restaurant nearby. It was nearly empty at that hour, with long wooden tables set along the wall. Perhaps I was too happy—who knows? Teddy Ballantine was talking to me with the fervent, absorbed interest that always transformed him from a slight, rather bored young actor to a glowing intense person whenever he talked of painters and painting, a subject in which he was deeply absorbed. Gene, further down the table, was half listening to our conversation, and I noticed an ironic look he sent in my direction. Gene didn't care or think too much about painting. He felt all this was a certain affectation on Teddy's part—a "chi-chi" attitude which gave Teddy a chance to be slightly superior. I know this wasn't true about Teddy— at times afterward we even argued about it. Teddy Ballantine had as fine an understanding of modern painting as anyone I have ever known. . . .

A little time passed and also a bottle. I saw Gene pouring a large straight drink for himself. I waited a few minutes, then got up and walked down to where he was sitting and squeezed in next to him, whispering in his ear that maybe we ought to go back to the hotel. He got to his feet, gave me a push that sent me backward, leaned toward me, swinging as hard as possible with the back of his hand, and hit me across the face. Then he laughed, his mouth distorted with an ironic grin. . . .

I can remember my horrible astonishment and despair at this performance, along with a crazy dazed feeling that it just couldn't be true—it couldn't have happened; and then I saw that everyone was taking it, as it were, with a grain of salt, as a Dionysian gesture. . . . They were watching Gene, not look- ing at me; and he stood there, ignoring me too, now quoting dramatically something from Ibsen: about "vine leaves in his hair." (Men, on occasions like this, seem to stick together, is all I can say!) But Stella Ballantine rose to her feet and in her deep acquired British voice told him what she thought of him —though perhaps with a vein of pity. Teddy was silent. Gene looked at Stella (whom he called the Duchess behind her back) without seeming to see her, although his next remark *was* directed at her. "*Get out of here—all of you!*" Harold Magee and his wife got up quickly and left. I put my hand to my face and thought, *This isn't happening . . . he'll be all right in a minute*. But it *was* happening. Gene gave me another baleful look, heartlessly implying, I suppose, that I should get out of there too, and the sooner the better; and Stella, her warm proud face very intense, put her arm under mine.

"Let's you and I and Teddy go to our place for a while. Teddy has to go anyway. He has a rehearsal in the morning!"

But Teddy, with that detached charm which reminded one that in his days as a London playboy he had seen so much that nothing could ever disturb him again, elected to remain—for a while at least.

I got to my feet, Stella grasping me firmly as if she did not intend to let me go. I did not want to leave—it couldn't end like this.

"Gene—*listen!*"

But he was not looking at me or hearing me now; in some way, almost physical, he had gone over, completely, to something else. I saw him as if in a haze, surrounded by those others as male and Dionysian as himself, one of whom, with an admiring look at Gene, produced another bottle.

Stella walked outside with me, talking calmly, never stopping her talk. "It means nothing, my dear, nothing! I've had the same thing happen to me—although Teddy, I admit, has so far never tried it! Genius is like that, my dear! Genius must have its outlet! Come to our apartment (it was just around the corner on Grove Street) and see some of Teddy's recent paintings." I told her I should go back—wait and go with Gene to the hotel, but she insisted that would only make matters worse.

"We will go back later," she said soothingly. "It is much better if you keep out of sight for a while. He didn't like you talking to Teddy—I could see *that*. My dear it was the same with my aunt Emma. I devoted myself to her for years, and yet she resented any little bit of attention that I received. . . ."

We went up to her apartment, and Stella with pride displayed Teddy's water colors, and then showed me some photographs of her aunt, Emma Goldman; but I hardly saw anything,

226

wondering what was happening to Gene. . . . Stella noticed this and decided to accompany me back to the restaurant. When we got there everyone had left. The Italian waiter shrugged when Stella asked him where they had gone. I waited while she telephoned the Hell Hole (the Golden Swan) and was insanely relieved when I heard her talking to Teddy, but Gene wasn't there! "My dear, where did he go? Haven't you any idea?" She paused. "Remember, there's a rehearsal tomorrow!"

Stella convinced me that Gene must have gone back to the hotel, expecting to find me there: we would take a taxi, she'd drop me off and go and pick up Teddy. "He's in *Redemption*, you know. I'll call you after I get Teddy tucked in bed."

Stella did call me (half an hour later) and I told her Gene was not there. I sat alone in the bedroom, looking at the brief case, carefully put at the end of the bureau the list of people he had to see that day, carefully placed near the telephone. . . . I heard the elevator come up, and footsteps coming along the hall. Once, twice—three times . . . but not *his* footsteps. The sound of the elevator ceased at last. I got up from the chair and pulled up the window blind: dawn was coming faintly along the tops of the buildings. Then I heard footsteps again. They were slow, unsure, and my heart began beating rapidly. It was someone wandering along the hall, past our door. Then the footsteps came back, stopped outside—silence. I hesitated, and slowly opened the door just a crack. It was Gene. He stood there, forlorn and without his hat.

"I walked up"—he hesitated—"I couldn't find our room. . . ."

I saw a sick man standing in front of me. His face sagged and his mouth was set in the old familiar tight line, pressed together to keep something in. This gave a look of bitterness to his whole face, as if he knew too well the taste of gall on the sponge. . . .

He came in, without appearing to see me, and sat down on the edge of the bed. He put his hands up, and his long spatulate fingers pressed against the skin of his forehead; bent forward, his elbows resting on his knees, he looked alone and unhappy. I went over and stood beside him, and put my hand on his head. He reached out and put his arm around me, holding me tightly and quivering.

3

Two things that I was to do often afterward in my life with Gene I did for the first time in that hotel, whose name I have forgotten. First (when we came in from the Fall River Line) the signing of the register—a ritual which was ever afterward observed. We went inside the hotel; Gene and our luggage remained near the door, as much out of sight as possible; I went to the desk and registered. Second—lying for him. He was sick, I was sick, or some story or other was invented to put off something he had promised to do, or someone he said he would see. . . .

4

The next morning it was obviously impossible for him to go with me up to see his parents. There was a washbasin in the corner of the room, and he stood braced over it for a long time, the water running from the tap. Then he came back, exhausted, and lay on the bed. He opened his eyes long enough to see if the brief case was safely there. . . . *"See if you can get a pint from the bellboy."*

I called up the Prince George about eleven, although I hated doing this, as I had never met his mother. Gene was sick—he had eaten some oysters on the boat, and they had poisoned his stomach. But the doctor thought he'd be all right by this evening—probably he'd be a little shaky. We'd come up after dinner, about eight o'clock. Was that all right?

His mother's voice was filled with concern over the telephone, tired and rather faint. "Will he be all right?" I wondered how much she knew, and when she asked me if *I'd* eaten any of the oysters I said I never ate oysters. I felt all right—perhaps just a little tired after the trip. She said how much they were looking forward to meeting me, and to be sure to take care of him and come up tonight, or his father would be very disappointed.

Gene was listening, lying on the bed.

"I think having the doctor up was a little too much, Gene, after all; I could have just said the oysters upset you. Now I've got to remember never to eat oysters when we're with them—and I love them!"

"I know Mama! She always said oysters were poisonous. Come and sit over here. . . ." He was feeling better already after two drinks. "Do you think they'll send some soup up from the restaurant?"

I sat beside him, and he put his head over on my lap. I stroked his forehead, and felt the throbbing of his eyeballs under my fingers. . . .

"The dream—it's back," he whispered. "I almost shattered it . . . you're here. . . . You and I always. *Us always!*"

5

We stood in the lobby of the Prince George, waiting for an elevator up to room 819. I was nervous somehow. I had been looking forward to seeing Gene's parents—but this was not the way we had wanted it to be. Gene stood beside me, tense and still pale: his healthy tan had a sallow cast, and his face was shaded and somber under the velour hat. He gave a sudden, half childish, half sickly smile.

"Buck up! We're here, aren't we?"

He held my hand surreptitiously going up in the elevator. We walked together down the thickly carpeted hall and stood before a closed door. Gene did not knock immediately. He stood there, waited; drew in a deep breath, looked at me . . . then his knuckles made a nervous tattoo on the dark, polished wood.

The door opened immediately—I think his mother must have been standing there behind it.

"Well! Eugene!" She stood back a second, looked at him and then embraced him and I saw them for a moment, his arms around her, her head close to his chest. Then she was speaking to me:

"Agnes!" and she kissed me, gently and affectionately. "Let me look at you—Eugene's wife!"

I smiled back at her. *She's lovely*, I thought gratefully. At once there was a bond between us (was it the bond of Eugene?) and I think we were both aware of it; that recognition of love and understanding. Then his father was there: he had risen from his chair and come to greet us; he seemed a little concerned but very pleased.

"Jim, this is Agnes!"

"How do you do, my dear?" He shook my hand, then bent and kissed me on the forehead. "Eugene, you've done well! Take off your hat, my boy—where are your manners? What's this about the oysters?"

Gene was smiling and in a teasingly ironic mood all of a sudden. He put his hat on a chair and slipped out of his topcoat. "Never mind about the oysters, Papa. Been poisoned from eating bluefish lately?"

"Never mind about bluefish! I still refuse to eat them. What about a little snifter?" he added, looking at his wife. She looked at me. I don't know what my expression was, but she said:

"Just as you like, James—if he wants one. Let me take your coat, dear," she added as I slipped out of it. "Are you sure it's warm enough for this weather? You should have something heavier!"

Gene and his father had moved past the long table in the middle of the room to a comfortable sofa and Gene sat down, his father standing. "You're sure you've had your dinner, Eugene? We can have something sent up."

We had eaten—nothing very much, it's true. "Maybe later," I said. "A sandwich and coffee, something like that." The older man nodded and turned to go into the bathroom. Ella O'Neill sat down near her son on the sofa.

"Come and sit down here, dear," she said to me. "Eugene, you look well. You look very brown—you've put on weight. And isn't it wonderful about your play! Your father is so pleased—he may not show it, but he is so pleased!"

There was a chandelier in the middle of the ceiling, with glass crystals which gave a soft but brilliant light. It was a spacious room, comfortable and homelike, with large easy chairs, a soft carpet, tall curtained windows opening on the street eight floors below. There were flowers on the long table; little silver dishes; a table with magazines and a sewing basket, a bookcase. On the wall hung some framed pictures and over another small table a group of photographs. The door into the bedroom was partly open, showing a shaded light beside the bed. Near the bathroom door was a stand on which stood a coffee percolator and some cups and saucers; and over the stand was a picture of a lovely nun, her face bent down, gazing at a crucifix in her hands.

From my end of the sofa I watched Gene and his mother as they talked. Every moment or so she would look at me and then back to him. *She is quite a beautiful person*, I thought. Although at first she had given me the impression of being quite conventional, there was a serenity and goodness about her that revealed itself as one listened and talked to her. My first impression had perhaps been caused by her manner of speech, which was slightly precise; or by her carefully waved white hair; the small matched strand of pearls that she wore around her neck; or the quiet elegance of her rather small neat figure. Her dress was black, of finely fluted silk, with long close-fitting sleeves and with delicate handmade lace at the wrists and neck; her shoes were exquisite, very fine lizard with some sort of an intricate knot at the instep. When one was close to her, one noticed a faint and elegant flower perfume—the perfume of a lady. Once when she said something to Gene she leaned over and put her hand on mine and I noticed this elusive odor. This charm or beauty of hers, which became more perceptible as one watched her, was partly because of her eyes, which were a deep dark muted brown, and her skin, which was amazingly smooth and soft and pale; and also because of the exquisite suitability of her clothes; her simple and very elegant taste—and, added to this, the calmness of her expression.

James O'Neill came back from the bathroom, carrying a tray with three drinks tinkling with ice and ornamented with lemon peel. He put them on the table before us, groaning a bit as he sat down himself.

"It's a little soon after dinner for me, but I'll have one with you to wish you luck, Eugene. I made one for you," he said, turning to me, "but if you don't want it, don't take it and no doubt your husband will have it himself—to save you from it, eh, Eugene?"

They began talking about the play then—*Beyond the Horizon*. The old man had some advice to give, some comments to make, and while this was going on, Gene's mother talked to me. She asked me where we were planning to live this winter and advised me not to let Gene take me again to the Garden Hotel. "It's all right for Jamie," she said, "but not a nice place for you." She suggested that perhaps we could take an apartment later; she had always wanted an apartment but nothing would do for James but the hotel. "We've been living here now for years except in the summer when we go to New London," she said. "But you wouldn't like it here—you should have your own place!"

Gene and his father were still talking, so she took me into the bedroom to see a coat that she had just bought. It was a beautiful full-length Persian lamb. "James grumbled—men always do," she said. "But I got it at last!" To my surprise she slipped it on me, instead of on herself. "You look well in black. You should make Eugene buy you one when his play goes on. I have a mink scarf——" she began, and then hesitated and said no more.

She sat down on the bed, and we talked about Eugene and

his health, and also how I must take care of myself, and put on a little weight: She didn't see why Eugene had to stay up in Provincetown in order to write—it must be lonely for me there. Then she asked me about my little girl. "I'd love to see her," she said. "You know I always wanted a little girl so much—and then I had three boys." I looked surprised. "One died when he was a year old—my own fault," she added sadly. "He might not have died if I hadn't left him; we had a good nurse, a very good nurse, and James wanted me to go with him on tour—he can't seem to manage without me. I think Eugene is going to be the same about you."

I asked her after a moment, if Jamie would be over that evening; we had not seen him since our arrival in New York.

"Ah, Jamie—yes, he said he'd drop in later. He looked so well when he came back from Provincetown. He likes you too. He enjoyed it very much in Provincetown."

We talked a while longer and then went back into the other room. Gene was rather restless, and after a moment or so his father asked if he'd like another drink. "But drink it down! I want to get the bottle out of the way before Jamie gets here!" he added rather bitterly. He did not join Gene this time; and Gene's mother apparently did not drink anything at all.

I began to sense a restlessness on the part of both Gene's parents. They kept glancing toward the door. At last there was a knock—and Jamie opened the door which had been left unlatched. He stood there with that Punch smile of his, aware that all eyes were on him. He was neat, compact, red-faced: the tan of Provincetown had been replaced by the tan of alcohol. . . .

"What ho! The prodigal returns. . . ."

I saw Mrs. O'Neill's face—it was kind, severe and sad. Her husband's face was stern and also sad. For it was only too obvious, as he moved slowly into the room and toward us, that Jamie was very potted. His careful speech, his slow movements, his fixed, ironic smile . . . I wonder what Jamie felt, with four of us sitting there, what his real feelings were—for he must have had some, even though alcoholic. One never really knew.

Gene's face lighted with a delightful grin. "What ho!" The old man did nothing else than pick up a newspaper from the table near his elbow and begin reading. Mrs. O'Neill fluttered nervously, her hands moving over her lap.

"Have you eaten, Jamie?" she asked reprovingly. "I told you to come here for dinner!"

"I have dined with the gods!" Jamie said. He carefully located a chair and sat down. "And I am in perfect shape, Mama, to join this joyous reunion with my brother and the wild Irish rose. You have eaten the fatted calf, I presume? Mama, have you presented your daughter-in-law with your mink scarf yet?"

Mr. O'Neill raised his eyes at once from the paper and cast a look of stern inquiry at his wife, whose pale skin, beneath this scrutiny, flushed slightly. I was embarrassed but Gene looked pleased.

"You are intoxicated, Jamie," his mother said, "and you promised me that tonight——"

James O'Neill turned on her angrily.

"Haven't I told you that his promises amount to nothing?" He slammed the paper down on the sofa.

"I hear that Jamie was a very good boy all summer." Mrs. O'Neill said. Her hand fluttered again; she turned to me. "Agnes—he says you're a good cook, my dear. I never learned to cook. . . ."

"Mama makes the best scrambled eggs in the world. She makes them every morning for her esteemed husband," Jamie said with malice. "My fond papa eats them with relish after his morning tot of whisky!"

"If you limited yourself to a drink before breakfast, as I do, you'd be doing well," the old man exclaimed. "It *is* medicinal —the doctor ordered it. Keep your dirty Irish tongue out of my business!"

"Now, now, James!" Mrs. O'Neill turned toward Jamie.

"How often have I begged you to come and I'd cook eggs for you here? You could have the whisky first too, if you wanted it."

"Not from me!" The old man growled. "Not a drop of my liquor!"

The brothers looked at each other and grinned. Then Gene said something in his low quiet voice, about the six-day bike races, while the old man went back to his paper, grim and quiet. Mrs. O'Neill was watching Jamie with silent anxiety. When she ordered some sandwiches and coffee sent up she ordered soup for Jamie; but he refused to touch it, and got an angry glare from his father. . . . We left sometime after this, and Gene's mother walked to the elevator with us, urging Jamie, who left with us, to come in the next morning and have breakfast with them. . . .

6

I had thought that after we left the Prince George Gene would want to stay and talk with his brother, possibly stop somewhere and have a drink with him; but instead of that we went back to the hotel, and the next morning, rather pale but determined, Gene went up to the Williams office. I don't know how it was that he did not go to see Mr. Nathan, who was anxious to see him and who was on Gene's list, but he did not, for that meeting did not occur until the following May. Gene came back to the hotel very quiet and sullen, for Williams, it seemed, was on one of his frequent absences; where he was seemed a mystery, and apparently he could not be reached.

But there was a bright spot—Mr. Williams' brother Joe, to whom Gene had talked. "He's one of the nicest guys I've ever met," Gene told me, "but sort of worried-looking!" Joe had informed him that Williams was still planning to open with the two Barrymores—as soon as John was free.

"Let's hope *Redemption* flops soon," Gene said gloomily. He was in a very gloomy mood about everything—money included. "I guess we'll have to go to your place in Jersey as soon as *The Cross* rehearsals are over; then I'll have to come back for *The Moon*—they'll make a mess of that unless I'm here."

The telephone rang. It was Jimmy Light to see Gene. They were going to start rehearsals for *Where the Cross Is Made* and he wanted to talk to Gene and then take him down to Macdougal Street. It seemed that some objections were already being made about the actual presence on the stage of the ghosts of the dead sailors. . . . When Jimmy came in he handed me a letter that had come to the theater addressed to me. It was from my mother. I glanced at it—and then forgot everything else. I went into the bathroom, closed the door and tore it open, the postmark on the envelope had shown me that the letter came from the small town in New Jersey where I had thought of going with Gene.

She had received my letter saying that we were leaving Provincetown for New York and that Gene expected *Beyond the Horizon* would go on that winter. She supposed that with the good news about the play we would be able to get a nice apartment, but meantime she was writing me care of the Provincetown Players as I suggested. She *should* have written before—but you know how things are! They had thought for some time that they didn't want to put up with another cold winter on the farm, and then Grannie had cabled from London that she at last had been able to arrange for a passage to the States. It would be, of course, impossible to have the old lady on the farm—she would freeze to death! So they had decided to spend the winter in the Old House (my mother always capitalized this). Everything is fine, she went on to say, and added that having the electricity put in had made a great difference. The tenants had left some things in a mess, but she had cleaned it up. I might have to get the windmill fixed later, as it was making a lot of noise. They were looking forward to having either me, or Gene and me, if he wasn't too busy, come down for a visit: or perhaps she would be able to get up to New York later. Grannie had arrived safely and looked very well.

In order to leave London with the war still more or less on, she had finally appealed to a cousin of hers who happened to be very influential in the Government at the time. He had arranged everything and now Grannie was happily installed in the upper nursery. Grannie, of course, after paying her passage hadn't a cent left, and Teddy had taken so long doing a miniature that had been ordered that she didn't know when he'd get it finished. *But try not to worry!* Things were all right so far, and she was designing some hooked rugs that she thought might sell. They had left the farm in care of a young man who was going to stay there for the winter in exchange for looking after the place. . . .

7

The curse of not writing letters when one should—*letting things slip!* Procrastination! What is it, anyway? Why does one procrastinate? Is it because that which one puts off is really disagreeable and disturbing even though one does not consciously know it? Or is it that writing letters is a real chore for those who do other writing? I wish I knew!

Now because I had put off writing to my mother at the farm I was completely baffled. I didn't know what to do. In looking back at it now the winter down in New Jersey certainly had its humorous aspects. I remember several incidents that are very funny, at least as I recall them. At the time I may not have seen them in that way, being always too much influenced by Gene's personal aspect—whether he looked gloomy or pleased. For example, the time we were sitting before the fireplace one afternoon and someone I knew appeared on the porch and then walked in; Gene didn't have time to leave the room but hid in the closet, listening with fury to the conversation, which I was trying in vain to terminate.

There was a lot of heartache connected with it however, at least as far as I was concerned. At the house, at the time she wrote me, and expecting to stay for the winter, was not only the whole family, but my mother's little dog Trixie, three cats, and a pet crow! And here was my husband—like Garbo, he must be alone—and I had promised him that. He had two important long plays to do and other work planned. . . .

Why didn't I admit the whole situation to him and let him know that we'd have to go somewhere else? But where else was there to go? I just couldn't do it—he had counted on me and the house and being quite alone. I was no doubt completely obsessed by my devotion to him and his work. And also, there was now beginning to be the question of money.

I had promised to go down to the Provincetown Players with Gene that afternoon (Jimmy Light after his talk with him went on uptown); but the next day I sat down and wrote my mother the letter I should have written in the first place—only now it was a problem that I didn't know how to solve and I didn't see how *she* could solve it either. . . .

But she did—and that was what led to a situation which must have seemed strange to various people in that New Jersey town. All right! she said, we could use the house, of course. Gene could have his solitude, with no one to bother him, although, she added, it *would* have been nice to meet him. But she would have to leave the cats and Trixie in the house and we would have to take care of them. The pet crow she would take with them, she had already gone down to the village and rented a small cottage near the sea for the winter: it would be up to me to explain to Gene about Trixie and the cats. They would be very crowded in the little house, but everybody understood except Grannie and she was going to have a hard time explaining things to that firm and opinionated lady, for if *she* knew we were there she would be marching right up to see us. . . .

They, at least, could keep out of sight, although my father had looked forward to meeting Gene, as he admired his work so much—he had been reading some of the plays published by the Provincetown people. And after all, she said, it is *your* house.

It was, and yet I knew she felt that in a way it wasn't. Or so it seemed now. When I came of age I had recieved a not too large inheritance from my great-aunt Agnes Boulton, for whom I had been named. There was a mortgage on the house, the man who held it wanted his money to use for something else, and there was difficulty in getting anyone to take the mortgage over. I had paid the mortgage and with what was left bought myself a little riding horse, which I had shipped down in a boxcar; got a new black suit and a couple of hats and an outfit for each of my sisters. Some time later on (a year or so before I met Gene I believe), there seemed to be talk again of selling the place. I don't know why this time, but I do remember everyone sitting in front of the fireplace and reading the advertisements in the Strout farm catalogue. Perhaps that had nothing to do with it—but my mother decided that she would turn the place over to me in payment of what I'd put into it, and she would take a second mortgage for the balance of the value of house and land. So Agnes Boulton Burton, short-story writer, became the legal owner. It was all rather complicated and what it amounted to was that except for the time it was rented, the family, or certain members of it came and went, lived there or not, according to what was convenient or expedient for everyone. I had not been there, except for short visits, for quite a long time.

So in one way, I was tremendously relieved—as far, at least, as Gene was concerned. And when soon after that I received another letter from my mother in which she seemed to think the whole thing was a big joke—they had all laughed so at the idea and at Gene's needs, all except Teddy, who said he understood; and Grannie, who didn't know. I must be sure and not let Gene know that they were there, as, after they thought it over, they were sure that it would be just too boring meeting him—he must be quite a disagreeable and morose man; when I read this letter and saw that even *that* sarcasm was more or less of a joke, I, too, began to feel less badly about it and wondered how it would all turn out. . . .

8

Gene and I took a bus downtown. The Provincetown Players had moved from 139 Macdougal Street to number 133, a few doors away, and there was a chaotic happy hammering and painting and moving around of scenery and stage effects going on. . . . Everyone seemed in a daze—but it was the absorbed daze of a fixed purpose. They were getting the place ready for their first bill. They were already more than two weeks behind in their schedule; if you spoke to someone, he answered you, but his attention was not on you but on a place on the wall where electric wires were being hung, waiting for a fixture; or on the shade of yellow paint that was being applied to finish the walls; or on watching burly truckmen carrying in more lumber, as if wondering if there was room for it somewhere.

Jig Cook—no one even thought of him by his formal name of George Cram Cook—was standing on the stage, which was piled with boxes, lumber, and half-filled pots of paint. Bolts of material lay on a bench made of rough planks laid on wooden sawhorses, and Jig was regarding them with speculative eyes when we came in. Someone tapped his shoulder and he turned around; his tired, absorbed face lit with joy and affection as he saw Gene standing in the aisle.

"Knew you'd be here. Thank God you are!" He had not seen Gene since the night of the welcoming party. He held my arm, squeezed it, and put his other hand on Gene's shoulder. "We'll start rehearsals tomorrow on *The Cross*—come hell or high water! I'm wondering what shade of cloth would be best for the ghosts—theatrical gauze, damp—come and look! But first, what do you think of our color scheme?"

The place had been painted since the first night we were there, all but the benches, which were now being hammered into place. The walls were a rich tawny orange, the ceiling deep blue, and the rectangular proscenium was a dark smoke gray.

"The benches will be black—and, by God, Gene, we're going to have them comfortable—*pad* 'em! We've put in an inclined

floor. I figured it out so that each seat is right, and everybody
in the audience will be able to see the stage!"

Jig was sweating, the perspiration in streaks on his unshaven
face. His hair, gray and dusty, swept in a massive mop just
escaping his kind and brilliant eyes. I don't believe he had had
time to take off his clothes since we last saw him; he was wearing
the same gray sweater and paint-stained trousers. In order to
save time and money (for they had begun their moving not
really knowing where the money was coming from, but carried
along by Jig's indomitable spirit and enthusiasm), Jig had con-
tributed the rent he expected to pay for an apartment; he slept
on the stage, ate whenever he could manage, and worked with
the others day and night.

Gene approved briefly of the color scheme—but his eyes were
on the stage, and a moment later he and Jig were up there, Jig
explaining, and Gene looked at everything with intense interest.
I pushed into a row of seats that had been finished, all but the
padding, and in the half-light watched two men hammering
away in front of me.

Behind me something else was going on—a switchboard was
being installed. A tall, light-haired woman was supervising this
operation, meantime doing a dozen other things—answering the
telephone, talking to people, selling subscriptions—all of which
did not interrupt her other job of putting the circulars into
envelopes for the new bill. I watched her. It seemed to me she
had become conservative, businesslike and quite distant. That
impression was probably due to the same absorption that I
noticed in everyone else. Eleanor Fitzgerald was a wonderful
warmhearted person. She stayed with the Provincetown
Players, giving to them everything she had—her health, her
time, her warm devotion, her *life*—up to the very end.

Suddenly I heard Jig call to the young man working on the
benches and a moment later they left their work and were
moving the boxes, paintpots and barrels away from the center
of the stage. Gene and Jig stood and watched, and soon they
were joined by others.

Gene came toward me at last, nearly an hour later, and sat down in the next seat. He looked pallid; his jaw and mouth were set in a determined line.

"Well, rehearsals start tomorrow—that's fixed! Tonight they'll read the parts—James Light as Nat, Ida as Sue, and Hutch Collins as Captain Bartlett—he'll be fine! As for the ghosts!"—Gene's voice was as quiet as ever, but as he spoke he was looking at the stage with angry determination.—"Jig's for it, but some of the others want to cut them out—say it can't be done! I'll show them if it can be done or not!"

At this moment the outer door opened, letting in daylight, and Ida Rauh and another woman came down the aisle. Fitzie had telephoned them that Gene was there. Ida went right to the point and without too much tact.

"You'll have to do something about the ghosts, Gene. The boys never *can* look like ghosts, you know it. The audience will simply laugh at them. . . ."

They waited for Gene to reply:

"Everybody in the play is mad except the girl. Everyone sees the ghosts except the girl. What I want to do is hypnotize the audience so when they see the ghosts they will think they are mad too! *And by that I mean the whole audience!* Remember—*"The author shall produce his plays without hindrance, according to his own ideas."*

9

At last Gene and I left for New Jersey. The rehearsals were over—thank God! Then there was a meeting. Gene went to that while Christine and I and some others sat in the Hell Hole and waited for it to be finished. It was all too much for me. I couldn't figure out what it was all about—the arguments and discussions and so on—except that this meeting, a very important one, was partly to decide whether or not they would give free tickets to the critics from now on. I was tired, and very anxious to get away before another opening-night party. Gene, absorbed in working with the play, the cast, the direction *and* the ghosts, had kissed me each time he started to a rehearsal. *"Don't worry —not a swallow of anything stronger than coffee today."*

We left the night before the opening, after the meeting was held, and I cannot even remember if Gene was for or against admitting the critics free. . . .

10

It was a drafty, dusty, two-hour trip, and it seemed to me that particular train stopped at every station on the way down. We got off at last—ours was the last stop—and took a local jitney, as they called them then, to go up to the house. The driver, clamfaced, greeted me coldly and never said a word, although when Gene paid him the fare, which was a quarter, and gave him a quarter tip he managed an inarticulate grunt.

We went into the house through the door of the outside shed, to which I had the key, and into the kitchen. As we entered the shed, my mother's dog Trixie leaped up at me, barking furiously with joy, and inside the kitchen Happy, the small gray cat, and a Manx tomcat looked up at us and began mewing piteously. It seemed Mother had expected we would be there in the morning, and the animals had been without food since then.

Gene looked so funny bundled up with a muffler around his neck, his brief case under his arm, his expression quite bitter and amazed, for the place was cold and the train trip had been more than we bargained for and it had made him very petulant.

"What the hell is this—a menagerie?" he said. He put his brief case down on the kitchen table and started to unloosen his scarf. Then he paused suspiciously. "Good God! What do I smell—cat mess?"

It was a dreadful moment. I could smell it too. The Manx cat was rubbing against Gene's trousers—he shoved it away. Out of the corner of my eye I saw what we were speaking about, on

243

a pile of newspapers in the corner, newspapers that had been put there next to some kindling wood to start the stoves.

"Come in the next room, Gene, I'll start a fire!"

Trixie, still in the shed, was barking. The cats sat on the floor, looking up expectantly.

"Better feed these animals something first, and keep them quiet!"

I had picked up a couple of clean newspapers and some kindling wood and pushed open the door into the next room. Gene followed me, taking his brief case, and the cats followed him. I pulled the cord of the light that hung from the ceiling, and knelt before the fireplace, rumpling the paper and laying the sticks across it. Gene would love the fire, and in a moment a small fire crackled behind the andirons. Gene stood watching me. He looked tired and thin, and yet relieved at being here. I smiled up at him—the ordeal was over, we were here, no drinking this time, thank God! I'd been a little resentful in the kitchen, when he acted the way he did—thinking that after all it wasn't my fault but *his* for not taking the train that we planned and arriving in the afternoon—but then, *I* had been tired, too.

Gene smiled back at me, a trusting warm smile, with that gaze behind it of love and intimacy that I always felt he kept for me alone. "That fire's fine—I'll put a log on. . . ."

There was a pile of cordwood against the side of the fireplace—that had been ordered ahead of time. Gene, still wearing his gloves, carefully laid one of the largest logs on top of the little blaze. Then he straightened up and pulled off his gloves.

"What's that? Never saw anything like *that* before!" he exclaimed suddenly.

He had seen a hand that appeared to be holding up the arch of the brick fireplace, as though from the inside of the chimney. It was once white plaster, but now pale yellow from the smoke of many logs.

"Oh—that's my mother's!" I explained, laughing at the expression on his face. "Don't let it frighten you. A friend of ours made a cast of her hand and later we thought this was an appropriate place for it and fastened it there with some cement."

I took his coat and my own and hung them inside the closet and closed the door—that old familiar door on which were marks cut with a penknife where each year my father had measured his four little girls as we grew up.

Gene was standing before the fire, holding his hands in front of the blaze, when I went back into the kitchen. I fed the cats out in the shed and closed the door upon them. On the shelf were the things I had ordered, and I opened a can of soup, made hamburgers and some canned green beans. The old coffee mill was still attached to the wall, and I was grinding enough for the two of us when my husband came in.

"What's that?"

"For grinding coffee," I explained. "Just a moment and everything will be ready!"

We carried a tray in and ate before the fire. Every once in a while Gene would look at the hand holding up the arch of the fireplace. It was warm and comfortable in the room now, and we ate our supper without talking. I wanted to sit for a while after we finished, and watch the flames, and the embers dropping into the ashes. But Gene was alert and curious.

"Let's look around and see what sort of a place you've got here." His typewriter, which had been sent ahead by express, was standing in a crate in the corner of the room. "I'd better decide where I'm going to work. This room"—he was looking at the three doors that opened from it—"won't do."

A year earlier he and I would have had to carry a lamp, going from room to room, upstairs and down; but now I proudly pulled the cords of the electric lights installed last spring. Briefly I recalled my father's telegram to the Garden Hotel—and our fantastic last days there. . . .

I suggested that we see upstairs first—most of the rooms were closed off, I explained. We could decide which ones we wanted to use. . . .

We climbed a narrow flight of stairs, and stood a moment

looking in the upper west bedroom, where we could dimly see a Victorian bed, a bureau, and a stove.

"That's enough now!" I told him shivering, and without opening the two other bedroom doors, took him through the big old-fashioned bathroom into the large upper nursery where we had slept as children. "There's no stove here, Gene, just a register from the room below. We can't use this room—it's too cold."

We went down the east stairs, and back to where the fire was burning. Gene looked thoughtful. I opened a door at the foot of the stairs that we had just descended.

"This is the lower nursery! There's a fireplace, but it never worked."

"It's a nice room—must be very light in the daytime." He carefully examined another large stove, set before the fireplace. It had a tin drum that went to the ceiling. "What's *that* for?"

"It's supposed to heat the upper nursery—the room above—but it doesn't do more than take the chill off it in cold weather."

"It's chilly in here—let's get warm again and then see the rest of it. Where do we sleep, dearie?" he added facetiously. "Hope you've got a lot of blankets!"

We put more logs on the fire and stood getting warm for a few minutes. Then I took Gene's hand and led him through the little front entry into the lower west room. I had looked in there before; the coal stove was banked, the room was warm and cosy, and I had opened the damper and put on the drafts to make it even warmer. A full coal scuttle stood beside the hearth. There was a double bed, neatly made up, a chest of drawers, and sofa. "This is nice!" Gene said. I noticed again that he seemed to be studying the stove, as if in some abstract speculation about it. Then he opened the door leading from the north side of the room. "What's in *here?*"

"The studio." I had really not wanted him to see my father's studio that night—not until tomorrow, when I'd have a chance to straighten it out. I was not sure where the light was; and as we stood there in the darkness inside the door, I noticed the faint, familiar odor of tubes of paint. . . . It was like the stage set of a ghost room; the familiar objects coming slowly into our vision from the pale translucence of the skylight, beyond which the stars shone in a dim and misty swarm.

I saw the cord for the light hanging from the ceiling and reached for it, feeling as if my father were there in the room with us. The light went on and Gene gave the room a careful inspection. He appeared to be pleased. The tall walnut wardrobes that had been sent down from Philadelphia after the death of my great-aunt gave off the sheen of old polished wood; against another wall canvases were stacked; on my father's big easel was a half-finished landscape. . . .

"What's *that*—another stove?"

"That's the 'coffin stove.' Doesn't it look like one?" I opened one end. "It takes eight or ten cord lengths of wood!" There was a pile of wood inside, laid on kindling and paper. I had asked my father to see that wood was there, and he laid the fire in case we should need it. "This is a cold room in the winter, Gene! It needs a big stove."

"Who's going to take care of all these stoves?" Gene asked; and I could see from the way he spoke that this had been on his mind all the time. "Let's get back to where it's warm. We're going to sleep in here tonight," he added as we closed the door behind us. "I'll bring the bags in and unpack."

I wondered, as I washed up the few dishes and straightened the kitchen, why he had said *tonight?* The lower west room was the most comfortable place to sleep in the winter. The family had a habit of changing the rooms and furniture according to the season—or even according to mood; the west room had been a sitting room, and (before my father added the upper and lower nurseries to the old farmhouse) even a lesson room when we were very small. But it had also been used as a bedroom—certainly in the winter it was the warmest room in the house.

I was feeling a little low by now, thinking of the family down in a small rented cottage by the ocean, and Gene and I here. Mother and Teddy had come up to the house and made everything ready for our arrival, and now there they were (hiding away, I thought to myself), no doubt wondering whether or not we had arrived. It was pretty sad and as my mother had suggested, rather crazy; but I tried not to mind. What *might* have made me forget it hadn't happened. Gene just hadn't been enthusiastic or even seemed pleased at being here. . . .

I began to wonder what was wrong. I just couldn't tell what it was. Whatever it was I would try to make it all right. I put the cats out and went into the next room, closing the door behind me.

The fire was blazing and my husband sat in an oak armchair before it. He had taken off his suit while I was doing the dishes, and put on a gray flannel shirt and corduroy slacks and a sweater, and I saw with relief that he *did* look contented and happy.

"I was thinking about this," he began. "Why couldn't we sleep upstairs, and, if it's such a job keeping the studio warm, I could use the west room to work in—I imagine it's quieter than that big room—you call it the lower nursery?"

"Well, it won't be warm, just the register in the floor, and you know you like to read at night!" I didn't add that upstairs we would hear the windmill at night. . . . "Do you like it here, Gene, or don't you?"

"Yeah, I like it. Got to get used to it, that's all. I don't know about the cats and the dog—suppose you can keep them quiet. And another thing—the stoves. How do we manage about them?"

"They have to be shaken down every day and the ashes taken out. Then coal has to be brought in—you can help with that."

"Sure. If I don't forget it!" Gene laughed. "I don't know anything about running them though, and I don't intend to learn—that's *your* job."

"I don't expect you to. . . ."

"It's good to be here anyway, and alone! God, I'm tired! Let's go to bed. We can decide about everything in the morning."

II

Something woke me early the next morning and I lay there wondering what it was. Gene was sleeping peacefully beside me—there was no sound anywhere; quietness, like a benediction . . . the bright, still sunlight outside. What was it? Something I had not done? Then I knew—I hadn't turned the windmill on last night.

You know why. You thought of it. But you were afraid it would start in the night and wake him up.

I dressed without disturbing him, put the draft on the stove, and went out to the kitchen. Trixie was asleep on her mat; she was not a young dog, so she opened one eye and went back to sleep. I had quietly closed the doors behind me, and now I picked up the iron shaker and as gently as possible shook down the ashes in the stove. But this required a vigorous manipulation back and forth of the stove shaker, which was very much like the old-fashioned crank used to start a Ford. A pile of fine ashes appeared in the opening below the firebox; when the coal was halfway down the grate, I looked at it, saw tiny blue flames appear, and, laying aside the shaker, proceeded to the next step, which consisted of getting on my knees and peeking up into the grate and with the poker dislodging the large "clinkers," as they were called. If this were done properly there would be a good fire all day; otherwise it would sulk and be moody, like a person who has not had a good bowel movement.

I stood up and straightened my back, lifted the stove lid and saw the coal beginning to glow and burn hot just as it should. Good! Next a couple of small shovelfuls of coal, the drafts open, and the top of the stove beginning to get hot. I debated whether or not to take the ashes out now. I was enjoying all this, so I decided to finish the job instead of doing it later—perhaps when Gene would be watching me and wondering what it was all about. I got the big coal scuttle from the shed and removed the ashes and put the kettle on. The cats followed me into the kitchen and I gave them some milk—when I looked for them again they had disappeared. . . .

Now—turn on the windmill! There was no hurry. Everything was still peaceful—there was no sign of any wind. So I stood at the kitchen window, looking out. Behind the three dark cedars near the barn an oak tree was a glittering, silent deep red against the blue of the sky. Not a leaf had fallen. Near it, the old wild-cherry tree was as bright a yellow as the oak was red; only the beach-plum bushes along the fence had lost their leaves and their branches were a tangle of misty gray. Beyond the fence, on the other side of Allen Street, the little pines stood still, waiting. . . .

But I could wait no longer. There might be a breeze any moment, and we mustn't run out of water. I didn't know if the tank in the barn was full—it might not be. I pulled on a sweater and ran around the back of the house and, standing under the tall and rusty and familiar old windmill, pulled down the wooden lever and fastened it down with the wire. There was a clank as I did this; the tail of the windmill swung out, the metal fan quivered and groaned and then all was still. I looked up anxiously. There wasn't a sign of a breeze—even up there.

But later, when I was getting breakfast, thinking that Gene was still asleep and that I'd have it ready when he woke up, he suddenly appeared at the kitchen door wearing his old blue bathrobe, his hair tousled, looking around in astonishment and anxiety.

"What on earth is that noise?"

I hadn't noticed—I suppose I was too used to it, and besides I'd been grinding the coffee. I listened. There was only silence, then it started again, a clank, a rattling groan, a whirring—brief but hopeful.

"It's only the windmill. It always makes that noise when it starts."

"It *startled* me—I thought I was in a stokehole!" he said gloomily and rather resentfully. He pulled the bathrobe more closely around him. "Also, there was a cat asleep on my feet when I woke up!"

12

The fact that he knew it would be necessary for him to return to Macdougal Street before very long to attend rehearsals of *The Moon of the Caribbees* made Gene rather moody. He really wanted to settle down to work on his plays. At times he even tried to persuade himself and me that it would be just as well if he attended only the last rehearsal or so and left the rest of it up to Jig Cook. But Jig was busy with Susan's play, *Tickless Time*, which was to be on the same bill—and after all, *The Moon* was Gene's favorite play. The Provincetown Players had never felt they could do it justice before; but now, with a stage nearly three times as deep as the stage at 139 Macdougal, there was a chance to make the production that Gene dreamed of—even though it seemed impossible because of lack of time and money to build the plaster dome that he so much wanted.

So he resigned himself to this, and during the next few days managed to occupy himself with things to do that would make it easy to start work when rehearsals were over. He was not going to let Christmas have its usual effect on him this year, he told me; by December twenty-third, the day after *The Moon* opened, he would be back here and at his desk, or on his bed, working, and Christmas could go to the devil. So, during the next few days, we changed some of the furniture around, started the stove in the lower nursery, walked to the village and bought a leather jacket and rubbers, and in the afternoon began taking long walks through the pines. Gene decided he would work in the dining room where the fireplace was; there was a big table there that he could use, and he liked the fire. The closet had always been piled up with dishes and glass; he took them out, put them in the kitchen, and put his scripts and books on the empty shelves. The bookcases in the studio were full of books that had been there for years; but there was a tall old rosewood secretary in our bedroom, with glass doors backed with faded pink silk, behind which were some shelves. One morning I heard Gene in the studio and found him carefully going through the books there and putting in a pile on the floor those he wanted to read. A little later he carried them in and arranged them in the secretary-desk, carefully and thoughtfully.

At night we went to bed early; he had fixed a long cord from the socket and made a reading light that hung on the wooden headboard, and before getting into bed he would choose a book from behind the faded silk of the glass doors of the secretary and lie reading for an hour, while I did the same; both of us propped up on horsehair pillows and very content. . . .

But every morning after breakfast, which we ate in front of the open fire, there was that period of silent expecting and waiting, which was to go on all winter and spring—getting more tense and at the same time more hopeless as the days went by. About a quarter past nine we would both look out of the front windows, where the road passed beyond the hedge at the end of the garden, to see if the mailman was going to stop at the gate. Sitting there waiting, I would sometimes think of our old mailman, who used to go by when we were still children, old George Hankins, who (like the present, younger man) took the mail to the next town three miles away and dropped the mail for a half a dozen houses along the way. Old George had one little red horse, very alert and full of spirits, and an old, gray lazy mare, and we would watch to see which horse would be attached to his old hooded buggy. . . . We didn't have a mail-box then: if there were books or magazines, he would throw them over the hedge; but if there was a letter he would stop the horse, yell loudly, "*Mail!*" and someone would go out and get it. I remembered when we were children how George Hankins, not so old then, would call out sometimes in the spring, on his trip back, "*Lil-locks, children*, lilocks!" and we would run out and pick up great flowering branches of early pale lilacs that he had broken off for us on his return from the other town. "*Them lilocks bloom earlier than yourn, Mr. Boulton,*" he would shout to my father if he saw him. "Real good earth up there in Herbertsville!"

Old George was dead, and we were waiting, not for lilacs, but for a letter from John D. Williams.

"You can't expect to hear—it's too soon," I told Gene every morning—hardly able to bear his gloomy and pessimistic expression as he waited to see if the mailman would stop.

One morning, in that mild Indian summer which was upon us, he walked out and stood at the gate. When he came back across the lawn, carrying only bills from the electric-light company and the hardware store, which he hadn't even bothered to open, he said as he came up to where I was waiting on the porch "What's the matter with that goddamn mailman? He just glared at me!"

I was disturbed by this—I couldn't understand it.

"Maybe they look at you and think you're one of them there furriners——" I laughed, remembering how strangely the jitney man had acted the night we first arrived. "So Agnes Boulton married an *I*-talian this time! What'll she be up to next!"

He didn't think this funny, but looked gloomily at the two bills.

"We've got to be careful of the money—— What's this? Did you buy something more at that hardware store?" he added, seeing the name and address in the corner.

I knew what he meant. "I'm not buying anything we don't need—it's probably about fixing the windmill." He looked at me suspiciously, and I knew what he was thinking of—an incident that occurred the afternoon that we went downtown to buy the jackets and get some things we needed at the stationery store.

My father, on arriving with the family and finding that there was the necessity (because of the circumstances) of paying rent, had hopelessly contemplated some small water colors he had done, debated about their chances of being sold, and then asked the proprietor of the hardware store, whom he knew well from the days when he was making many purchases there, if he'd give him a job. This was done, at ten dollars a week, and so every day from seven-thirty in the morning until six o'clock at night he stood behind a counter, sorting hinges for customers, weighing nails, advising perplexed women what sort of door-knobs, or latches perhaps, would be suitable. And—the stupid situation being what it was—I had to slip into the hardware store if I wanted to see him, and, in fact, even if I wanted to buy something, without Gene. I did this a few times without arousing much suspicion; then, that afternoon, when he insisted on going in to find out if they sold punching bags, I became so nervous and acted so strangely that he grew very suspicious and unpleasant, insisting I must be going in to talk to some admirer who worked there.

Gene put the two bills on the mantelpiece, went to the closet, and took out the unfinished script of *Chris*. He looked through it, still morose, and put it back and went to the window and stood there, as if still waiting for the mailman and hoping for a letter. I knew what the trouble was; he wanted to get to work. This was the hour he had accustomed himself to working, and he was struggling in a sort of vacuum of frustration. . . . Somehow things didn't seem right: he couldn't put out the *Chris* script on the table, sort it, concentrate, begin to plan. I felt that it was something about the room itself that was wrong; the doors and windows; the fact that it was really a room through which the traffic of the house passed, even though now it was only the traffic of two people, and I was worried about that and asked him about it.

"No, it's all right—I like the big table. I don't want to start on *Chris* or *The Straw* and then have to leave it for rehearsals, that's all. When are *you* going to start working?" he added in a sarcastic tone. "We spent more money than you may realize in New York. I not only have to sit here and worry about *Beyond* going into rehearsal, I've got to begin worrying about the damn money angle too. You know we can't count on *In the Zone* going on much longer. Perhaps you're too absent-minded to recall that I telephoned Lewis and Gordon about that the first week we were in New York, and they were pretty damn uncertain about it, even then. I should have heard from them—wonder why I didn't?"

"I'm going to start working right now," I said, suddenly furious about everything, "if that's what you want me to do! I thought this whole plan, being alone here and everything else —your goddamn solitude—was so *you* could work! We have to go up to rehearsals—that stops you from getting started, but I have to put my nose to the grindstone—is that it?" I flew into the lower nursery and stood rigidly clenching my hands. The old Oliver typewriter was on the table, and furiously, so he could hear me, I inserted a sheet of paper into the machine and pushed the carriage, making the bell ring. I was going to sit down and bang away on the keys, making as much noise as possible—but I couldn't. I suddenly felt foolish and weepy and sad, and stood there silent, listening.

There was not a sound in the other room. . . . Then I heard the front door close and saw Gene walk down the path. I ran back through the dining room onto the porch.

"Gene—come back!"

But he refused to answer me, and I stood there desolate, watching him as he walked down the road. . . .

So there I was alone, no longer angry but unhappy and confused. What was happening to us? Instead of seeing the situation as I had done only fifteen minutes ago when I had realized that Gene wanted to work and couldn't—or wouldn't— I was seized by a host of thoughts (none of them completed), which flew through my mind like besieging bats. We had acted as though we hated each other. What was it we had said in our anger? Money—but didn't he realize that I was doing everything I could? At least I wasn't spending anything much except for food. It was *he* who wanted the leather coat, and he who had insisted that I buy one too. Was it possible that after all his talk he *did* need people; that it was too much being alone with me? And the room—he insisted it was all right, he could work there, but was it? and what could I do about it? Was it sex—was *that* it? I had been tired at night lately, and gone right off to sleep . . . but couldn't he understand that? And I realized then, with something of dread and dismay, that he hadn't seemed to feel that way either. . . . All this was going through my mind; but behind it and overcoming it at last was just the longing to have Gene back, to throw myself into his arms and have him hold me tight and tell me that he loved me. . . . But it wouldn't happen—I was sure of that. . . .

But it did happen—just that! I was going crazy—had he taken a train? Had he bought a bottle? Had he hitchhiked off to some unknown place? I wandered from the kitchen to the dining room; looked out of the windows; got my coat . . . but if I *did* go after him, he might come back and I'd be gone! Then he might leave again . . . and . . . all the while the two cats and Trixie were anxiously watching me, as if they knew something was wrong.

Then—the door into the dining room opened quietly and Gene stood there. I had not heard him, so silently had he come up on the porch. He looked cold and pinched, and he shivered and cast on me a reproachful, sad, and yet tender look.

"Gene—*darling!*"

"Aggie—my own wonderful little wife!" We hugged each other and clung together and sat before the fire so he could get warm; he in the oak chair and I on his lap, his arm around me, pressing his damp tender skin against my face.

"I walked to the ocean and back," he said. "Maybe it did me good. We mustn't ever have this happen again—these horrible, searing, destructive fights. Never again, darling, do you understand?" And taking his face away from mine he gazed at me tenderly. His face looked thin and tortured—and very humble. And I remember feeling, without any explanation of it, a faint incredulousness. . . .

"Let us promise each other that, my own!"

"I promise, darling!"

"Let's forget the bills and the money and Lewis and Gordon and J. D. Williams—and everything. Except ourselves!" He stood up and pulled me close to him. "Let's get in to bed and get warm!" And he carried me in his arms into the bedroom, sat me on the bed, and began taking off my shoes. . . .

13

This letter I found among others, the paper thin and worn, the handwriting faint. It was written the day before *The Moon of the Caribbees* opened, which was on December twentieth of that year:

Dearest,

I'm not coming up. Not unless you send me a wire when you get this. (You ought to get it Friday A.M. early.) There was a letter from Lewis and Gordon and things seem doubtful about *In the Zone*.

So, much as I want to come, it's better to wait. I'll mail the story to Sonia (it's finished) and you'll have to tell me about *The Moon*.

But dear dearest heart, come home Saturday. I won't be able to stand another day longer than that without you. It's such a thin shadowy world, very still, just waiting—for you. All the reality is gone, and it's only when I shut my eyes and think about us, about you, that I'm something real —something still too, but with that stillness of the stars— something deep, something complete. . . . How futile words are!

Dear dearest, it's so silly to tell you that I love you (millionth time). Do you mind? I just wanted to say it again.

You've never forgotten to say it to me, heart of mine. You are so beautiful, dearest, all of you.

I wonder if I'll not be able to take that train? I'm lonely!

Your very own wife,

Aggie

14

Gene had gone to New York without me, protesting about it and predicting disaster for both of us but having to accept it, for, as so often happens, the mechanics of daily living blocked our intention to go up to the rehearsals together. It was impossible to leave the house alone—and that was all there was to it. The stoves had to be kept going or the pipes would freeze. The animals had to be fed—and I saw Gene give Trixie a vindictive look when I mentioned this; for he had never grown used to her, even though the little dog adored him. I *had* promised that if it were possible I would try and get someone to look after the fires, the animals, and the windmill, and join him in a few days.

The letter saying he must come up immediately had come sooner than he expected, but it was urgent; Jig Cook wrote that he had to come at once. If there had been time I might have arranged to have someone keep the place warm while I went up until he got settled, but not on that short notice; and to be truthful I was glad to be there alone for a short while.

After our quarrel I had taken the time to think things over very seriously. What I thought over was of course not myself and my family and our problem; but Gene—and myself in relationship to him. I recalled what he had said, and made an effort to find out if he was right in what he had said and how he'd said it. I tried to discover what, if anything (except the fact that he would soon be called to New York), was responsible for his inability to sit down after breakfast, even if he didn't do much actual writing, and spend some time working over his ideas, looking over his script, or something—as he had always done before.

I felt guilty because I was convinced that it was something to do with the house or his surroundings. I remembered what he'd said that first night—he'd wanted the west room to work in—until I'd explained things. I decided that I'd get the stove into the upper nursery, and we'd sleep there; the west room would be his study—leave the bed for him to lie and write on—have a long table there; another table for typing, near the west window; the secretary-desk was where it had always been, in the corner; and the Franklin stove, which was stored out in the barn, would keep the room warm, and be almost like an open fire. . . .

This idea I had kept to myself, as I felt it was too much of a project to impose on him at that time—and also the problem that I felt this would solve *was* solved, temporarily at least, the very afternoon of our quarrel, when we returned to the house after a long walk.

We had started out late that afternoon, intending to walk to the ocean; then Gene decided it might be too far, as he'd been down there once before that day. So we took a road that Gene hadn't seen before, and came to a house. The fence was down; the bare sandy yard was full of trash—old kerosene stoves, broken chairs, pots and pans, and small, dirty, healthy-looking babies. A red-faced man was stretched on a hammock; a woman was hanging out quilts on a line; and there were three young girls, all blond and beautiful and all pregnant, sitting or walking in the sun in this front yard.

"Who are *they*, for God's sake?" Gene asked me. I told him that they had just appeared out of nowhere, no one knew from where, and taken the house, which had been empty for some time because of its bad state of repair. And there they had stayed and still no one knew where they came from or even what they lived on; for although the mother occasionally took in some washing, the big red-faced father never did a day's, or even an hour's, work, but sat inside or outside the house, depending on the weather, drinking cheap whisky. The queer thing was that the seven daughters were all fresh-faced, innocent-looking, healthy and blond—but each girl in turn became pregnant, usually having to leave school for this reason. No one knew how this happened, for they talked to no one, this family; and no one talked to them. They were the town outcasts and didn't seem to mind it or even to realize it. As to what happened to the girls after their babies joined the little group of other unidentified babies, I hadn't been able to learn, but it seemed to me I had heard that they just vanished, and nobody knew where. . . .

After supper that night, which he ate in silence, apparently very absorbed, Gene went into the bedroom and lay down on the bed. Then he came back, and took paper, pencils and his writing board from the closet.

"I've thought of a one-act play—a peach! I'm going to outline it now and go ahead with it tomorrow. I should be able to finish it before I have to go to New York."

I was tired that night—between the quarrel, the reconciliation, our walk, and my various duties I must attend to every day, I didn't have much energy left. I went to bed earlier than usual, leaving Gene at the table before the fire, working. . . . The next day I woke up as usual and, still feeling tired, went back to sleep for a few minutes. I was awakened by a noise from the kitchen. Gene was not in the bed. I usually got up before he did, and, thinking it must be very late, I looked at the clock—to find that it was only seven-thirty. I put on my bathrobe and went into the kitchen.

Gene was there, holding the stove shaker in one hand and the poker in the other. He had removed the stove lid and he was staring inside with a puzzled expression on his face.

"Darling—*what* are you doing?" I had surprised him, and he turned to me, smiling ruefully.

"Something happened—there doesn't seem to be any fire left!"

I looked. The grate was empty. "You shook it too hard! The grate opened and it all fell down below!" I couldn't help laughing at him. "Now we have to start another fire!"

"You go back to bed and rest. I know how to start a fire. I've made up my mind to give you a hand with these stoves. Go on back to bed for a while and leave me alone!"

He looked so determined that I stifled the impulse to tell him what to do next and obeyed him. But I left the door open and listened to every sound—paper being crumpled, kindling snapping as he broke it, the roar of flame up the stovepipe, and then the sound of coal being dumped on the blaze. *My darling Gene . . .* I propped the pillow behind my back, then had a horrible thought. *I bet he forgot to open the damper!* I rushed into the kitchen again.

"Did you open the damper?"

"Think I'm that stupid? Go back to bed, you crazy little thing."

After he started on the one-act play in the dining room that morning he forgot all about the stoves—even forgot to watch for the mailman. I sneaked out and brought back a letter from a little theater that wanted to do one of his one-act plays, and kept it in the kitchen until he was through his work.

He worked on the play, which was based on the family we had seen, for two or three days—for some reason he didn't want to show me this play until it was finished and typed. It took him another day or so to revise and then type it. He was going over his script, getting ready to read it to me, when the postman brought a special delivery to the door. It was that letter from Jig. *Please come up that afternoon if possible, if not next day at the latest.*

"We can go tomorrow morning," Gene said. "*Don't look so concerned—relax!* Listen to this; I think it's pretty good. . . ."

I'm not going to mention the title of that one-act play here, but it is listed among Gene's lost plays, and I don't think that a copy of it exists today.

He left the next afternoon (as I said before) and I was alone in the house during rehearsals; and near the end of the time that

I was alone I wrote the letter I have mentioned. That was on a Thursday morning. An hour or so later I wrote another letter:

Same day!

Dearest Gene;

I just sent you a letter and now it seems to me it wasn't a very practical letter and that you might want to know more definitely about Lewis and Gordon. So—I'm enclosing theirs. I did not intend sending it or telling you what they had to say until you got back, as I was afraid it might give you the blues; but on thinking it over perhaps you will want while in town to phone him and find out something definite. So here it is.

Don't be discouraged. Now I'm here and not so worried about things I'm going to support the family for a change. I have started a story and know I can do a lot. I always can when it really gets down to brass-tacks. You said just about that a week or so ago, and it's true. Only you didn't say it in quite that flattering way. I will simply do Harold de Polo's stunt for a while—look over old copies of the magazines I'm writing for and dope out some plots. . . . The reason I haven't sold stuff this summer is, as you know, I was getting in too much of the other, more serious—or anyway, attempted serious style.

Wrote two letters for you. I'm getting a lot done while you're away—have to keep busy, so as not to miss you too much. Having stove put upstairs etc. Finished typing story. Under the circumstances I ought to stay here, and get things started . . . stories I mean. So please Dearest don't fail to be down. Come earlier Saturday if you can. By getting your mother to phone Penn station you can get time of trains and wire me if you take other train than the one leaving three something. I'll meet that one Saturday evening, with jitney, as I have some shopping to do. Love to all.

Au Revoir, my own dearest . . .

If your write me on getting this I'll get letter Saturday A.M. or noon. Please do.

But, late on Saturday afternoon, a boy arrived at the house on a bicycle, knocked at the door, and handed me a telegram:

I will not come home until you come up.

Eugene

15

Without bothering to think what the consequences might be, I locked Trixie in the shed, the cats in the kitchen, left them food and water; banked the stove, and turned the dampers; extinguished the fire in the fireplace with half a bottle of water, got a jitney, and took the next train for New York.

After I bought a return ticket and gave the man at the ticket office a wire to be sent to Gene telling him that I was arriving, I found I had very little money left—less than a dollar in change. As the train pulled out of the station I realized that I had forgotten to turn off the windmill. . . .

Gene was not at the Provincetown Theater, when I arrived about two hours later, and no one seemed to know where he was. Yes, there had been an opening-night party the night before! I talked in whispers to Fitzie, for the play had already started and there was an expectant silence in the small theater. For a moment I stood there watching the play and listening to the lines spoken by the actors—those words that had come out of Gene's heart, out of a lonely and somehow embittered past. A feeling of unspeakable sadness and beauty came over me as I stood there with Fitzie, holding tightly to her arm; my throat constricted and I felt tears in my eyes.

Fitzie led me outside, and we stood a moment longer in the street. She explained to me that Gene had intended to leave for New Jersey . . . why didn't I go and see if he was at the Hell Hole? If he wasn't there, I must come back and tell her. . . .

I walked around the corner and down Fourth Street and pushed in the back door of the old Hell Hole. I saw Gene at once, sitting at a table with Jamie. There was a good-sized white dog lying at his feet. The back room was full of people —I recognized several of Gene's old friends, the Hudson Dusters. Scotty Macdonald was there; James Light, and his wife Sue Jenkins, with whom I afterward became great friends, Harold de Polo, and Edna St. Vincent Millay.

Harold saw me first and, as always the most polite of men, pushed through the crowd and took me by the arm.

"Agnes, my dearest! We've been expecting you!" This, I soon found out, was a polite subterfuge on Harold's part, as Gene had not received my wire. Harold seldom showed his liquor, but that night his eyes were glazed. In one hand he held an empty bottle firmly by the neck. When we reached the table where Gene was sitting I realized that my husband was reciting *The Hound of Heaven*. Harold and I stood watching. Gene did not notice us and continued in his low voice:

> " '*Yea, faileth now even dream*
> *The dreamer, and the lute the lutanist;*' "

"Shall I go out and get you a wreath of vine leaves, Gene?"

He saw me, got to his feet, and I felt his arms around me. He made me sit down next to him. "No vine leaves, my own, not tonight! I knew you'd come at last. The Hounds of Heaven have been on my trail . . . wait a minute! Or was it the Hound of the Baskervilles? Anyway, here's a hound for you—*our* hound. I'm bringing him back with us—a playmate for Trixie!"

Jamie, who had risen to greet me, sat down. Harold went to bring me a drink. "Make it a double one, Harold!" I said. Jamie leered at me and patted my hand affectionately.

"*The boys from Brooklyn are coming over the bridge to-night, wild Irish rose! They'll be sitting on the end of my bed, dozens of little men all staring at me . . . !*

"Ah! that's what we'll name him—'Brooklyn Boy!' " Gene leaned over and patted the white dog, who sat up and licked his hand. (*Poor Brooklyn Boy!* Little did he know that he'd be murdered before the winter was over! Nor could I know that Trixie, too, would be lying beside him in a grave under the cedars.) He was a wonderful dog, somehow; I don't know what it was, but he certainly had something. He looked rather like Bowser—funny old Bowser, who had attached himself with such devotion to Jamie last summer.

At that moment I caught Scotty's eyes fixed on me with a complacently malevolent expression, a look of satisfaction that caught me unaware and confused me. The dog put both paws on Gene's knee and tried to lick his face. Gene put his arm around the dog, and there they both were, looking at me.

"How do you like our new dog, honey-puss? We're taking him home with us," Gene repeated, as if he wanted to be sure that I understood. I knew that we couldn't take the dog with us, and decided it was just an idea of Gene's that he would forget after a while, so I said nothing. "*God, baby*, I'm glad you got here!" he went on. "You surely let me down this time, promising to come up. Never again! You come with me next time."

Jamie sat there abstracted, paying no attention to us, as if he were remembering the other white dog and the brown freckle-faced girl and the flats where the fiddler crabs hid in their shells. Harold de Polo brought up a chair and began a vivid conversation, telling us how he had bottled a milkman who woke him soon after dawn one day demanding payment for his bill. Obviously he did this to intimidate two burly, tensely silent Hudson Dusters who stood nearby; for as he talked Harold gesticulated with the large whisky bottle, which he was holding firmly by the neck, and I was sure that at any movement on anyone's part that did not meet with his approval he would smash the bottle against the wall and, armed with his favorite weapon, begin an attack on the enemy. But, alas, this time Harold was not able to indulge in one of his favorite sports, for the Hudson Dusters, it seemed, were fascinated by Gene and unable to take their eyes off him. They knew him well and looked on to him as a two-fisted drinker, one of their own kind;

but Gene had given them tickets to the opening night of *The Moon of the Caribbees* and the reason that they couldn't take their eyes off him was that they were trying to figure how all that they had seen and heard on the Provincetown stage had come out of their friend Gene. . . .

Edna Millay, chaste, silent, and mysteriously discreet, sat at a table with two admiring male friends, watching all this. Her play, *The Princess Marries the Page Boy*, had been on the previous bill and she had heard the story that on leaving the party after the show (to which Gene had also invited them), the Dusters had picked up a copy of *her* play, thinking it was Gene's, and taken it off to read. She had been brought to the Hell Hole to hear, if possible, what the Dusters thought of *her* play. Scotty managed to get to her and tell her that they had thrown it down the toilet, and soon after, she and her friends left.

Gene knew by this time that we had to take the train that left at midnight (known as the Owl), the last train leaving that night. He seemed anxious to catch it and not spend another night in town. At least this is what he told me, managing to convey to me at the same time that he wanted to be alone with me and tell me everything that had happened—after he'd had just a few more drinks. He already had a bottle of Old Taylor in his topcoat pocket to take on the train.

There was still enough time, but I began to get uneasy as Gene made no movement to leave. Scotty, who had disappeared a half hour before, suddenly appeared again, holding a leash and dog collar. Gene took it and put the collar on the dog. Jamie's glazed eyes went from the dog to Gene and back to the dog again.

"We can't take the dog, Gene—are you crazy!" I said, and added—thinking I must have made a mistake and that Scotty would take the dog—"You *weren't* thinking of doing that, were you?"

He did not answer, and I knew that he had gone into that

abstract state where no answer was necessary to anything. But I kept on talking, after one glance at Scotty's face.

"Gene!" I pleaded. "It's bad enough taking care of Trixie and the cats and feeding them. We *can't* have another dog there!"

"What do you mean, we *can't?*" He heard me that time, even though his big dark eyes had been moving aimlessly around the room.

Scotty agreed immediately, though Gene did not seem to hear him:

"Of course y' can! There's plenty of room, from what Gene told me, and plenty of pine trees, too, for him to lift his leg and pee on!"

"Gene, let's go!" I was getting angry now. "We'll get a cab outside and drop Jamie off. Don't you realize that we cannot take the dog on the train? There is no baggage car on the Owl."

"I won't take a train then—is that clear?"

"Jamie," I said, "let's go! Maybe we can leave the dog with you."

I put my hand on his shoulder and Jamie got slowly to his feet.

"Leave him wherever you like, my dear! What's Hecuba to me or me to Hecuba?" He hiccuped and looked at Gene: "C'm'on, old timer . . . let's get goin'!"

Somehow we persuaded Gene to leave the Hell Hole. Jamie, Gene, the dog and I stood on the corner waiting for a taxi, and how we got even that far I don't know. I was beginning to think it was all very funny and wondering what would happen if Gene tried to take the dog through the train gate. A taxi picked us up, and we started up to the Garden Hotel, where we were to drop Jamie. I decided we shouldn't take the dog as far as the station, and whispered in Jamie's ear that we would put the dog off with him. . . .

But Gene must have heard me or read my mind; for when we next stopped for a traffic light I saw him set his lips firmly and just as firmly grasp the dog's collar. I didn't realize what he had in mind, for he was clever enough to wait until the light changed and our taxi started. Then with a swift and adroit movement he picked up the dog, opened the door, slammed it shut behind him, and stepped into the oncoming traffic. It happened before I could stop him, or stop the taxi, and as we moved on I saw through the back window that he had reached the curb and was starting rapidly back downtown. . . .

Jamie didn't seem to know what had happened. There was no use going back—we'd never find Gene. But when we stopped at the Garden Hotel, Jamie refused to get out of the cab. The driver shrugged and told me we were going to miss the train if we didn't get going. . . . So we started again, Jamie sitting beside me. By this time I began to think I was living one of Strindberg's dramas myself, a sort of *Spook Sonata* or *Dream Play*, maybe, for neither Jamie nor the driver seemed to notice that Gene and the dog had disappeared. The driver began to sing in a very melancholy and very loud voice, making it impossible for me to think what we would do when we did get to the station—should I take the train, go back and look for Gene, or what?

Gene had all the money in his pocket—all I had was my return ticket and twenty-five cents. When we pulled up in front of Penn Station Jamie got out of the cab and began fumbling in his pockets to pay the taxi driver. I knew he had some money and I tried to get him to get back into the cab and return to the Garden Hotel. There was a sort of slow-motion scene there under the lights of the entrance between Jamie, me and the driver—with me trying to push Jamie into the cab, knowing that words would be of no effect, and the driver peering around to see what happened to the other passenger with the dog.

"So long! De odder guy was wise to leave!" he exclaimed, having at last realized that fact; he gave Jamie his change and drove off, again singing his melancholy song about his old gal Sal. . . .

I told Jamie that I had to hurry and tried to say good-by, but he grasped my arm and hurried along with me. When we got to the gate and he found that he couldn't get through without a ticket, or without buying one, he began fumbling for his money. I heard the conductors calling *All aboard* and saw the train begin to move, and ran down the steps just in time to get on the last car. As I got on I saw Jamie, who had at last sorted out enough money to pay his fare, walking like a somnambulist down the ramp toward the moving train. . . .

16

There was always someone waiting at the station to pick up any passenger who might be on the Owl. Old Clarence Hall saw me step off the train, waved to me glumly and opened the door of his cab. Halfway up to the house his peculiar nasal voice drifted back to me. "Saw your paw today. He hain't lookin' very well!" and I saw his lean jaw close like a trap. No more was said—not even good night.

Everything must have been all right at the house. I only remember dragging myself upstairs and getting into bed in the upper nursery and lying there watching the reflection on the ceiling from the stove until I fell asleep.

It was still dark when I awoke, reluctantly letting go of some dream as I tried to identify whatever it was that had awakened me. I was sure that I had heard the sound of a heavy vehicle stopping outside and I tiptoed to the window and peered out. Yes, there was something outside the back gate. It looked like a large truck. I turned back, listening, for I had heard something else—voices talking somewhere—and after a moment, standing at the head of the stairs, I discovered that these voices came from the kitchen. I pulled on my bathrobe, pretty frightened by now, wishing Gene or someone was there, and crept silently downstairs. The door into the kitchen was closed. I listened—and couldn't believe what I heard. *Gene* was talking, and he was interrupted by another voice almost as low as his own.

I pushed the door open. Gene was sitting on one side of the kitchen table. Across from him was sitting a man wearing a pea cap and a heavy jacket; between them on a chair, eating canned beans out of a dish that Gene had put before him, was the Brooklyn Boy. In the center of the table was an open pint of Old Taylor.

Gene rose, a smile of intoxicated good will and satisfaction on his face. I'm not sure that he really knew that it was I who was there. Then he swallowed, looked at me unsteadily, looked again, and came over to me.

"My wife, Hank!" he said, putting his arms around me. "Aggie, this is Hank. He's on his way to Atlantic City with a truckload of frozen geese. He's brought me and Brooklyn Boy down from New York."

17

Gene brought a turkey along with him that night. Hank, the truck driver, had helped him buy it somewhere in Newark. I suspect that we ate turkey for a week or so; but I have a folded piece of thin typewriting paper, and on one side of it is written down in not too orderly fashion what I also bought on a trip to the village the day before Christmas.

½ lb. bacon,	.14	Typewriter ribbon,	.75
½ butter,	.35	Post & papers,	.10
3 eggs.	.21	Trunks, express,	.50
Wesson oil,	.37	Stove pipe,	.25
Bread,	.10	Dogs,	.22
6 oranges,	.26	Paper, cig,	.09
Hamburg,	.35	Pluto Water,	.20
Sausage,	.20	Cup coffee,	.05

A couple of items help me to remember, even more vividly, that this Christmas was like past Christmases for Gene and not as he had wanted it to be; but also that he *was* trying to get himself straightened out. He had decided that a bottle of Pluto water was good to take before going to sleep—when (as he explained) he wanted to start thinking about not drinking; the next day if he changed his mind, and wanted to stop thinking and start drinking, it still was a help. And the *Post* (was the *S.E.P.* ever five cents?), which he must have asked me to buy for him, shows the same thing. . . .

The other side of the paper might be a diary but isn't; I wasn't keeping a diary then. I had put the list in the kitchen drawer, and, finding it when I was alone in the kitchen before going to bed, I wrote down (for no reason, perhaps, except that I was feeling sorry for myself) just what I had done that day; the day before New Year's, for it is dated at the top of the page, December 30, 1918:

> Got up about ¼ to nine, got breakfast and at 10.30 started to work on THE HAT SHOP at twelve the dogs had been raising such hell, and G. just discovered that Happy made another mess. So was too nervous to work longer. Swept living-room and dusted it, mopped up all four cat messes, got lunch, only mush, and after lunch just had time to dress with Gene and start downtown. He walked as far as P.O. with me, where I got "Wharf" back from the Metropolitan with a letter from Sonia Levine, and a letter from Arthur Jones saying unless I paid note he would put it in the hands of a lawyer. Walked on to village by myself, very tired. Met Mrs. Q——. She is very attractive and wants to meet Gene as she has heard much of his work and admires it. Left her, did other shopping, arriving pretty tired, got supper, liver, bacon, potatoes, tomatoes, and tea. After supper laid down a while, then fixed damper in stove-pipe, very hard job, tidied kitchen, put up stove-pipe. Then felt very blue, it being last of 1918 and for other reasons.

Gene had brought with him a few copies of *Thirst*, the small book of one-act plays which, to encourage his son, James O'Neill had paid to have published. I was consoled and amused looking at the inscription that Gene had written when he gave me the book for a Christmas present. It was not as intense and full of meaning as some of the inscription to me in his later plays—but I loved it.

> *To Agnes—*
> *These first five Stations of the Cross in my Plod up Parnassus——*
> *"I, also have been afraid—but I know now that I had been gazing at the sea too long, and listening to the great silence."*
>
> *"Thirst"*
> *also—(It is four bells and the scoff-summons yet unheard) —"I think I am a little out of my head. I am very weak. We have not eaten in so long——"*

It was dark long before six o'clock on New Year's Eve, and although I had in mind some sort of a little celebration for the two of us (creamed turkey, probably, and a pie, and the remaining liquor decked out somehow in a bowl with lemon peel), on observing Gene's laconic look as the evening approached I quickly gave up this foolish idea. I was relieved when I realized that he would only be bored by anything of the sort, for I was not really interested in doing it either. So we both settled down for the evening, Gene with a severe and dour expression as he picked up the *Saturday Evening Post* and finally got started reading it after a few necessary drinks.

I poured myself a couple of good straight ones too; feeling that I should bid farewell to the old year in some manner even though Gene chose to ignore it. I gave Trixie and Brooklyn Boy each a big slice of turkey, and cut up some turkey breast for poor Happy, who it appeared, was going to have kittens before long. She was a very sensitive cat; one of our trials during the past few days had been that (not being used to liquor or its effects on human beings) she got uncontrollable diarrhea when

Gene was drinking. I was never able to figure out if it was fear or sympathy. . . .

After my second Old Taylor, (with neither lemon peel nor ice), seeing from Gene's expression that he was not interested in talking, I had a remarkably nice time getting into a real O'Neill mood all by myself. I evolved a little drama which seemed very significant to me, and after the last distant noise of the New Year had died away I left my seat by the fire and went into the next room where Gene was lying on the bed.

"Listen, Gene: *There is a little country village, overhung with the indifferent moodiness of a somber night. At twelve o'clock midnight all about in isolated spots indicating taverns, churches and farms there is a comical medley of sounds which sound unutterably futile against the night's silences!*"

Gene put the *S.E.P.* down, vaguely frowning.

"*Comical* medley?"

"You're right—no . . . it's another word. I don't know how to pronounce it—don't know how to spell it, either. It means ——" I stopped.

"Cacophonous?"

"That's the word!" and I continue: "*Guns firing, an old horn, a dinner bell or so . . . a revolver . . . a voice raised in a drunken hurrah!*"

Gene picked up the *S.E.P.* but I kept on.

"*In a farmhouse where poverty or ill luck—or something— have brought—er—my hero to the point of despair, these shots, signifying to the world only good luck——*"

I could see that he had gone back to that story that he always liked about a tractor, but I continued to read, raising my voice.

"*. . . These shots which signify to the world a greeting to the New Year have bloodily and at leisure closed the human comedy for one small family!*"

"You mean *us?*" said Gene, but his eyes were following the dilemma of the salesman and a client for the tractor.

"Of course not!" I said. "*This is tragedy!* This man because of his guilt at being a failure, and utter disgust at life, kills his wife, his children and himself. Didn't you hear the gunshots a while ago? I should think *you* at least could understand!"

There was silence, then Gene raised his dark somber eyes to mine, and I understood that for some time he had not heard what I had been reading, nor getting much sense from the story before him, but had been absorbed in profound self-disgust. . . .

He glanced at the clock, closed the pages of the *Saturday Evening Post* and let it drop to the floor beside the bed.

"Life's a tragedy—hurrah!" he said sarcastically. "No, I heard neither bells nor gunshots. I was insulated from time—the past, the present, and the future—by the liquor, one half of which now remains, my darling, in the bottle on the floor beside the bed; and by the involvements of a salesman with the home office, a client, and what became to me a strangely important female impersonation—a tractor!"

He got up, and for a second I saw the crazy, laughing light in his eyes; then I was caught and pulled tightly against him, his arms embraced me almost with desperation. I seemed to feel a tremor in that body against which my head rested, and then I felt him kiss my hair as he whispered in my ear:

"Forgive me, darling—and happy New Year! We will make it *our* New Year this time!"

I lay awake with Gene asleep beside me in the quiet room, and thought of tomorrow—a new day—and of the week that would follow, and the carpenter who was coming to make a typewriter table and a long writing table with two drawers for correcting manuscripts. We had decided on this, and Gene had made a rough sketch of the table. I thought also of my hurried trip in a jitney to the cottage near the sea the day before Christmas, while Gene was home and I was doing my shopping. I had taken a few small presents; it was Grannie's afternoon to go to the library and no one was there but my sister, my mother, and my little girl. I could only stay a few minutes, for I knew Gene would be restless at home. When I embraced my child she had seemed astonished and detached, and then mildly pleased at my present. When I left she was regarding it with increasing interest and paid little attention to my farewell. For some reason I had brought her a bouquet of flowers, arranged by the local florist in circles around a little glass angel, and as I went off to sleep the bouquet of bright flowers appeared and floated for a moment before my eyes, with the little, smiling, expectant angel in the center. . . .

18

Not long after that, when I asked Gene if he wanted me to get the *Saturday Evening Post* and he said *no!* I knew that the holiday season was over.

Our life among the little clowns assumed a routine that can be recalled without much effort. For everyone there is a pattern of days, no matter what the circumstances: a waking up and a going to sleep, a time to eat and a time to go out and to stay in. . . . We had breakfast, waited for the mail, and then Gene went into the west bedroom and in that abstraction that signaled the approach of work, sharpened pencils, neatly piled up paper, put a glass of water on the table next to the bed, and, with my father's drawing board propped against his knees and a pillow behind him, looked absently at the sheet of white paper on which (in his tiny handwriting) there would soon come to life one of those *others* who shared the days with us in the Old House.

We ate a silent and often uninteresting lunch. (When I saw that word *mush* in the middle of that day's record I must admit it gave me a shock. What, *mush!* I felt that I couldn't leave the word there for everyone to see. I was tempted to add the word *fried*, so that anyone reading it would think of tempting crisp corn-meal squares, and there would come the connotation of crisply fried bacon; for I surely could do no less than that with a genius on my hands! But *mush* it said, and *mush* I left it, even though I was rather annoyed at having to admit having *mush* in the middle of the day!)

Our silence at this midday meal was not, however, because of our fare—for whatever we did eat, I don't think Gene would have noticed it, being still absorbed in the work which he had been doing for three or four hours and to which he would shortly return . . . nor did I particularly want to talk then or bother myself with trivialities, though probably interested in what it was like outside—if there would be sun or not for our walk in the afternoon, or even what I'd have for dinner. . . .

It was a joint and uncomplicated silence; for I, too, would have in my mind some part of that work (whatever it might be) which for the morning occupied me; or even more often I would be in that peculiar and probably lazy state known as *not thinking*, into which would drift ideas having no relation to who we were or what we were doing.

Gene, after taking time out for a look at the sky, would return to his room and again occupy himself with work. I am quite sure that at the Old House in New Jersey he did not take the nap after lunch which, everywhere else, I remember he did take. Why, I don't know—but he didn't. An hour or so later he would appear, stand there watching whatever I was doing, and say: "Aren't we going to take a walk?" if my duties were at the moment domestic, as they often had to be in the afternoon; or if I had my jacket and scarf ready: "Let's go while there's still some sun!" and he would get his things from the closet, and pick up his thorn walking stick; sometimes put a leash on Brooklyn Boy's collar, and sometimes leave him in the house while we set forth to find a different road, somewhere among the little pines. . . .

A pot of tea when we came back; sitting before the fire, talking or not talking, according to which was most pleasant; the lights on and the shades down. After supper, a sort of absorbed drifting around, or looking at a newspaper or a magazine, or writing a letter or so; or, now was the time (if it was to be done) for him to be sarcastic about certain people, or

circumstances connected with the *Beyond* situation, or with
the Provincetown Players. Then a book and two or three hours
of reading before the fire, or sometimes in bed, until he finally
turned off the light.

19

So went the pattern of our days, so much I can recall, but
as if in a void—two small figures moving like silhouettes against
an emptiness, an undramatic background, where there was only
the silent waiting of the little pines, the dark, spiked, expectant
little clowns.

Later, it is true, things happened there at the Old House
that stirred those emotions concerned with the dramatic aspect,
or, let's say, the intensity of living—as happened many times
during our years together. But always elsewhere these incidents
or events seemed to occur against a landscape that lent itself
to what was going on, or in a house or dwelling place that in
some way participated in or even aided the general effect.
Peaked Hill Bar (which has become the legend of an old
abandoned coast-guard station, though it was much more than
that), Brook Farm . . . Spithead . . . a room over Polly Holliday's restaurant in Greenwich Village . . . or that strange place
where Spanish Willy lived and moved and had his being;
everything had a setting that emphasized events, and, now as
I think of it, emphasized Gene himself.

20

For Gene dramatized Nature and made her useful for his
plays and only loved her as she dramatized himself. There
was nothing in that flat New Jersey landscape that he could
identify with any part of his own personality. Even the ocean
appeared uninteresting to him, with its waves breaking monotonously on the sand close to the old wooden boardwalk, the
decrepit summer hotels and the flimsy summer cottages, and

before long he stopped walking down there. He never went into a bar and seldom into a store, and after our daily walks would return to the fireplace, his books, and his tidily arranged script with something like relief.

He was comfortable there, but I do not really think that comfort itself ever meant much to Gene. To him a house was a house. He had no particular taste or feeling about them, only as they expressed that person whom he saw as himself. He would have been happy in a huge ugly Victorian villa had he seen himself as a second Disraeli; or, had he not forseen himself as a successful playwright, but visualized himself as ending his life as a beachcomber, he would have been perfectly happy in a shack in Papeete, Tahiti. He was not uncomfortable in the Old House, but (as with the landscape and the sea) he could not dramatize himself against that background—and this trait on his part was not any outward ostentatious thing, but something quiet, deep and a part of himself.

21

During the winter and spring, perhaps because of our solitude, those *others* I spoke of were a part of our life and at times seemed even more real than ourselves. Chris Christopherson; Eileen Carmondy who lived and nearly died in *The Straw;* Steven, her belated fiancé; her father; a nurse or so in white uniform; and, of course, old Chris's daughter, who took the trip on the barge that was to alter her life.

Anna seemed very aloof from us, being at that time a very proper young lady from Leeds, England, who spoke most correctly and whose ambition was to improve her position as a typist and probably become a secretary—rather uninteresting, I thought, though Gene did his best to make her speeches sound convincing as he read them aloud. I used to secretly wonder how old Chris had ever come to have such a daughter. She didn't like herself either, it seems, and even then was secretly rebelling and a year or so later became a prostitute, changed her birthplace to Michigan, and demanded another lover (big romantic Mat Burke) instead of the rather ordinary first mate, Mr. Anderson, whose ambition was to become a captain. . . .

Old Chris—how real *he* was! It was Chris that Gene really knew and loved, and old Marthy too—and the bums and outcasts in the first act down at Johnny the Priest's saloon on South Street in lower New York; the longshoremen, even the mailman —they all came to life there in that house.

There was a man who sat at one of the tables in Johnny's saloon and wouldn't leave, though he didn't seem to add anything to the play—and I even asked Gene once when he said the play was too long, what he was there for—an uninteresting traveling salesman on a drunk, whose only purpose seemed to be to annoy the others, having run out of money. But he stayed there. Who could have known that one day he would kill his wife and turn Jimmy the Priest's upside down as Hicky in *The Iceman Cometh?*

Eileen Carmondy joined us also, and a man I never cared too much about: Steven Murray. Gene seemed to know these people as he wrote and thought about them; but they, at least Steven and Eileen, became rather unreal toward the end, as they were forced into certain words and actions. But, after all, he had brought them to life and it was only fair that they should help him by acting in a manner that would prove whatever theme he had in mind, rather than following their own destiny. It appeared to be Eileen's destiny to die; and I'm sure that she would rather have slipped out of life at the appointed time than have had the newspaperman, Steven, come back to the sanatorium and dangle a belated love before her—Steven, who didn't even know he loved her (or should love her) until he held a rather ambiguous conversation with a head nurse. . . .

Whatever it was that Gene was trying to say then, to the world and to himself, it was certainly convincing at the time to him and to me, for we both loved *The Straw* and for a long time the lines, near the end, speaking of the "hopeless hope" in life itself had meaning for both of us. I think at that time he was striving for some perfection in his own life; some dream or hope of a relationship with "one other"—that *other* of whom he had spoken to me one day in the back room of the Hell Hole. . . . There was that in him which desired this—and that in him which denied it. I suppose he was haunted by the God whom he had discarded. But there was neither sentimentality nor regret in his attitude toward that God and the religion in which he had been brought up—rather a robust, humorous mockery, a personal challenge and a delight in that challenge itself. There was always in him a persistent sense of the reality that lies behind what *is*, what seems to be. He could find nothing of that in the God he knew and whom he had outgrown; nor could he really find it elsewhere—either in love or in idea. So he saw life as a tragedy and had neither the desire nor curiosity to go beyond the limits of his own vision. He loved his own tragic conception of life and would not have given it up for the world. He even saw it at times as humorous, and would laugh at himself for it; but he would never permit any knowledge or idea, or discovery of science that would interfere with it, to enter his mind. *His* index was as rigorous as that of the Catholic Church.

At the same time, it was necessary to him as a man to conquer this fate, this worm that gnawed in every apple, and firmly convinced that he could not alter that heavy hand of Fate, he must believe that it *was* possible—even if it were never to be possible. *The hopeless hope*—"Life's a Tragedy, hurrah!" *He* must triumph—even if he didn't! Ego must outwit God.

At times, however, Gene must have achieved briefly a sense of that expanded consciousness in which the self, forgotten, becomes one with whatever is behind the veil; he speaks of it in a prose poem the next fall, which he gave me as a gift; and perhaps, in those beautiful and moving lines that Edmund speaks near the end of *Long Day's Journey into Night*— those lines that end: *"It was a great mistake, my being born a man. I would have been much more successful as a sea-gull or a fish. As it is I will always be a stranger who never feels at home, who does not really want and is not really wanted. . . ."*

22

Something happened to us before long, which had the elements of a small tragedy—to which could not be added a *hurrah!* Gene loved our white dog from the Hell Hole, and so did I. Too much, perhaps, for our own good, for one night when we let him out before going to bed he did not return. We did not worry until the next day. That night, again, he did not come back. The next morning I was getting breakfast in the kitchen and Gene appeared at the door, wearing his bath-robe and slippers, his face a ghastly, sick color. A moment before, he had paused at the front window to look out at the day, and now he could not tell me what he had seen. . . .

There was a moment of confusion, without words—of fear. I thought he was going to be sick. Somehow he let me know; and I looked out of the window and saw on the front lawn the poor stretched-out body of Brooklyn Boy, but not that alone. Not death alone—but malice. His throat had been cut from ear to ear, and he was laid there so that his fatal wound could be plainly seen.

The mystery of Brooklyn Boy's death was never solved, although I heard from some small boys in the neighborhood that he had been seen the day before, lying dead among some huckle-berry bushes at the side of the road. But Gene and I saw animosity behind it—some of the same animosity that I had noticed in the jitney drivers; perhaps this was due to the fact that people there, possibly people I didn't even know, were going over in their minds (as they went over everything in those days) the fact that my family, settled there for the winter, had suddenly left the house and moved out, while I and a strange, silent man whom they couldn't understand or place moved in.

There was an old woman living along the road, and sometimes I would stop and talk to her as she worked in her garden; or go inside while she showed me her seed catalogue and told me what she was going to plant when spring came. One day she asked me a question that so astonished me that I did not at first know how to take it.

"Doesn't your husband take drugs?"

This was put in such a naïve cheerful manner, much as she might have said doesn't he smoke cigarettes, or chew tobacco, that it took me only a moment to recover and realize how extraordinarily naïve her attitude was. No, I explained, he didn't —what made her think so?

"Those walks—those long walks! It ain't natural, a man walking like that. I thought you had to go along to take care of him. I've passed him looking so quiet, you could tell he wasn't drinking, so I calculated he must of been taking drugs."

Gene and I laughed at this, and he said it reminded him of those long solitary walks in Provincetown which resulted in his being accused of being a German spy.

23

The afternoon walks were not enough exercise for Gene, it being almost an obsession with him to go through every day a certain, regular routine of building up, or stretching his back, his arms, his shoulder muscles. Behind the Old House, near the edge of the grounds, stood a weathered two-story building know as the "barn"; and Gene, after looking it over, decided that here was where he could get that extra exercise that he needed. He cleared a space of some fifty feet on the east side of the building, bought some tennis balls, and either before lunch or after our walk he threw the ball against the side of the "barn" for half an hour, running to catch it as it bounced back, and throwing it back again with increased vigor.

He liked to have me watch him do this, but one afternoon, tired of watching him, I unlocked the padlock on the barn and went upstairs. A crate of empty mason jars blocked the top of the stairs, but I stepped around it and stood looking at everything piled up in that large, cobweb-hung place. It seemed to me that every object for which we had no future use had been piled here: old shutters, a broken bench, pitchers and wash-basins of heavy white china; old kerosene stoves, harness for the horse we once had; toys with their paint faded, dolls with distorted arms, piled on an old hammock. . . . Here also was some of the heavy walnut furniture—wardrobes, a chest of drawers, a sofa, and Victorian chairs—that had been sent down from the house on Fortieth Street in West Philadelphia when, on the death of my great-aunt Agnes my grandmother had broken up housekeeping. Aunt Agnes' beautiful Victorian bed had been given to me; but the heavy velour curtains from her bedroom were here, wrapped in the brown paper in which they had arrived some twenty years ago. Some of her books were piled next to them, covered with thick dust. A large poison-ivy vine, which had climbed up the back of the barn, had thrust its tendrils through the window and, since I had last been here, a strong growth of brown, poisonous tendrils had twisted over the shelves and attached themselves to the dried leather of her books—all books on religion: sermons, hymns, and prayers for the living and the dead, and a set of the New Testament, each Gospel bound separately. . . . There was no room for them, anywhere else: the attic in the house had for years been piled high with the leather-bound contents of the library on Fortieth Street, and this was the overflow that had not found a place anywhere. I remembered sitting on the floor by the tiny attic window after picking out something I liked, and when it got too dark, lighting a candle. What would become of all these relics of a past? What would be done with them? In the pale dusty loft I caught sight of the clay water jar that my father had brought back from Mexico; and, going over, I removed it from a nail on the rafter where it hung on a heavy cord. It was made of beautiful heavy porous clay; I would take it back to the house, perhaps hang it in the kitchen. What had happened to the other things that he'd brought back from Mexico and given to my mother before they were married—the heavy bracelets of woven gold wire, the blue-fringed rebozo, the rosaries of carved wooden beads . . . ? I had not seen any of them for a long time; and, sitting for a moment at the head of the stairs, holding the water jar, I thought of some pictures that my father had done while he was in Mexico—they were somewhere in the house, in a portfolio. He was such a gentle man—so kind, my father. And yet—he understood! There was one pen-and-ink drawing, beautifully executed. Had he done it while he was in Mexico or after he came back? There was (in the background of this picture) a great building of stone, or as I learned later, probably of adobe; a palace or government building, early Spanish, perhaps built by Cortes or his followers; there was a great arched entrance; and before that entrance, blocking it, stood a little man. He held a shotgun. He was small, weak, insignificant, yet he held the shotgun firmly in his hands. His dress was inconspicuous, and he had a wispy mustache, and somehow one got the impression that his sad patient eyes were watering. But there he stood, before the monumental architecture of old, despotic Mexico, with a gun almost as big as he was; underneath, in my father's fine lettering were written the words: "They shall not pass!"

No; it wasn't a machete—it was a gun, and as my father was there I suppose he knew. Perhaps *he* was something like that little man himself—slight, kind-eyed; he, too, had a gentle mustache. But he defied his family, refused to go into their shipping business and instead studied painting under Thomas Eakins, who was the greatest and most original painter of his time. Eakins was fond of my father (I heard later that he considered him his most promising pupil), for when Eakins went to Camden to do the death mask of Walt Whitman it was my father who went with him and helped cast the mask.

For a long time Teddy kept some photographs that he had taken with Eakins not long before Whitman's death. . . . *Dear Teddy!* I picked up the water jar and went downstairs to where Gene had just finished throwing his last ball against the wall of the barn.

"Where were you?" he asked me curiously.

"Oh—just looking over some old junk in the top of the barn!"

24

I must have caught a cold up there that afternoon for I had to stay in and couldn't go walking with Gene.

The first day that I stayed in bed Gene came upstairs with Trixie and told me he was going to take her along. I was up, a day or so later, much better (but still drinking lemonade and taking aspirin), when Gene came in, put his stick in the closet and hung up his coat. I was in front of the fireplace, bundled up in his woolen bathrobe. He came and sat in the chair on the other side of the hearth. He had not spoken, not even to answer my greeting, and I saw at once that there was a disturbed and severe expression on his face. Trixie came and put her head on his knee.

"Is something wrong, Gene?"

He told me then. He had come home along the river, and, taking a short cut through the pines, wasn't sure where the house was. He saw an old man, one of the natives, chopping wood. Trixie ran up to him, wagging her tail. The old man put down his ax and patted her, and Gene asked him where our house was.

"I had quite a talk with him," Gene said, looking at me sternly. "What's the idea of not telling me your family was here?"

25

I told my parents what had happened and they felt (my father in particular) that as Gene was working, and his work demanded solitude, this should be respected; about this time, also, they were all taken with light attacks of the influenza that was still causing so many deaths. It was a windy and damp time of year, and even the little clowns seemed to be longing for a good clean snowfall. Gene working on *Chris Christopherson*, and, at times frustrated by his slow progress, grew daily more gloomy. No definite news came about John and Lionel Barrymore being cast in *Beyond the Horizon*. I was working on a short story, hoping I could sell it to the Sonia Levine at the *Metropolitan* magazine, as it seemed to me important now to try and sell to the magazines that paid more money.

I was typing this story in the lower nursery one afternoon. Gene, who had finished work, lit a cigarette and was looking over what I had done while he waited for me to come to the end of my page so we could get our things on and go for our afternoon walk.

I heard a knock at the kitchen door, left Gene sitting on the couch and went out to find two of my sisters, gay and laughing at having decided to beard the lion in his den. We giggled and talked a moment or so in the kitchen—the girls wouldn't take off their coats, and said they couldn't stay; but I felt that this *was* the time, if ever, for them to meet Gene. . . .

The door to the dining room was open, and there was no way for him to escape. I knew he was still where I left him. I went past the stairway to the lower nursery, my sisters following me.

"Gene——!"

But he was not there. The room was empty. The windows had not been opened; they stuck, due to the damp weather; it required not only effort but a hammer to get them open.

"Oh——" I said lamely, "I thought he was in here."

My sister Barbara gave a sarcastic look at the door of the

closet in which, years ago, we had kept our toys, books and dolls.

Barbara by now had given up the idea of being a lawyer, but her attitude then (she was two years younger than I) was at times that of a wary detective ferreting out clews. She had started wearing an enormous pompadour at the age of fifteen, with her hair tied in a ribbon at the back, and for some unknown reason refused to change this way of doing her hair; now she pushed her pompadour up, shrugged her shoulders under the heavy blue knitted sweater, and pointed silently to the tightly closed door. We all knew how the various doors worked in the old house; and that door could not be shut tight from the outside. The truth was that Barbara, as a painfully shy child, had always run into the closet and pulled the door behind her when we had a visitor.

My youngest sister Margery (who was, some six or seven years later, to do much of Gene's secretarial work and typing at Brook Farm in Connecticut, and in Bermuda) tried desperately not to laugh. I could see the bright color rushing into her cheeks. Margery at that time looked very much like the portraits of Lady Hamilton, while Barbara, with her pompadour and lordly profile, was supposed to look somewhat like George the Third of England. (I might add that the family joke was that I looked like Great-uncle John Boulton, whose portrait, with one hand inserted in his frock coat, and wearing a huge white stock, hung in a large gold frame on the wall.)

There was a pause—no sound anywhere. Barbara could not avoid making some slightly sarcastic remark about how badly she felt at not meeting her new brother-in-law; but I got them out of the room, and all giggling and laughing together, walked with them to the back gate. They knew, of course, how Gene had hidden in the closet when my cousin Elizabeth came in unexpectedly with a friend one day earlier in the winter, and I think they were rather delighted that he had done the same thing again that day. . . .

When I went back Gene had his coat on and his cane in his hand, all ready to go out. He only said he didn't know who it was, and thought it might be someone he didn't want to see. . . .

26

Not long afterward we had another visitor—a charming woman who had written a letter to Gene. I rather nervously served afternoon tea in front of the fireplace, for she was the sister of an English essayist and philosopher whom Gene and I had long admired.

I need not have been nervous, for she turned out to be a wonderful woman—a really free spirit. We laughed and talked and drank tea. She talked to Gene about his plays, which she had read and seen produced at the Provincetown Players; and she talked also to me, very interestingly about herself and her idea of life. Gene was charmed and moved by her eloquence; but as she left she made a remark which, although we tried not to show it, was a dreadful bombshell to both of us.

"Mr. John D. Williams has your new long play, hasn't he?" She had not been over very long from England; she did not know anything of the situation in regard to *Beyond the Horizon*, for she added: "I hear he did such a fine production of *Redemption* with the Barrymore brothers! He started rehearsing the two of them last week in a new play, *The Jest*. I am sure he'll do a wonderful job with *your* play when the time comes!"

27

We made a trip to New York after that—I remember that we were there when Hutch Collins died, and how much it affected Gene. Hutch had been (as were so many newspapermen in those days) a steady consumer of alcohol, and although he never appeared intoxicated to us, or at the Provincetown

Players, where he played various roles so effectively, he was persuaded (or it may have been some latent feeling within himself) to give up alcohol entirely. We saw him a couple of times, and he and Gene went for a walk through the village and stopped at the Hell Hole, but Gene told me that Hutch wouldn't even take a glass of beer.

It rained, and Hutch was wet and chilled when he left Gene and went home. Gene never saw him again. Within a few days he was dead. Gene was bitter about Hutch's death, and particularly when we were told that it was the lack of alcohol after so many years of being used to it that weakened his resistance and perhaps caused his death. He died of pneumonia.

I thought of that cold night in the village when Hutch had invited Gene and myself to his friend's apartment; and how Scotty had found Gene there; and how understanding Hutch Collins had been, and I, too, felt a great loss in the death of this young man whom I had never known very well. . . .

Once again, trying to escape that fear of death which seems always to have haunted him, Gene wore the vine leaves in his hair. . . .

We were about to return to New Jersey; but once again Gene felt it was impossible to leave, to take a train, to depart anywhere but into that oblivion where he could be free of fear. . . .

Edward Fisk, the young painter who later married my sister Cecil, had arrived in town the day before. He had enlisted in the Navy as a first-class seaman during the war. Fisk and Gene had been very close friends during the summer of 1917, and he and Gene and I sat in Polly Holliday's restaurant, talking of war and love and death—Gene doing most of the talking, and he and Eddie imbibing from a flask which the young painter had brought along. There was no longer any thought of taking the train for the country that night; and Polly suggested that we take our bags and go up to her apartment upstairs over the restaurant. She had an extra couch or so, and we could take the train in the morning. Eddie came with us, for he and Gene were still talking, and brought along more liquor to celebrate his return.

Polly gave us the key to her place. I sat on a sofa, and, rather tired by now, took a cushion from another couch to put under my head. Behind the cushion, to my astonishment, was a large pile of five- and ten-dollar bills. . . .

Polly had money hidden everywhere; under bowls; in books scattered about the room. Once or twice during the evening she came up with pocketfuls of dollars, which she put in new hiding places—saying they were safer there than in the restaurant below.

I went to sleep toward morning, still hearing the low voices of Gene and Eddie as they talked on and on.

It must have been an hour later when Gene woke me. He sat on the edge of the couch and I saw his face, fixed in an expression of anger as he looked at a large vase of dying gladioli on a low table before him.

"*I can't stand that lousy odor!*"

Eddie had gone to sleep, and Gene was speaking either to himself or to me.

Disgusted with the odor of the dying flowers, Gene suddenly sprang up and tore them from the bowl, with the intention of flinging them from the open window into the street below. But Polly (in a hurry to get back downstairs, and knowing of no safer place), had used this spot to conceal a lot more one-dollar bills. He stared at the wet bills, thrust for security among the stems of the flowers, and, fascinated by some secret symbolism disclosed only to him by all this, his eyes sought a mirror as if desiring to find a companion who could understand him—for he was paying no attention to me. But, earlier in the evening, on one of her trips up from the restaurant, Polly had removed the mirror from the wall when she found Eddie standing before it, weeping.

Poor Eddie, now sleeping—his navy-blue sailor's uniform was still fresh, but his face was very tired, pressed in sleep against one of Polly's knitted pillows.

Gene looked at him, but it was no use.

Then—how can I describe that look of ironic humor?—he went to the window as he had first intended to do: not now, however, to drop the white gladioli, still flowering bravely from the top of their pale stems, all at once to the street below. He dropped them one by one instead; and then, returning to the bowl, he lifted out the mass of dollar bills, and with the smile of a boyish and delighted Olympian, dropped them also one by one to the pavement, where belated whores and all-night beggars of the underworld (for it was only just dawn) had already stopped to look upward at the gladiolis coming from God.

Gene came back from the window, his eyes seeking first the sleeping Eddie and then returning to me.

"They looked at last for a moment at the sky!" he said with triumph in his voice.

28

I suppose that we took the train back that day. . . .

Gene really wanted to get back. He was bored and restless, particularly as after going to William's office on our first day in New York he had been unable to find out anything regarding the production of *Beyond*. He also decided that he needed an agent; and I believe it was about this time that the American Play Company took over the handling of his plays.

I, too, was restless, and frequently feeling tired. When he asked Scotty to return with us for a few days, I did not have the energy to object; particularly as it was understood that there would be no drinking after the pint Gene took along was gone. Scotty agreed, but I think he blamed this restriction on me rather than on Gene's desire to get back to work and complete *The Straw* before summer arrived. Scotty had heard of the death of Brooklyn Boy and worked out some sort of intricate malevolent mystery plot, in which he dared not involve me as part of the villian force, although it was evident to me that he hoped Gene would not forget how antagonistic

I had been that night in the Hell Hole to the very thought of Gene adopting the dog. If this came across to Gene, it only amused him, for Scotty did not know how attached I myself had been to poor Brooklyn Boy. Probably to Scotty, the white male dog (now dead and vanquished) represented masculinity —and Trixie (small, brown and a lady dog) represented the unwanted and inferior feminine species. Whatever it was, he was quite contemptuous of poor little Trixie, and indirectly managed to have Gene join him in the attitude that Trixie was no suitable companion and a nuisance; as I have said, she was attached to Gene, who by this time was quite used to her.

Whatever was in Scotty's mind, the results worked out satisfactorily to him. On Sunday we all took a walk. We started off on our old sand path through the pines, Trixie running here and there, having a good time. Scotty didn't much like the pines or the sand and the leafless huckleberry bushes, so we came home along the highway which ran a block or so away from the house. There were not many cars in those days, and the three of us were walking in the middle of the highway, Gene and Scotty talking, and I, tired and bored, wanting to get home. Trixie was on a steep incline above the road, racing around. We heard a truck come up behind us, and moved out of the way. Trixie would have stayed where she was, but Scotty, with pretended concern, called her, and she came —rushing down the incline to join us on the other side of the road—just in time to be run over and be killed by the truck.

29

Soon after this, my grandmother Williams came to see us, and this time Gene was not able to hide in a closet. When we left the Old House late that spring there was a friendly relationship between Gene and the rest of my family, a mutual liking which continued during our marriage. But my father and mother put off visiting us until later. Grannie (as she insisted we call her) was, however, of a different opinion.

Grannie was an extraordinary woman, tall, vigorous and handsome at seventy. She had a strong and yet simple mind, and her contact with various brilliant people during her life had in no way changed her liking for the novels of Ethel M. Dell or Marie Corelli, nor did it ever occur to her that, for example, the Russells, whom she knew quite well, or at the other extreme Mr. Sinnet of the Theosophical society, would question her liking of these sentimental writers to whom she often referred. She was the daughter of a librarian at Oxford, and, strange as it seems now, this, and the fact that as a young woman she gave piano lessons, was, in the caste system then prevailing in England, the first obstacle to her marriage with my grandfather—whose family probably felt he should marry someone with a name and money. The second obstacle was that Robert Williams held a fellowship (he was among other things a distinguished Greek scholar) at Oxford, which he would lose if he married. Grannie waited, meanwhile meeting (more or less briefly), many of his friends, including Swinburne, the Rossettis, and Lady Wilde, mother of Oscar.

My grandfather died and all that remains now are a few photographs and a yellowed clipping from an English weekly, the *Freelance*, dated 1902; "*Gone also is 'Bob Williams' that mad scholar, once of Christ Church Oxford, then fellow of Merton, who coached Lord Rosebery for the Oxford schools.*"

Grannie had not been happy in London during the World War. Her youngest beloved daughter, Margery Bianco, was in Italy with her two children, one of whom in the years after the war was to become a famous child prodigy, Pamela Bianco, whose pictures hung in the Tate gallery in London, and was spoken of by Gabriele d'Annunzio as the "child with a name like a flower." For some reason, Grannie could not join them and she made up her mind to come to the United States. But there were no passenger boats allowed on the high seas, and for a long time she was not able to leave England. It was characteristic of her that she went to a distant cousin with whom she had not previously bothered (probably thinking him rather uninteresting) and insisted that he get her a passage somehow. This kindly man, Sir William Bull, by then having become Privy Councilor to the King, was able to arrange passage for her on a transport. If he hadn't, I'm sure she would have kept after him until he did.

So, having learned from my mother that Gene and I were living at the Old House, she immediately arranged a visit. Hearing that Gene worked all day and walked most of the afternoon, and accepting the habits and idiosyncrasies of artists and writers (though a most conservative person herself), she sent word that she would be up on a Saturday evening "after tea": spend the evening with us, and leave at ten.

Gene couldn't get out of it. He was very gloomy, brushed his hair, trimmed his mustache, and put on a coat, not knowing what to expect; for I was not able to describe Grannie to him, any more that I was able at that time to give him much idea of the rest of my family—one reason being that he wasn't really interested. He did know that she was over seventy, and seemed astonished when I told him she was going to walk up to the Old House, a distance of over two miles.

After supper the wind began to blow from the south. It was dark by then, and Gene went out on the porch to look at the sky.

"It's raining—and it's going to get worse," he said. "She won't be up—thank God!" And he took off his coat and picked up a copy of Aeschylus which my father had left in the studio, and began reading.

I smiled to myself as I took the supper dishes out to the kitchen. He didn't know Grannie! At a quarter to seven there was a firm knock. Gene hastily slipped into his coat and I opened the front door.

"So, this is Eugene—an Irish face definitely—*black* Irish!" said Grannie. She removed a knitted muffler and handed it to Gene, after shaking hands with him.

Gene laughed and helped her out of her long ulster; then she held onto me while she kicked off her galoshes. Her face was wet with rain. She was still handsome in spite of her seventy years and gray hair. Her skin, colored slightly from the wind, showed no wrinkles, only a certain looseness in her cheeks—she did not seem old at all.

"Well, my dears, I see you have a nice fire! I hope you are burning up all the old dead trees around the place and not paying for wood!"

Gene laughed—already I could see that he liked her. He had been doing just what Grannie said—sawing up old branches and dead pine in the late afternoons. He offered her a cigarette.

"Just one! I don't approve of this constant smoking! Your *mother*, my dear," she said, turning to me, "used to roll her own—do you remember? Duke's Mixture, I believe it was called—it came in little white bags. *I* never allowed my daughters to smoke, but after she married your father she smoked like a chimney!"

Grannie allowed Gene to light her cigarette, but this did not interrupt her conversation:

"I came over from England, if you remember, when you children were small. Your father had spent every penny coming to him—he was working on a portrait that someone had ordered, trying to bring in something more, having spent everything on those elaborate chicken houses when he decided to go into the chicken business. Your dear mother would run out of Duke's Mixture and be very cranky without her smoke, and you children would cross the road and hunt through the woods and under bushes for empty pint whisky bottles that drunkards had flung there. . . ."

Gene grinned—he was enjoying this.

"What did the whisky bottles have to do with cigarettes?"

"Ah!" Grannie smiled too—she was feeling very much at home. "After they found *five* empty whisky bottles they would take them to old Fet, who ran the hotel, and get a penny apiece for them and buy a bag of Duke's Mixture for their mother. No —I don't approve of smoking becoming a vice!"

But she had one cigarette after she got into bed—then, she

added, she always took a stiff glass of brandy and hot water before going to sleep.

Granny talked about the war; the United States of America; President Wilson: impending Prohibition; loose morals; skirts getting shorter—and so on. Gene was delighted. His plays and the theater were never mentioned; though once they got briefly on the subject of poetry, and she told how her husband had once taken her over to meet Algernon Charles Swinburne in a restaurant—a horrid little man with messy hair, greedily eating a huge dish of boiled cabbage and pork shins!—and *that*, she told Gene, finished her with poetry!

It was still raining and I wondered if Gene would walk back with her. They were now on the subject of life after death, and the astral plane—how that came about I don't know—and Grannie, her eyes alight, was telling Gene how much she was looking forward to going there when there was a knock at the door and Grannie rose. She had ordered a jitney to come for her exactly at ten o'clock.

30

Spring came, and I was by turns depressed and happy. I sometimes walked alone along the old boardwalk on the ocean, feeling the east wind or the fog on my face, remembering the times I had walked there as a girl. I tried not to think of what I should do or what I should not do. Gene, deeply absorbed in *The Straw*, talked to me only about that, or read scenes aloud, nor did I want to disturb him about anything. I typed his letters for him, and forgot my own work and my desire to make some extra money, and moved about the house silently, in a sort of hushed and expectant and yet reluctant daze.

For quite a while I had thought certain physical symptoms were the result of a chill from the wet weather or tiring myself with the stoves, or being a little rundown physically—or even from my worry over Gene's work and *Beyond the Horizon. . .*

Both of us felt that having so firmly thought out the pattern that was to be our "aloneness" it should never be disturbed. Even then, it was not disturbed (from his point of view) by my family; and if I was beginning to feel that it might eventually be disturbed by the various tentacles reaching out more and more to wrap themselves about him—tentacles of the theater, and the mishaps of production before his work could be seen, or judged—it had never occurred to me that he and I would have a child. Now I began to think that it might be possible.

I knew at last that I could no longer procrastinate. I walked down to the village and went to the office of the kindly old physician who had taken care of us when we were children. He said there was no doubt about it, I was pregnant. He did some thoughtful figuring and told me we could expect the baby about the first of October.

"Now"—he patted me on the shoulder—"you can go home and tell your husband the good news!"

Perhaps because I was confused and inaccurate when he asked me for information, Dr. Carrigan's calculations were wrong—little Shane was not to arrive until next to the last day of October; or perhaps, because he saw trepidation and unsureness in my face, he added a month so there could be no question of anything but acceptance on my husband's part. For I had talked with him when I first went in: I told him my troubles; my husband was working hard on a play: we were not too secure financially, as the production of another play had been long delayed. We had, I added (the thought coming to me suddenly), no place to have a baby. . . .

"What's the matter with the Old House?" he said sternly. "I brought two of your sisters into the world there!" And I realized then that there was no use trying to explain anything to him.

But where *would* we have the baby? Gene wanted to go back to Provincetown not later than June. He had already written John Francis to keep his eye open for a small cottage or a summer shack out on the Truro hills—where, I thought to myself sarcastically, I suppose we will live like two sea gulls—and at the end of summer have another little sea gull!

I did some shopping that afternoon, stopped at the post office, found a letter there for Gene and walked home, feeling alone and alien from everything in the world. It was a damp and chilly day, and Gene had made a fire in the fireplace. He was sitting there waiting for me—and for the afternoon mail. I gave him the letter and went into the kitchen to make some tea. Walking home I may have felt myself alone; but now I was saturated, like a sponge, with a quiet and almost welcome melancholy. My eyes swam with tears, and as I put two cups and a teapot on a tray I did nothing to wipe them away.

"Aggie—*here's a darn nice letter!*"

Gene called to me from the other room. When I did not answer he came in, holding the letter, and saw my tears.

"What's the matter, Aggie?" he said tenderly. "That damn walk downtown is too much for you. God damn it, after this take a jitney home! Listen—here's some good news even if it doesn't mean money!" He picked up the tray and carried it into the next room.

The letter was from a well-known critic, Barrett Clark, the man who later became Gene's first biographer. The handwriting was distinguished and scholarly; it was sent from Briarcliff Manor, New York. Gene looked at it again.

" '*Dear Sir!*' I'm becoming important in this cockeyed world!"

The writer informed Gene that he had been following his literary career for some time, and waiting for an occasion to do his part. He was looking forward to the publication of the new volume of Gene's plays, and wanted to write a special story for the book section of the *Sunday Sun*. He asked Gene if he would be good enough to give him some data relating to himself. Gene read it aloud as we sat before the fire drinking our tea.

He was very pleased, but I could see that he had something else on his mind—he kept looking at me and smiling.

"Now—more good news! I wrote those well-known words *The Curtain Falls* while you were downtown, darling! Surprised? I wanted you—needed you *here*—to hear my triumphant yell as I finished *The Straw!*"

I could not tell him then what I had learned from the doctor that afternoon. He sat down at the table and on a sheet of yellow paper, slowly and with much thought, began to put down dates and places and events concerning his past life. He had read Barrett Clark's *European Theories* and felt that this was critical opinion at its best.

But that night, lying awake, I decided, now *The Straw* was finished, that I would tell him the next day.

31

I was surprised to find that without knowing it (and certainly without our discussing it) I had somehow conveyed to Gene that there was a chance of my being pregnant, for when I began —by telling him that I'd been to the doctor the day before—he seemed to know why I had gone, and said at once, anxiously; "Well, what did he say?"

I told him. His first reaction was that the doctor had made a mistake; his second reaction was silence. I could not tell what he was thinking about. I was miserable, imagining what he *might* be thinking about. He was withdrawn, deep in himself, not hostile, not even perturbed, so far as I could see. But there was no contact between us and I was miserable because I could not follow him, could not understand . . .

Then one of those utterly silly and absurd things happened that make one wonder if the comic gods do not top the downcast gods of tragedy. Later, we were in the lower nursery, which was sunny and warm that spring day. Little Happy began making noises and wailing meows in the next room. Gene, who was standing at the window looking out, did not even hear her. I (brooding on the couch) saw Happy come to the door. There was a beseeching look in her frightened eyes.

We had been expecting her kittens any day. I had laid an old shirt of Gene's in a basket in the dining room closet for her.

I picked her up, took her in and put her down in the basket for the big event—her first kittens. She purred. I stroked her, and left her there.

But a moment later she returned—she was not going to be left alone. This time she went straight to Gene, looked up at him, and again gave that beseeching meow. Gene turned, looked at her and began to swear. I could not help it, I began to giggle hysterically.

"She wants you to hold her paw while she has her kittens!"

It was true. Happy simply refused to stay in her basket and have her kittens unless either Gene or I were beside her. So we took turns sitting on a stool by the basket until the first one was born. Gene insisted that she preferred *him*, and became very interested in what was happening. After the first kitten (a black one) was born, Happy purring loudly and Gene singing a sea chantey which he said helped her labor pains, we left her, thinking now she would take care of herself.

No! Happy, after cleaning the first kitten (purring gratefully meanwhile) came out and again demanded that Gene be with her for her second—definitely *Gene* this time, not me! Perhaps she liked the sea chanteys. The first kitten was born to the tune of "Whiskey Johnny," and the second, Gene decided should have "Blow the Man Down."

A little later I was in the kitchen, doing something or other, and I heard Gene go again into the closet, and then the refrain:

> *"I put my hand upon her knee,*
> *Said she, young man you're mighty free . . .*
> *I put my hand upon her thigh,*
> *Said she, young man you're drawing nigh.*
> *No more I'll go a roving,*
> *With you, fair maid!"*

"There!" he said, coming to the kitchen door. "I've named them already—'Whiskey,' 'Blow' and 'Drumstick,' "—and he came over and laughingly put his hand on my thigh, to illustrate what he meant, and then gave me a long and devoted kiss.

32

One day in May a package arrived at the house from Gene's publisher, Boni and Liveright, containing six beautifully printed and bound copies of *The Moon of the Caribbees and Six Other Plays of the Sea*. Gene wrote an inscription inside one of them and gave it to me. It was a quotation from *Ile*, one of his sea plays. . . .

"To *my* wife——

"No man ever had a better Annie (only in this case it ought to be Aggie). Gene, *her* husband."

We were planning to leave the Old House before long, and Gene was writing letters and already making appointments in town for the middle or end of May: with George Jean Nathan, whom he had not yet met; with George Tyler, the theatrical producer who was an old friend of his father's; and with (he hoped!) John D. Williams. Gene and I had already sat down and composed a letter to his parents telling them the good news.

There was a lot to do that last week: books, scripts, the typewriter, some of our clothes and all our personal belongings were packed and sent by express to Provincetown. Gene was wonderful at packing in those early days—I had almost forgotten that! He was careful, slow and neat about it—much better than I was. He seemed to enjoy it now that there was no more work to be done on the plays and gave it the same concentrated attention that he gave his other work.

John Francis, to whom we were sending these things to hold for us, wrote us that he had two houses in view for the summer rental—but in his quaint, kindly way he added that he didn't see why Gene didn't buy the old coast-guard station at

Peaked Hill Bar for his home. "It is for sale now, very cheap . . ."

Gene meditated over the price—which was far more than we had. He even wrote asking if it would be possible to make a small down payment and the balance later—or could we possibly rent it for the summer?

John Francis replied that it could not be rented, only sold. It had to be all cash, as the price was more than fair.

So Gene and I decided that the little house in the rolling hills of North Truro, not too far from the outside shore, would be the one we would take when we arrived in Provincetown. Beyond that, we made no other plans for the future.

Gene left for New York a day or so ahead of me and took a room for us at the small hotel where we had stayed in the fall. His parents, and Jamie too, had already gone to New London for the summer, after sending us a wonderful telegram saying how happy they were that there was to be a grandchild—their first. I packed my small suitcase, saw the doctor again, gave the keys of the Old House to my mother, and said good-by to all my family. I felt sad at leaving them. It was understood that they would go back to the Old House, and I left "Whiskey," "Blow" and "Drumstick" (whom Gene at first had suggested shipping to Provincetown!) to their kindly care.

I stood at the kitchen window and, while I waited for the jitney to take me to the station, I saw my "little clowns" still lined up there, waiting, and for a moment I was sad, thinking of our walks along the old sand roads—roads made a hundred years before by the early settlers and now forgotten—somehow knowing that Gene and I would never take those walks again.

33

I do not remember much of our time in New York that spring —except Gene dressing himself very carefully one afternoon for his meeting with George Jean Nathan. He had not taken a drink since coming to New York, and he stayed away so long that afternoon that I began wondering what had happened. But he returned at last, very pleased and still without having had anything stronger than ginger ale. This had amused Mr. Nathan, but Gene said that he had understood. Gene told me in detail about his visit; about Mr. Nathan and their conversation, and that he had been both delighted and impressed. I had the impression that his meeting with Mr. Nathan had been so stimulating that it left him without any desire for a drink.

The trip to Provincetown must have been uneventful, for I remember nothing about it. Gene was probably tired; he had taken care of several things in New York; and, alas, he had still found out nothing definite from Williams. *The Jest*, with the two Barrymores, was a great success—it would close for the summer and open again in the fall, and there seemed no prospect of their being free to play *Beyond the Horizon* for a long time.

But when at last, after that long trip by the Fall River Line and then on the slow train down the Cape, we arrived and talked with John Francis, who was waiting at the station for us, we were the happiest people in the world.

Peaked Hill Bar was ours—it was incredible, but it was ours— our own house, our home! John Francis had received a check for the entire amount from James O'Neill, and the deed was to be made out in the name of his son, Eugene Gladstone O'Neill. . . .

A Red Cape and Some Holy Images

I

Peaked Hill . . . how many memories come back, the sand, the dunes, the great pink-flowered rosebush that spread over a dune near the house—a seedling or plant that had drifted in from a Japanese ship wrecked off the shore, and, blown to the dune, had established itself there. . . .

A tax sale, put through and printed in a local paper to define the boundaries and protect our rights to the property, which read: *'Bounded on the East by land unknown . . . on the South by land unknown . . . on the West by lands unknown . . . bounded on the North by the Atlantic ocean. . . .*

. . . The time a whale drifted in to our front yard and lay there decomposing for weeks and Gene and I hoped each day for a strong breeze from the South, to blow away that morbid odor. . . . The morning we got up to find a barge cut loose from its tug and wrecked on the beach. . . . I remember, too, the sunny morning a coast guard brought us a wire saying Gene had won his first Pulitzer prize and how he and I looked at each other, wondering what on earth the Pulitzer prize was.

And the strange story of a cat, whom Gene threw down the outside toilet, and the events that led up to it . . . and the morning I will never forget—more because of the chaotic week that followed—when, going down to the beach to swim after Gene's work was finished, we saw something shining in the sun, reluctantly being rolled in by the waves. On inspection it turned out to be a five-gallon kerosene tin, new and evidently heavy. On closer inspection it showed many pinholes, from which, when the waves retreated, tiny streams of what what looked like water came out, but which turned out to be 100 per cent pure alcohol—dropped into the sea, we found out later, by a rumrunner who was pursued off the shore by a government boat that night. Gene hesitated; we looked at the bright tin slowly loosing its contents and at each other . . . then he grinned and went up to the house, coming back in a moment with two pails, a wrench, some bottles and a funnel. He was always very thorough about everything! He had unscrewed the top and was pouring out the liquid when there was another shining glint in the waves a few feet away and another kerosene tin began rolling in. Altogether we emptied some dozen or more tins, and by two o'clock the house reeked of alcohol even with the windows open; pails, pots, a big dishpan and two washtubs were full. The rest of it Gene put in the bathtub, after being sure the spigot wouldn't leak. He walked across the dunes to get help and spread the news to his friends while I waited, wondering what was going to happen.

Gene was happy at Peaked Hill, writing, living life as he wanted it, and always rather sad when it got too cold to stay any longer and we would return to Provincetown with our things in the big farm wagon pulled by two horses. We both loved the place, but after we separated I was told that he made out a deed giving it to his son Eugene. Soon after this I received a letter in the mail; and on opening it found a picture of the house cut from the rotogravure section of the New York *Sunday Times*, just as I remembered it but now drifting off to sea. It had torn itself, in a big storm that came along, from the dune where it had spent so many years; and now is, no doubt, lying among the many wrecks that have gone down in the dangerous currents off of Peaked Hill Bar.

2

We went out across the dunes in a farm wagon loaded with rope, shovels, picks and food for the day, taking three Portuguese fellows with us. I sat on the wagon in the long red cape that Gene had bought me in town, while he and one man started digging the sand away from the door and two others started at the south windows. The wind blew Gene's hair about and every once in a while he would turn to me and grin with happiness. There was a sort of pagan air about him as he threw the shovelfuls of sand into the wind, digging out his future home. It was exciting and primitive So a cave man might have excavated a home for himself thousands of years ago, while his wife and unborn child waited wrapped in animal skins,—so he told me laughinglly.

During the following week Gene went out every day, sometimes with a helper, or one of his friends, and kept digging the sand away from the house. The shovels and picks had been left in one of the outbuildings on that first trip, so he walked out and back, sometimes discouraged, but enjoying it all. At last he said that we could move in—the gasoline pump that Mabel Dodge had installed was started; there was water in the house; and the plumbing was in shape. We began getting ready. . . .

3

It had been a great relief to the elder O'Neills when Gene and I were married and he had now more or less settled down. When they heard that I was to have a baby and that even the strange Eugene seemed to be looking forward to it, James O'Neill began to think of what he could do for his son. Somehow, up in their pleasant, homelike suite in the Prince George Hotel, an idea came to them that was to give Gene some of the happiest and most productive days of his life. Mr. O'Neill paced the floor of their living room, turning over various practical plans in his mind, thinking of the little grandson to be born in the fall. . . .

Mrs. O'Neill, as she told me later, was also thinking of the coming baby, except that it was a little granddaughter that *she* thought of. Already she was planning a layette in pink for a girl child and thinking of the expensive long baby dresses, sacques, caps, capes and bootees which she would manage to charge (in spite of her husband) at Lord and Taylor. What connection there was between this and the perfect idea of a gift to Gene that suddenly came to her I never knew, but she said to her husband that she knew what would make her son happier than anything else—that place which was for sale now out on the beach at Provincetown, and though he may have been surprised and grumbled a little, her husband finally consented. So it was that we received a deed to the old station and the land surrounding it. Gene had often spoken longingly to them of the place; but he had never imagined that one day he would own it and be living there

It was not long before, one morning, we left the town behind us to live at Peaked Hill. The two strong horses, plodding through the sand; the heavy wagon creaking under the load; I seated on the wagon beside the driver and Gene walking. It was a bright, windy day and although we had been warned that it was too early in the spring to move to the "outside," there was no chill in the air, and we were both of us happy and excited. Gene had carefully packed all his manuscripts in a suitcase, which he had placed on the wagon where he could keep his eye on it. We had our books with us also, carefully wrapped in newspapers; photographs; files; letters. . . . These things Gene had packed himself. His clothes too he had packed, wrapping some of our small treasures in tissure paper and using them to fill the space between sweaters, T shirts, old slacks, and his two suits, worn but still good. Two blankets we owned; two we had borrowed.

The horses stopped now and again for a rest and Gene would look up at me with deep affection in his eyes. I was going to have the baby in October, but no one would have known it and I felt wonderfully well and strong. We both looked forward to the long summer together, lying in the sun, swimming, watching the sea and the ships that went along the horizon, taking long companionable walks. He had his working hours planned, writing on his play, and reading, his exercise and rest, and once a week or so we would walk back across the dunes to Provincetown and see the people we knew and hear the latest news. It was a relief to Gene that we would be quite alone, and neither of us thought that I would need any help around the house.

We had three or four big boxes on the wagon full of food and supplies put up by John Francis, whose gentle soul was greatly delighted by new adventure. I had gone over the list three or four times to be sure that nothing was forgotten. At last we were there, and Gene unlocked the door and then helped me down from the wagon. Our driver thought it was all a big joke; and, looking at me, he kept shaking his head. I really believe that he thought Gene was quite mad. He began untying the ropes that held our belongings together, and meanwhile Gene and I pushed open the door.

It was an incredibly happy moment when we stepped inside and looked around. Instead of the former light into which I had peered before (a light which gave the effect of the whole interior being submerged in an opalescent quietness at the bottom of the sea, with objects appearing unreal, or as if swimming in nothingness or shadow), there was brightness and sharpness and beauty. One of the friendly coast guards had come over early that morning and opened all the windows, letting in the sun and air. He had started the engine for the pump and even brought a bouquet of flowers which we found upstairs afterward—evidently he thought it more appropriate to put them in the bedroom.

We stood for a moment in a long, white empty room. Two big doors made one end of the room; they were open onto the dunes, letting in the sunlight to lie in a large patch on the blue floor. Through those doors, Gene told me, they used to take out a lifeboat on rollers when there was distress at sea. At the other end of the room, near where we entered, was the kitchen, a large room with casement windows opening on the sea. Neither of us could quite believe it—what Mabel Dodge had done or how she had done it. Copper pots and skillets hung against the wall, which was a soft white like all the other rooms in the house; the floor was a deep blue linoleum, highly polished. There was a dinner service of old, heavy willow ware in soft blues and white; bowls; platters; a tureen—everything. Rows of glasses of different sizes, translucent and all the color of the sea; a copper teakettle; Italian trays and Mexican silver; everything beautiful and unusual and useful. A long table made of wood from the beach with its top rubbed to a velvety luster stood next to a modern white sink. The casement windows, through which the sound of the waves came in, as if they were just beneath us, were curtained with yellow linen, which blew and shifted in the breeze.

The other end of the kitchen (separated by a small partition) contained a kitchen range; a huge white icebox; low lockers with cushioned tops which lifted up, revealing space for storage; and *closets*—closets for everything needed to run a house, several of them fully equipped with tools and gadgets needed for that purpose, in fact, everything anyone could want; for Mrs. Dodge, besides her many other talents, was evidently a most practical and efficient person. She believed in beauty and order and non-cluttered living. Everything to keep the house in order was "*of the best*" and probably the most expensive.

Gene watched with delight my dumfounded pleasure, ecstatic silly smiles, murmurings and little cries at all this, for his pleasure was as great as mine: but *he* had known about it all week and kept it as a surprise for me—even letting me bring an old iron frying pan and a couple of battered pots along when I insisted I must have something to cook in. I had thought him rather mean, in fact, not to let me buy a few things to cook

with, and was secretly provoked at his insistence that we'd
manage all right with cooking frankfurters and other things
on sticks, and baking potatoes in the ashes of a driftwood fire,—
though I'd forgotten all about it when we started out in our
farm wagon.

Tony Sousa, the driver, was bringing in the boxes of groceries, and we showed him where to put them; then Gene said,
"*Now!*" and, taking my arm, opened the middle door from the
kitchen.

We stood on the threshold of a large, wide, long room—*our*
living room. At the far end was a fireplace with casement
windows on either side and great wood boxes, used as seats,
below. The ceiling was painted white, and held together by
strong wire cables; in fact the entire room was white, except
the floor, which was blue. But white and blue does not describe
it, or perhaps gives a wrong impression, for Mrs. Dodge had
something more than whiteness there, or blueness. She had
achieved a depth, a patina, a quality that was perfect. She
had put seven coats of white paint (with time between for complete drying) on the walls and ceilings and when it was finished
it was something more than paint—it glowed, it soothed, it was
just right. The blue of the floors—she had the walls and the
floors the same all through the house—was a *different* blue, not
dark at all, not too light. I have tried to get that same blue in
other places and never succeeded.

Along each wall was a heavy white wooden table on which
stood tall Italian pottery lamps with yellow shades. And against
each wall was an enormous couch, covered in blue linen and
piled with comfortable cushions in blue and yellow linen.
Above the tables and couches hung great round pottery fish-
plates, each with a different and fascinating design of strange
fish. There were heavy straw rugs on the floor, a cushioned
chaise longue of woven reed, other chairs of soft reed and—two
great comfortable Morris chairs, painted with the seven coats
of white and with blue cushions, arranged for reading at the
end of each table under the tall lamps.

Again I was speechless, and wandered around, went from one thing to another, touching things, looking at things, sitting for a moment here, and getting up and sitting there, just to see how it felt, trying to get used to it, Gene opening the wood boxes to see what was inside, lifting up the big blue blotters on the tables to see if anything was left beneath them, pulling the lamp nearer to the Morris chair and turning the wick. . . .

"*Kerosene!*"

Yes, we had forgotten to bring kerosene—no lamplight, no cooking without it, for the kitchen range had been equipped with a kerosene burner inside the firebox. We had plenty of gasoline for the pump stored in one of the big outhouses; but now we had to send the driver to the coast-guard station to borrow five gallons of kerosene. But it was early and we didn't care, though Gene did say, with a frown, that now the driver would have to make another trip out this week. . . . He lit a driftwood fire outside, and we made coffee and ate sandwiches for lunch, for we were hungry by now; and I found myself a little tired because while the driver was getting the kerosene Gene and I unpacked, carried in, and arranged the contents of the boxes and bundles that had been piled outside the door. There were blankets and sheets to be taken upstairs, the bed to be made, clothes hung up and shoes unpacked. Gene carried in his books and arranged them on the shelves, took his dumb-bells and what other equipment he had of that sort into another room that we had discovered next to the bathroom (which was downstairs).

He took off his clothes in there and came out barefooted in his bathing trunks. Every once in a while he would go to the window and look out at the sea. Then he would go back to work, helping me put things away in the kitchen, or carefully arranging what he wanted to keep in the table drawers in the big room.

After a while he began to get chilly, for the early June day was not too warm. So he collected wood and kindling, and we had a fire in the big fireplace. I lay on the wide blue couch, comfortable, and watched him.

That night we slept upstairs in a big white-enameled iron bed, which was very cold at first, even the sheets chilly, listening to the sea and the slow rising of the wind, his arm around me and my head pillowed against his chest. I could hear his heart beating, and the sound of his heart and the sound of the sea were confused but peaceful as I drifted off to sleep.

It was there, that first summer at Peaked Hill, that Gene told me of how he first got himself into the writing of plays, trained himself, I was going to say, because in one sense it was that—a training of the senses. He wanted to write plays, that is understood. He may have even written a few of the earlier ones, which didn't amount to much. But he was undisciplined, he told me, not only in working habits, but in writing itself, what form to use and how. Then he began consciously to use a method which he kept up for over a year. He read nothing but plays, great plays, melodrama. . . .

Before long he was thinking in dialogue, talking to himself in dialogue, and answering his own thoughts more or less aloud in his low voice, seeing life in scenes and acts—with the curtain going down, perhaps, as he went off to sleep.

There were always periods of working and not working with Gene, as with every other writer. Long periods of work, of course, depending sometimes on the length of the play. Nothing to stop him, no going to parties, no going out in the evenings or making trips away from the house. When a play was finished he relaxed, sometimes just swimming and lying in the sun, or seeing and talking to people he liked. It was harder in the winter, of course. Sometimes—but now I am remembering Peaked Hill—I think perhaps it was that first summer out there that he finally settled into the general routine that he followed faithfully when he was working as long as I knew him—long walks on country roads taking the place of sun and swimming, if we were where it was cold. . . .

Every evening after dinner Gene sat down in the white

Morris chair and, under the light of the tall Italian lamp, took his book and read until eleven. At midnight he would go to bed, and at Peaked Hill he seldom had trouble sleeping.

After breakfast, which he always ate silently, he was glum. He said some people were and some weren't; and he was one of the ones that were—so not to mind it. He told me that when we were first married. Sometimes I wonder when we did talk, but I know we talked a lot. He talked about his work with me before he wrote it, while he was writing it, and after it was finished.

4

Upstairs there were two long rooms, separated by a stairway, and they too had been given their seven coats of white paint so that they glowed luminously, even in the darkness. We slept in the room that looked out, through two small sand-glazed windows on either side of the chimney, on to the sand dunes behind the house, that first year in a white iron bed with a driftwood table beside it for Gene's cigarettes, the tall kerosene lamp and his book. Above us the beams of the ceilings, tied with iron cables, rose to the peak of the roof; and on windy nights we could lie there and listen to the sand beating with a sharp needlelike sound on the windows, and on the roof above us, and the sound of the sea. Gene had all he wanted there, me in his arms, the sound of the sea, and he would go to sleep at last, with my head on his shoulder.

The other room faced on the sea, so that the windows almost overhung it, above a narrow strip of sea grass which broke sharply into a cliff above where the ocean lay stretched out to the horizon. Here Gene had his driftwood desk, with several large drawers, and a gray weathered top on which he kept his manuscript neatly arranged. There was a captain's chair, a couch covered with dark blue denim, and a horror of a clothes-horse which he insisted on keeping there. Along the walls of this room he hung some old nets with weathered floats, and there were some pieces, too, of driftwood encrusted with barnacles. When the windows were closed the sanded glass shut the room off in a solitary and opaque light.

When he went up there to work, after breakfast, the door at the foot of the stairs was shut—the whole house was quiet and peaceful. At intervals a coast guard would pass on his way along the shore, and sometimes he would come up and leave some mail.

Gene always read the mail eagerly. Sometimes his comments were extremely sarcastic; and although he wished to live with me in solitude, he kept a close and shrewd watch on the progress of his plays. But he never looked at the mail until after he was finished working. At one o'clock there would often be a cry of pleasure or relief, and the playwright would appear, sometimes with the dream still in his eyes, embrace me if he was happy about what he had finished that morning, or go to the larder to make a small sandwich if he was perplexed or troubled.

Whichever it was it didn't last too long, for now was the time for his exercise. In good weather this was a run up the beach, his head thrown back, full of exuberance and joy, then a dive in the sea and a swim, from which he was apt to emerge a little cold and blue, ready to lie in the sun until lunch was ready. If it rained he would go into the back room and vigorously attack the punching bag for half an hour, then take a book and sit reading until we were ready to eat.

After lunch he always lay down and took a nap. Then he got up and went silently back to work alone and preoccupied, going over what he had written in the morning and often typing it out for the first draft. But soon he would be in the west room, punching vigorously at the bag again, wearing only his swimming trunks, and coming out with his brown lean body shining with sweat, ready for another plunge in the sea.

It was that summer that Gene meditated most, and was most alone with and even sometimes absorbed into that reality which for him lay behind outer appearances—and which he was always, perhaps even later, seeking. In the warm peaceful afternoons we would walk along the beach, rousing little flocks of little sandpipers, who scattered as we approached; and sheltered by an old sand dune, Gene would remove his swimming trunks and lie naked in the sun (which warmed his closed eyes) his face turned upward, his eyes closed, at peace at last with the sun, the sea, and the earth. Sometimes he would get up and do a strange jungle dance, and then plunge, laughing, into the sea. This laugh—for it seems to me I saw it more than I heard it— was a half-pagan, half-ecstatic cry of himself to God.

I sat there, not too close, alone, too, with the dunes and the sky! But I think that I sometimes admitted a solitary sandpiper or a gull into my solitude and happiness; or looked wonderingly at strange small tracks in the sand.

5

Gene was beautiful that summer, tall and brown and tender and smiling, working all morning, lying for hours in the sun, absorbing life and courage and hope from the sea. . . . I too, felt strong and well and happy; full of a sort of creative joy and well-being, a physical at-oneness with life and nature, with the sea, the sand, the dunes and the ever-changing sky. The days went by; at night we walked along the edge of the vast friendly sea in the darkness, holding hands, our feet on the damp sand, in a mysterious world to which we both belonged.

Each day was the same and yet divinely different; we ate breakfast on a card table covered with a blue cloth, drinking coffee from the cups with the willow design, the morning sun slanting in across our faces, the gentle sound of the breakers outside. Whenever I fixed poached eggs I waited with silent joy for the moment when Gene would cut off the edge of the toast, and then solemnly put the entire egg and toast into his mouth. I never understood how he was able to do it. We made sandwiches for lunch, and with tea, always about five o'clock and always ready for it, devoured dozens of biscuits imported from England, for we were very hungry. We made strange concoctions, sometimes, for our evening meal, trying to think, as the end of each week came and we ran low on stores, what shipwrecked sailors would manage with. I remember Gene insisting once that we experiment with stewing a horseshoe crab with onions and marjoram; but at this I balked and made curried duck eggs instead, with rice flavored with marjoram, as he seemed to like this herb very much at that time. He decided that it was a prenatal craving on his part and seemed rather disappointed that I didn't crave marjoram too. Sometimes he would cross the dunes alone to town, and always when he left he would ask me if there wasn't something I craved, so he could bring it back to me. I would say no—only *him!* and he would laugh and say that I was easily satisfied; but when he returned, besides what we needed, he would always bring something special—preserved ginger in a little gray jar, or one of Mrs. Avellar's famous blueberry pies.

Once, after a walk to town, he came back and very seriously inquired why I wasn't feeling sick at my stomach every morning. John Francis had told him how, when *his* wife was pregnant, he had morning sickness every day, just like his wife—and I'm almost positive that John Francis told him that when her labor pains began he, too, began getting cramps in his stomach. Gene began to wonder if this wasn't the way all husbands should be if they really loved their wives.

We grew quite fond of the large, prehistoric-looking horseshoe crabs—there were always two or three near the house or on the sand—and of the tiny sandpipers that ran in droves before us as we walked up the beach, rising in their flight and curving back to us again to pick up their food as the waves retreated, and even of the sea gulls that screamed around the top of the house.

One day I was sitting on the sand, watching my husband's dark head as he swam further and further out to sea, going under the water and emerging again, when I saw another dark head swimming beside him. I thought I was seeing double at first; but as Gene began swimming nearer shore again, I saw I'd made no mistake. Then the second dark head disappeared; and a few minutes later Gene came through the surf and up the sand to where I was waiting, breathless and laughing. He told me he had been swimming underwater and when he came to the surface a beautiful sleek young seal was gazing at him with luminous friendly eyes. Not only that, she (we decided, of course, it was a *she*) swam along with him, under the water and on the surface of the sea, finally submerging as he came nearer the shore. For a few days after that his little seal remained off Peaked Hill Bar, waiting until he came out, when she would appear at his side, with the same curious, friendly gaze. Gene said he talked to her, and she seemed to understand; but something must have happened to her, or perhaps her husband came along and reproved her; for soon after that she left; we never saw her again.

6

Once a week, Gene carrying my red cape, we would walk into town in the early morning and return to Peaked Hill in the afternoon, with the big wagon and team of horses laden with food and necessities for the week. We saw our friends in town, stopped at Susan's house, talked with Hutch Hapgood, and if Mary Heaton Vorse was not working, stopped in there. Often we went to the Ballantines', where Stella would make a delicious lunch for us, evading little Ian's furious attacks as she cooked, and managing to talk to me and also listen to Teddy and Gene discussing the theater.

People were wonderful to us that summer. I think everyone realized how happy we were, and responded to it. Mary Vorse spoke later of how Gene had that look of security and sweetness that made him so lovable. As for me, she would look at my expanding red cape when she met me in town, and say that pregnancy was very becoming to me. Mary came out sometimes to see us, for she loved the dunes and the outside shore, and understood them better than anyone. I remember one night she kept us awake telling us the legend of a great white stallion who had once roamed the dunes and, when they tried to capture him, swam out among the breakers and disappeared.

Other people came out to see us, but not often, as it was a long walk; the coast guards were very friendly, brought our mail, and apparently worried about me when a storm came up and lashed the water against our house.

7

My mother offered to come to Provincetown to be with me when the baby was born, and this was a relief to Gene, as he was uncertain as to what to do about such things, and also not sure about how much money he could spend for a nurse. There was nothing coming in now from *In the Zone*, and we were running a little low. By this time, the trip across the dunes and back the same day tired me, and Dr. Heibert, who was taking care of me, insisted I stay in town overnight whenever possible. Dr. Dan Heibert was big and young and kindly—and, strangely enough, though he was now married and practicing in Provincetown, he had been at Harvard when Gene was studying playwriting there with Professor Baker. It seems to me that Gene boarded with his family.

Late in August, I suppose I went in for an examination, for I sent a note out to Gene by the coast guard:

Dearest Gene: There was a telegram from Mother saying they arrive tomorrow via Fall River, so I guess I better stay in tonight and ride out with them—and the wash. I'll try and catch the life-saver, send out bread, and this—and mail. Only this letter from Madden so far. Wish I wasn't going to stay in. . . . I feel so awfully lost. The doctor says I must be in by the tenth. Francis says we can have Happy Home for September. Stella send out what New York Times she has . . .

8

Once again memory blocks out certain things, certain times and events. I know that my mother and Gene got along very well; and that my youngest sister, who came with her, was there for that last week or so at Peaked Hill; but a month that she spent with us a year or so later blocks out that earlier visit, except for a vision I have of her among the dunes, and by the sea, almost a part of sea and dunes herself. One memory I have of my mother, who was a bit of a gourmet herself, is of her eating snails from a large platter, extracting them carefully with a toothpick and urging Gene to join her. Where she got them, I don't know; another is one day when Stella came over with young Ian Ballantine, aged five. I was sitting, or probably reclining, on the couch, when Ian, after eying me curiously for a few moments, made a sudden swift dive at me, saying he was going to give that big football I had inside me a good kick—and my mother, in spite of Stella's look of consternation, took him by both ears and locked him outside the house.

Gene was working out an idea for a play; writing letters to managers; and, I am sure, looking forward with gloomy dread to having to leave Peaked Hill for Provincetown and Happy Home. He told my mother he *couldn't* work there—he was sure of that; and, as she would be with me, he would walk across to Peaked Hill after we moved in, work there all day, and return in the evening. She came up with an idea which I think he may have entertained himself, but didn't like to mention. It was a time of transitions anyhow, she said, so ordinary solutions to a problem shouldn't be considered. The simple solution was that Gene should stay at Peaked Hill and work, and she would stay with me in town. Gene was grateful to her, not only for making this suggestion, but for insisting on it; and I too was pleased, expecting that the baby would arrive before the end of the month, and no longer having to worry about Gene taking that daily trip to get his work done. . . .

We went in by the tenth of September—but not to Happy

Home, for Stella had taken a great liking to my mother, and insisted we stay with her. My sister had to return to New Jersey; but before she left, my mother was already sterilizing torn linen and newspapers in the rather primitive oven at Happy Home, where we were to go later on.

The warm languorous days of Indian summer came—the days of quiet sunlit peace arrived. I walked with my mother, or sat watching her as she picked up shells along the harbor shore. The coast-guard wagon went by about noon, and occasionally they would stop with a message from Gene. He walked across the dunes nearly every day to see how I was, but sometimes he sent a note or a message in this way instead, and I sent what mail there was out to him. One morning, the wagon stopped and Stella came down to the beach with a note. Inside was only a typed sheet of paper with "*For You*" written on the outside. I opened the thin paper and there in the sun, with a little wind that was coming across the water of the harbor rustling it so I had to hold tight, I began to read the long prose poem that he had sent me. The last part of it I read twice, then folded it carefully and put it inside my blouse, near to my heart, wondering if I would ever forget those words. . . .

But the wind that had tugged at the sheet of paper that morning grew stronger by afternoon, and colder. Dark clouds gathered and hid the sun, and that night Stella had a driftwood fire going to keep warm. . . .

9

Indian summer was over. The leaves fell in a golden dance and lay in piles of matted gold along the pavement; the skies turned to a brighter and colder blue, and the waters of the harbor glittered in restless excitement. Every morning I listened within myself, waiting for some sign. My mother had to leave; she did this regretfully and with some sadness, but she could stay no longer. Gene closed up Peaked Hill and came in, with a suitcase full of books and scripts on the coast-guard wagon, when

Mother left, and stayed a day or so with me at Stella's house. For some reason that I can't now understand or remember, we did not move from Stella's into Happy Home, but into another house, right next to the water, called Sea Captain. This was a gray-painted house, rather austere but comfortably furnished, and with a room looking out over the harbor, where Gene could write. . . .

But everything was ready at Happy Home, ready, but not exactly comfortable. Happy Home was a small cottage, hidden back from the street, behind the house where Susan and Jig Cook lived. It had heat and could be kept warm, whereas Sea Captain had only a fireplace and couldn't be kept warm during the winter. One of our main reasons for choosing Happy Home was that it was very close to the Cooks—so close that I could call to them from the window. We both knew that it would be necessary for Gene to go to New York after the baby arrived.

Every morning after breakfast I walked across the street (for Sea Captain was nearly opposite) opened the windows, sat down, and on cold mornings started a fire in the obstinate little kitchen stove. There were three rooms—a small kitchen, through which one entered the house; an even smaller sitting room, with a couch and three chairs; and a larger bedroom—containing a huge double bed. There were dark velour curtains in the sitting room and a little Franklin stove. Gene ordered wood, which was piled up in the kitchen, next to the range. Sometimes in the afternoon Gene and I would go there together. I would look once again at the bureau drawer full of baby things, at the pile of little blankets, and at the blue packages of unopened absorbent cotton and pads on the shelf in the small bathroom, while Gene read a book in that sitting room which seemed to me almost too small for him. Then I would take a last look at the walls of the bedroom, which were covered with large, colored holy pictures, each in a gilt frame. On the wall at the end of the bed was a picture of the Holy Mother, wearing a bright blue veil, and holding in her arms a pink-cheeked Holy Child. Next to that, a verse in Portuguese, with angels in gold surrounding the lettering; then not one but two large pictures of the Sacred Heart bleeding great drops of blood. There was another picture, the Virgin alone this time, with her heart transfixed with a sword, and a serpent under her feet.

Dr. Heibert was puzzled; Gene began to worry; and still nothing happened. Sometimes Gene and I walked out on the old Atkins-Mayo road where the dunes began, and sat a while in the sun, in that wash of wild color that comes over the Cape in the fall—the purple-red of wild cranberry vines; the yellowed beach plums were dropping their leaves, and the wild briars' leaves had turned to gold. There was a smell of bayberry and the sweet, spicy wild fern in the air.

10

I somehow got the idea that if I climbed into the jerky jolty bus every day and rode from one end of the town to the other, this would help matters; and as the doctor didn't advise against it, every morning, wrapped in my red cape, I took this trip, while my husband worked or wrote letters. *The Dreamy Kid* was already in rehearsal on Macdougal Street. I was getting heartsick and impatient, for I knew that Gene would have to leave soon; he wouldn't leave until everything was safely over. One day getting off the bus I met Hutch Hapgood, and he insisted on having a talk with me and telling me I should be doing a book right now—a book about just how it felt to be having a baby. It could be, he felt, an important document; and when he told me, after having led me back to Sea Captain, that I reminded him of nothing so much as a certain little white horse in a painting by Henri Rousseau, I felt rather confused. . . .

I was gay and lifted up as always after my encounter with Hutchins Hapgood, but afterward, sitting alone for a while in the tiny kitchen at Happy Home, I was overcome with a strange intangible sadness. I felt very alone. Although Gene was just across the street, working, it seemed to me that he hardly existed, that he had gone from my life and I was an alien here in the kitchen and in the town. Who was I, where did I belong? It was a pointless yearning—for what, I did not know; an emptiness that I could not seem to face. After a few moments I got up from the chair where I had been sitting, went into the bedroom and pulled out a drawer to look at the pile of baby clothes carefully put away there. A child was coming into the world . . . I seemed to be faced with an impenetrable mystery; not the fact of the child and its arrival, which was strange enough in itself, but the fact that all over the world even at that moment people were coming together in the sexual act and new human beings were being born. This was the important thing then. What did it mean? Why was it so? I saw the face of the gentle Israelite on the wall, with his sad eyes and his bared heart bleeding drops of blood. . . .

Only a night or so after this I was very restless and, as Gene was reading, decided to go for a walk by myself before going to bed. As I stepped outside I was aware of something curious and strange in the light—a crackling as of electricity in the air, an unusual brightness and burnish in the northern sky.

That night in later October there was a phenomenon so unusual that people stood in silent groups in the street, wondering and unbelieving. Great spears of light rose from the horizon and met and crossed and tangled in the high obscure depth of heaven. . . . The northern lights astounded and mystified Provincetown with a display that I have never seen equaled before or since.

Gene came and watched and was astonished too; but after a while he went back to his reading. I stayed outside a while, listening and looking, and then, tired, went in to bed and to sleep.

II

I awoke suddenly that night. There was a pale light in the room that came in past the windows from the night outside, and I lay there, frightened and not knowing what it was that

326

had frightened me. There was an extraordinary stillness in the room—a hush, almost of expectancy. I listened; for what, I didn't know; and then became aware of the slow, solemn beating of my own heart; a heart that seemed to be preparing itself for something, as the slow rhythm grew louder in my eardrums. I was aware of the inertia of my heavy body and a sort of trapped despair rose in me. I wanted to be free of my body and drift off into the night where it could not follow me. Then I heard another sound—the slow, almost snoring breath of my husband as he lay deep in sleep on the bed beside me. I listened. How selfishly he slept! With what egotism he lay there, unconscious of me, untouched and unaware! I pulled the chain of the small lamp beside the bed and looked at him with some sort of dire vengeance in my mind, sort of a primitive and animal-dumb fury at this man lying asleep so calmly beside me. I imagined, watching him, that I could see nothing in his face but a heavy sullen moroseness, lying there in a living death.

"*Gene!*"

He did not even hear me. I pushed him and cried his name again, more angrily. This time his eyes opened, he stared up at me in the dim light and now I cried out in rage and fury at him—I could definitely see a sullen, sour look at being so abruptly awakened from sleep.

"What on earth's the matter with you, waking me up like this?"

There was silence; then he leaned up on his elbow and looked frightened.

"*Are you having the pains?*"

"*No—no, of course not!*" That was the truth. There was no pain, not anywhere, nothing but inertia and some silent, secret stress.

"You're sure?" he said more gently. Then he groaned and looked at the clock. It was after two. "You'll be all right—go to sleep. It's just the electric storm—the northern lights!" He turned over and a moment later I heard him breathing evenly and knew that he was asleep again. But I could not bring myself to turn off the light and lie again in the dark. Gene was right probably—it was nothing to worry about, there was nothing going on in my body at all, only silence and my patient, anxious heart. I kept my eyes on the clock and saw the hands moving with exasperating slowness on the pale face of the clock. . . . Suddenly I could stand it no longer.

"*Gene!*"

"What is it now?" He woke more quickly this time, quite impatient at me.

"I'm going over to Happy Home! I can't stay in this room one minute longer!"

He stared at me, angry now himself, for he saw the antagonism in my eyes. For a moment we were two creatures out of the past—primitive man with a club, if one had been nearby, and primitive woman, half clothed and bulging in uncomfortable ugliness—wishing too, no doubt, that she had a club to eradicate the male who had brought her to this, and who now only wanted to be left in peace! I made a quick movement from the bed, caught at the table, overturned the lamp, and uttered a cry—but of sharp pain this time, not of rage.

"*Good God, Aggie!*" Gene leaped from the bed and caught me, holding me as I bent over. "I didn't realize . . ."

"It's all right," I said, a moment later, sitting on the edge of the bed. "I—something has happened. Perhaps you'd better get Heibert. I'll go across the street——"

"You'll stay here. Get in bed, *get back into bed!*" Gene was trembling voilently himself, pulling on his trousers. There was a telephone downstairs and I heard him hurrying down in the dark, bumping into furniture and cursing. I looked at the clock: it was half-past three. Then another pain, worse than the first, caught me, moved fast and stayed long, twisting and tearing inside me. . . .

"Gene!"

It wasn't more than a couple of minutes since the first pain. I could hear him talking downstairs on the telephone. He ran up again at my call, looking very pale.

"Heibert says to get you over to Happy Home. Do you think you can make it?"

"Yes," I said, looking in anguish at the clock. I knew what was happening—there would be no rest, no interval between the pains—a quick birth. Then all at once I felt calm and strong. There was a quietness in my body, a long moment of peace and relief. Gene was looking at me now with such torture in his face—and such love.

"Put your coat around me," I said. "We'll go over. You'll have to light a fire. . . ."

He got my red cape from the closet, wrapped his coat around me, over it, and, kneeling, couldn't find my slippers.

"*I can't wait!*" I cried, "never mind them!" I held his arm as he helped me down the stairs, and then down the steps of the porch across the lapping water.

12

The street was empty and silent; there was no sound of any car coming. The coldness of the pavement was grateful to my feet, and I walked proudly, not minding the sharp pressure of the tiny shells as we went up the path and I saw again the trembling light in the northern sky.

Gene held my arm, turned his flashlight on the door and unlocked it. I sat in a chair while he put a match to the paper and kindling already laid in the small kitchen range. The flames roared up the stovepipe and I went in and lay down on the bed, which had been carefully prepared long before by my mother, and in which Gene and I had never slept.

The pain really started again. It is too much, I thought, I cannot bear it, and I forgot Gene and the doctor and myself and became engaged in that animal-like struggle to bear down and bring forth that within me which, without ceasing, was causing me such torturing pain. I held the cotton quilt in my hand, pulled it and bit it desperately in an effort to stifle my cries. Gene stood there, a white and broken wreck—not knowing what to do or where to turn. Then there was another face there—the calm, smiling face of Dr. Daniel Heibert, looking serene, as he moved about gently. I begged him to help me, *do something*, and he did. . . . I felt his hand go firmly over the moving tense flesh of my body, and heard him say to Gene, *"Not long now!"* and that was the last I heard there in that room, and my own moans were no longer in my stifled ears. There was peace and quiet and a quietness, and I was lying on the edge of a large and darkly clear lake that rippled out from its center in quiet, gentle, waves that made a gentle sound as they reached the shore. . . . Then the sound of the waves seemed to grow louder, and the lake faded slowly, but half remained for a few minutes after I opened my eyes; and the rhythm of the lapping water continued but now it was the rhythmic cry of a human being—a dark, long, angry ten-pound boy being held upside down by the grinning, triumphant young Dr. Heibert.

Seeing me awaken, the doctor handed him without apology to his astonished father, who held him gingerly, and then looked at him with intense and delighted admiration.

"Blime—a tough bird, eh?" I heard him exclaim as the doctor bent over me. *"Shane the Loud!"* and a moment later as the doctor brought fresh pads and hot water from the stove: *"Where do I put him, Doc? He's kicking me!"* Dr. Heibert looked around vaguely and then bent over me again, too busy to pay much attention to Gene, who, a moment later laid the baby gently beside me on the bed. "God damn it, I knew we'd forgotten something!" he whispered as he bent and kissed me. "A crib for *him!*"

It was not too long after dawn when the doctor left, saying everything was fine and he'd be back later in the day. Gene lay down on the couch in the little sitting room, covered with his coat, asleep—I really hoped this time—at last. The doctor had left the small night light on, but I reached out and turned it off, for I wanted to see the light of morning coming into the room. My little black Irishman lay beside me, snuffling a little, but otherwise quite independent, once in a while moving his foot in a mild baby kick. I was remembering—thinking of what Gene had said to me after the doctor had gone and we were once again alone. He had pulled a chair beside the bed, and, sitting there, held my hand tightly in his, his face soft and tender, his eyes on the fuzzy black head of the baby beside me. . . . "It'll be *us* still, from now on," he said. "Us—alone—but the three of us——" and he laughed as a thought came to him. "A sort of Holy Trinity, eh, Shane?" he said; and when he bent over to kiss me good night he kissed the little black head too, and I saw a real tenderness in his eyes.